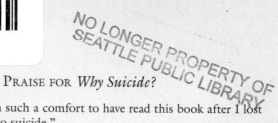

PRAISE FOR *Why Suicide?*

"It would have been such a comfort to have read this book after I lost my husband Edgar to suicide."
—Joan Rivers

"I opened this book and said, 'Where was this when I needed it?!'"
—Judy Collins

"*Why Suicide?* is one of those books that sounds too good to be true—but in fact delivers: it poses, and answers, every kind of question you wanted to know about suicide and were afraid to ask. In an arena full of heartbreak and puzzles, *Why Suicide?* gives valuable answers just when they're needed."
—Christopher Lukas, author of *Silent Grief*

"Eric's personal experience with the suicide of his father at age twelve gives this book both its passion and its authenticity. His writing is clear, his research is extensive, the need for this book is obvious. *Why Suicide?* is a must read for anyone who is a student of life."
—John Shelby Spong, author of *Eternal Life*

"[In this] well-researched, encyclopedic compendium . . . written in a crisp Q&A format Eric Marcus has provided the ultimate distillation of what experts know about the thorny issue of suicide."
—Leroy Aarons, *The Advocate*

"[The author's] responses [to his] . . . well-chosen selection of questions . . . reflect not only a knowledgeable and well-informed consideration of suicidology but also empathetic treatment. The typical response aims to educate by giving factual information and/or practical advice as well as to console by providing personal stories from suicide survivors. A marvelous addition to suicidology collections as well as a solid choice for bibliotherapy."
—*Library Journal*

"Educators in pre-K through college, school administrators, guidance counselors, pediatricians, social workers, and mental health professionals will all find this book to be an invaluable resource in the practice of their profession."
—Mary P. Lefkarites, Ph.D., associate professor,
Hunter College of the City University of New York

Other books by Eric Marcus

Why Suicide?

Questions and Answers About Suicide,
Suicide Prevention, and
Coping with the Suicide
of Someone You Know

REVISED AND UPDATED EDITION

Eric Marcus

HarperOne
An Imprint of HarperCollinsPublishers

HarperOne

HarperCollins books may be purchased for educational, business, or sales promotional use. For information please write: Special Markets Department, HarperCollins Publishers, 10 East 53rd Street, New York, NY 10022.

HarperCollins Web site: http://www.harpercollins.com

HarperCollins®, ▩®, and HarperOne™ are trademarks of HarperCollins Publishers

FIRST HARPERCOLLINS PAPERBACK EDITION PUBLISHED IN 1996

Library of Congress Cataloging-in-Publication Data is available.

ISBN 978–0–06–200391–1

10 11 12 13 14   RRD   10 9 8 7 6 5 4 3 2 1

For Martin Stephen Frommer

Contents

ACKNOWLEDGMENTS

I am especially grateful to Jennifer Finlay, who searched high and low for information on every possible aspect of suicide for both the first and second editions of *Why Suicide?* Her curiosity added enormously to this book, and her sense of humor was indispensable. A special thanks also to Linda Alband and Linda M. Finlay.

While Jennifer and I drew material from scores of resources, we relied heavily on George Howe Colt's *November of the Soul: The Enigma of Suicide*, which was invaluable. Colt covers all aspects of this issue with unparalleled clarity and thoroughness. I am extremely grateful for his work, and you will see excerpts from—and references to—his book throughout this one. I highly recommend *November of the Soul* to anyone who wishes to further explore the issue of suicide.

Many thanks to my original editor, Barbara Moulton, for helping shape the idea for this book, and the late Jed Mattes, for helping me find a home for it. Thanks also to assistant editor Lisa Bach. And thank you to my agent, Joy Harris, as well as to Gideon Weil, Maria Brock Schulman, Amanda Wood, and Michele Wetherbee at HarperOne for their work on this new edition.

Thank you also to the many people who shared their stories, suggested questions, offered sage advice, provided support and encouragement, and/or read all or part of the manuscript. These include Mark Burstein; Miriam Freifeld; Posy Gering; Joanne Harpel; Dr. Richard Hersh; Leslie Longenbaugh; Kit Lukas; my late mother, Cecilia Marcus; my late grandmother, May Marcus; Mynette Marcus; Richard Marcus; Lou Martarano; Vanessa McGann; Sandra Rockman; Phil Roselin; Stuart Schear; and Marian Young. I could not have completed this book without all of you.

And finally, a very special thank-you to my partner in life, Barney Karpfinger, whose advice, support, and love have brightened even the darkest days.

INTRODUCTION

I'm sorry that you have any reason to read this book. But the sad fact is that almost everyone is touched at some point in life by suicide, whether it's the suicide or attempted suicide of someone we know or our own passing self-destructive thoughts.

No matter what the circumstances, there are always questions for those of us who are affected by suicide. When I was twelve, my father took his life. His death was devastating, the circumstances painfully perplexing and embarrassing. I was hurt, angry, guilt-ridden, and ashamed, and I didn't know why. I had *so many* questions, but there was no one who could provide the answers and perspective I desperately needed. The adults in my life didn't have the answers to give and, as I later learned, had few places in 1970 to find them even if they had looked. And to be fair, most of them were devastated themselves and had little emotional energy or wherewithal to consider what was going on for a well-behaved and outwardly brave little boy who didn't shed a tear at his father's funeral.

From the start of my writing career, I was determined to create the kind of book that would have enabled my family to help me cope with the circumstances of my father's death. I also wanted to write a book that could serve as a broad resource for anyone whose life has been touched by suicide.

Inevitably, the experience of writing the original *Why Suicide?*—and then revisiting the book fourteen years later to prepare this new edition—has helped me find answers to many of the unanswered questions about suicide that I carried with me for years. Writing this book gave me the excuse I needed to ask the questions I was afraid to ask and to find answers when there were answers to be found. And it certainly gave me the excuse to talk to family members, track down my father's old friends, and subsequently fill in as many blanks as I could about what was going on in my father's mind and in his life at the time he killed himself. Through my research I also had the opportunity to speak with many people who have lived through a similar experience. Perhaps that was most comforting of all—to discover that I wasn't alone, that there are plenty of people in the world who understand in a visceral way what it is like to live through (and with) the trauma of a loved one's suicide.

I don't pretend to be an expert on the subject of suicide. And I'm not a psychologist, psychiatrist, or social worker. I'm a journalist by training. So in researching this book I did what journalists do and interviewed a lot of people, including many experts. I read magazine and newspaper articles, scanned the pages of numerous books, and searched the Web. I also watched educational videos and documentary films about suicide.

What I learned about suicide, you'll find in the pages that follow. I've included a broad range of questions, from the very basic to the extremely specific. In response to these questions, you'll find brief answers, long answers, anecdotes, opinion, and conjecture. A few questions will leave you with more questions, because I've included some that don't yet have definitive answers. And in the end you may not find the answers you were looking for because, as I discovered in my own search for answers, it's almost impossible to find satisfying or complete answers to the question of why someone we care about would take his or her life.

You'll meet many different people in *Why Suicide?* Some give answers to questions; others provide stories that help support a point. When I've used quotes or anecdotes from experts and those whose stories have already been made public, I've used complete names. When I've quoted private citizens or used their anecdotes—some of which are composites drawn from several different people—I've used only first names and altered identifying characteristics when asked to protect the privacy of the people I'm quoting. (Several of the private citizens I interviewed were perfectly comfortable using their full names, but I wasn't comfortable putting them in the public eye.)

Why Suicide? includes scores of questions, but not all the possible questions are here, nor are all the answers. My goal in writing this book was to create a resource that would be easy to read, easy to digest, and not overwhelming in details or length. There are plenty of other books on this subject that provide in-depth and very detailed information about suicide, and many of them were very useful resources for me in writing this one. (For a list of these books, please have a look at the bibliography). But if there's a question I've missed that you would like answered, or if you have an answer to a question that I didn't have an answer for or that you feel I didn't answer adequately, write to me at eric@ericmarcus.com or through my Web site, www.whysuicidebook.com, and I promise that I will write you back with the information you need or recommend a resource that can be of help.

I hope that the questions and answers in *Why Suicide?* bring understanding and comfort for all of you who have in some way been touched by suicide.

—Eric Marcus

Chapter

1

THE BASICS

I began my search for answers to basic questions about suicide during my lunch hour on a spring day in 1987. As an associate producer for ABC TV's *Good Morning America*, I spent part of every day in our cramped, windowless library searching through the extensive clip files, preparing background information for the stories that were assigned to me. (This was back when actual newspaper and magazine clips were sorted by subject and kept in huge filing cabinets in the heart of a long-gone office building on Sixty-sixth Street and Broadway in New York City.)

I had already decided by then that I was going to write a book about suicide and figured the best way to start was to see what we had on file. I wasn't looking for anything specific. And I wasn't counting on finding anything that I thought would help me sort out why my father had killed himself seventeen years before. I was simply doing what a journalist does when he sets out to write a book or an article. I was after the five Ws: Who? What? Where? When? Why?

But as I started pulling articles and, for the first time, reading stories about suicide—about people who took their lives, suicide prevention, theories, statistical analysis, history, religious views—I found something I didn't expect to find. Comfort. For one thing, I could see that I was far from alone in my experience. And I also found that with each bit of information I gathered and every heartbreaking story I read I was able to begin filling in some of the empty spaces in my understanding of my father's suicide and my own experience in the aftermath of his shocking death. I've come to accept that in life there are many mysteries, but my father's suicide left mysteries that plagued me. So by learning about suicide in general, I began demystifying my father's death in particular.

Not everyone will want to know every answer to every basic question that you'll find in the pages that follow. And I can't claim that the information I offer is anywhere near exhaustive or complete, but once you've read this first chapter you will probably know a lot more than before you started, and I hope that will be as helpful—and comforting—to you as it was to me when I began my search for answers.

What is suicide?

Suicide is the act of killing oneself on purpose. The word "suicide" comes from the Latin *sui*, meaning "self," and *caedere*, which means "to kill." But this definition is deceptively simple, because in reality suicide is many things to different people: tragic, shocking, horrifying, enraging, mysterious, a relief, shameful, stigmatizing, a shattering legacy, a cry for help, a release from pain, selfish, heroic, insane, the last word, punishment, revenge, a protest, a weapon, a political statement, tempting, desperate, upsetting, unsettling, a mistake, infuriating, hurtful, dramatic, a cop-out, devastating, and unforgivable.

In the pages that follow, you'll see how the act of taking one's life can be so many things, and more.

What about someone who drinks himself to death? Is that suicide?

Some people call this type of suicide *indirect suicide* or *slow suicide*. Other forms of behavior that could be considered indirect suicide or slow suicide include refusing to quit smoking if you're an emphysema patient or ignoring dietary restrictions if you have diabetes.

Is it considered suicide to refuse medical treatment?

It really depends on the circumstances and your perspective. For someone who has a treatable but potentially fatal condition, refusing medical treatment is a decision that many would view as suicidal. But for someone who is in the end stages of a terminal disease, refusing treatment may very well be a rational, appropriate choice, especially if treatment will simply extend life, yet not improve it or even maintain its quality.

What is suicidology?

Suicidology is the study of suicide and its prevention. The word was coined by Edwin Shneidman, who along with Norman Farberow conducted pioneering research in the 1950s and 1960s on the subject of suicide that challenged long-held assumptions.

How many suicides are there in the United States every year?

The official number is approximately 33,000 people a year, but the real figure may be higher because some suicides go unreported. At one time it was thought that up to three times as many people took their lives as reported, but I'm inclined to believe the experts on this subject, who now say that the official number is fairly close to the actual number.

Statisticians also speak in terms of the "suicide rate." By this they mean the number of people per 100,000 who take their lives. In 2007, the most current year for which suicide statistics were available at the time of publication (from the Centers for Disease Control and Prevention), the annual suicide rate for all Americans was 10.8 per 100,000 people. For that year suicide was the eleventh leading cause of death in the United States (between blood infection in tenth place and chronic liver disease in twelfth).

I have to admit that I am no great fan of suicide statistics, though some of them are objectively fascinating. It's also helpful to know which groups of people are more at risk for suicide so that prevention resources can be allocated accordingly. And statistics on suicide, like the ongoing multi-year decline in the overall suicide rate in the United States (see the answer to the next question), suggest that something is working when it comes to suicide prevention efforts and better treatment for depression.

But I also often find the statistics related to suicide confusing, especially when no one is able to adequately explain changing trends and so we're simply left with more unanswered questions. Because statisticians by necessity look at large groups of people, statistics can also be misleading. For example, we may speak of women as being a discrete group when we consider suicide rates, but within that single group rates vary by age, geography, ethnicity, and so on.

Statistics are also abstract and can feel especially meaningless when it's your loved one who has died by suicide even at a time when overall suicide rates are declining. So while I feel compelled to quote statistics and I attempt to explain what some of them mean, you'll find that I don't dwell on the numbers and prefer to focus on the experiences of individuals.

Please keep in mind that statistics regarding suicide are updated annually, so for the most current statistics please consult the Web site of the American Association of Suicidology (or any one of a number of organizations that I list in the appendix).

Is the rate of suicide in the United States the same as it was years ago?

The suicide rate today—which is just under 11 per 100,000—is a little higher than it was at the turn of the nineteenth century, when the reported rate was approximately 10 per 100,000 people. During the years in between, the rate fluctuated depending on economic conditions and war. During the two world wars, as "personal woes [were] overshadowed by the larger conflict," the rate went down. For example, George Howe Colt notes in *November of the Soul* that "during World War I the rate dipped from 16.2 in 1915 to 11.5 in 1919. . . . During World War II the rate sank to a low of 10.0." During times of economic hardship, the suicide rate has gone up, as it did during the Great Depression of the 1930s, reaching a high of 17.4 in 1932.

Between 1985 and 2004, the suicide rate dropped 13 percent, although since 2004 the rate has remained flat or edged up. The economic crisis that unfolded in the United States and around the world beginning in 2008 is expected to result in an increase in the rate of suicide as well—at least that's what researchers (including David Stuckler and Sanjay Basu) at the London School of Hygiene and Tropical Medicine and at Oxford University believe. Their report, published in the July 8, 2009, online edition of *The Lancet,* estimates that increased stress stemming from job losses could lead to a 2.4 percent rise in suicide rates in people under the age of sixty-five. The report's summary states: "We noted that every one percent increase in unemployment was associated with a 0.79 percent rise in suicides at ages younger than sixty-five years." Their report also offers ideas for how governments could respond in ways that would reduce the "adverse effects" of increasing unemployment during economic hard times.

Why at one time were suicides not reported?

In the not too distant past, doctors, medical examiners, and coroners sometimes spared families the added grief, stigma, and shame of having suicide listed as the official cause of death. This is, in general, no longer the case. The vast majority of suicides are now reported and counted in official government statistics.

In my father's case, his official cause of death in December 1970 was pneumonia. Technically, this was true. But it was also true that the pneumonia and concurrent multiple organ failure were a result of an overdose of a prescription medication (the sedative Librium). Because the true cause of death was not listed, my family did not have to deal with the public stigma and shame of my father's suicide, at least as long as no one talked about the true cause of his death. And for years no one talked.

Do life insurance issues have anything to do with why people do not want suicide to be the official cause of death?

Despite what many people think, when a person dies by suicide his life insurance policy is not automatically voided. Typically, as long as the policy has been in effect for more than two years, it is incontestable. In other words, it will be paid. If, however, a person takes his life within two years of the date a policy becomes effective, the amount received by the beneficiary will—in the case of whole life insurance—be limited to the premiums paid in, plus interest.

How many people attempt suicide?

Although there are no official domestic or international statistics on the number of attempted suicides, the American Association of Suicidology (AAS) estimates that there are as many as 25 attempts for each death by suicide. This estimate suggests that if we accept the official figure of 33,000 deaths from suicide in the United States each year, there are as many as 825,000 attempted suicides in the same period.

Among young people, researchers estimate that there are 100 to 200 attempts for every completed suicide. By comparison, among the elderly there are only four attempts for every completed suicide. For more information on these subjects, see chapters 3 ("Teen/Youth Suicide"), 4 ("Suicide and the Elderly"), and 5 ("Attempted Suicide").

Is suicide against the law?

The specific laws regarding suicide vary by state, but whatever the variations, people who attempt suicide are not punished under the law in the United States.

Is it against the law to help someone kill himself?

Although the specific laws vary from state to state, in general it is a crime for one person to intentionally aid someone else in killing himself.

In Oregon and the state of Washington, however, under very specific and highly regulated circumstances, doctors are permitted to hasten the death of a terminally ill patient when the patient has requested such help. Both the Oregon and Washington laws, as reported in the *New York Times* on May 22, 2009, "allow terminally ill patients who are at least eighteen and have been found mentally competent to self-administer lethal drugs under the prescription of a doctor." In the United States, this is most commonly known as *assisted suicide* or *physician-assisted suicide.*

Are the laws regarding assisted suicide different in countries other than the United States?

Yes, and these laws vary by country, although only a handful of countries have specific laws on the books that permit assisted suicide. For example, Switzerland permits assisted suicide under set guidelines, but in Great Britain providing assistance to someone who wishes to die is a criminal offense.

That prohibition has led scores of British citizens who wish to end their lives to travel to a clinic in Zurich, Switzerland, that helps people die. The clinic, run by a group called Dignitas, was first established in 1998 under Swiss laws that permit such clinics to provide lethal drugs. In general, these drugs are provided to people who are terminally ill. However, in a case that left me feeling very uneasy (although some of my elderly married friends found it touching and inspiring), a famous British conductor— who was not terminally ill—and his terminally ill wife took their lives together at the Swiss clinic.

As reported in the *New York Times* and the *London Daily Standard* in July 2009, the conductor, Sir Edward Downes, who was eighty-five, and his wife, Lady Joan Downes, who was seventy-four, traveled to the Zurich clinic with their son and daughter. Lady Joan was in the final stages of terminal cancer, with only weeks to live. Her husband, according to a statement released by their children, was "almost blind and increasingly deaf."

In an interview with the *Standard*, the couple's children said that they watched, with tears streaming down their cheeks, as their parents drank "a small quantity of a clear liquid" (which contained a lethal mixture of barbiturates), before lying down on adjacent beds, holding hands. "They wanted to be next to each other when they died," their forty-one-year-old son Caractacus Downes said. He described what happened next: "Within a couple of minutes they were asleep and died within ten minutes."

In an earlier statement released to the press, the Downes children explained: "After fifty-four happy years together, they decided to end their own lives rather than continue to struggle with serious health problems."

When news of the joint suicide was made public by the Downes children, the British police launched an investigation, but in the end no charges were brought against them. And none of the other known cases of British residents seeking assistance in dying in Switzerland has resulted in arrests.

Assisted suicide is an exceedingly complex and fraught issue, one that I do not cover in this book beyond this and the preceding question. For those seeking information about assisted suicide, there are many resources available in print and online.

What is murder-suicide?

Murder-suicide is what it sounds like. A person commits a murder and then kills himself. For example, I recently read the story of Eusebio Salazar, a seventy-six-year-old barber from Queens, New York, who killed his fifty-one-year-old wife and then himself. And he did all of this in front of his understandably horrified mentally disabled son. As reported in the *New York Daily News*, neighbors said that Salazar and his wife had "showered affection on their son, who is in his twenties," but that Salazar had recently suffered a stroke and had been depressed. In chapter 4 ("Suicide and the Elderly"), under the question "How common is it for elderly couples to kill themselves?" I offer another example of murder-suicide.

Is suicide a sin?

This is one of those subjective questions whose answer depends on your personal moral and religious beliefs. Given my own beliefs, I think suicide is a lot of things, but I don't think it's a sin.

What does the Bible say about suicide?

I just assumed that the Bible both condemned and prohibited suicide. But I was wrong. As George Howe Colt states in *November of the Soul*, "Considering Christianity's nearly two thousand years of intense opposition to suicide, it is surprising that neither the Old nor the New Testament directly prohibits the act." The Old and New Testaments combined tell only a handful of stories about suicide, and these are told with no judgment passed one way or the other.

What do Christianity, Judaism, and Islam have to say about suicide?

Traditional Christian doctrine has for centuries judged suicide to be a mortal sin. But as Rita Robinson explains in her book *Survivors of Suicide*, "Most religious communities, while not condoning suicide, empathize with the deceased and offer love and compassion to the survivors." She goes on to note that this wasn't always the case and that well into the twentieth century the Catholic Church, for example, considered suicide a public scandal and forbade burial within the church.

Dr. Aaron Kheriaty, assistant clinical professor of psychiatry and human behavior at the University of California–Irvine and founder of that school's Psychiatry and Spirituality Forum, concurred that Christian views toward suicide "were at one time very harsh. . . . Luther claimed that suicide was the work of the devil," he said. "But over the course of subsequent centuries, there was greater understanding of mental illness and the role of mental illness in suicide and that has led to more compassion and more acceptance of the idea that people who take their lives may have been impaired by depression and other illnesses. So in practice, at least in terms of Catholic moral theology, God can have mercy on people who take their own lives and an individual who claimed that a person was going to hell because of their suicide would be rejected. This isn't the reversal of an old teaching, but a nuanced understanding of suicide in light of what we now know about mental illness and suicide."

Joanne, a devout Catholic whose teenage son killed himself,

assumed that her church would take a harsh view. "From what I learned when I was growing up," she said, "committing suicide was a mortal sin, so you can imagine how that made me feel. It was awful enough to lose my child, and in that way, but the burden of knowing that he couldn't have a church funeral tore me up."

Joanne's worst fear was never realized. She recalled that, "the day after Kevin died, my priest came to see me at home, and he was wonderful. He told me that Kevin wasn't in his right mind when he did this, and for that reason what he did was not a sin." The priest officiated at Kevin's funeral, which was held at the family's church.

In Judaism, as Isaac Klein explains in *A Guide to Jewish Religious Practice*, "the rabbis ruled that no [mourning] rites whatsoever should be observed for a suicide. . . . Suicide was considered a moral wrong. Deliberate destruction of one's own life was rebellion against God." That said, Klein goes on to explain that virtually all suicides are not actually considered suicides, based on rabbinical interpretation of what in fact constitutes a suicide.

As Klein says, "The only suicide for whom mourning is not observed is one who killed himself out of a cynical disregard for life; this excludes one who killed himself because he could not cope with his problems." Klein continues: "Nowadays, since it is known that most cases of suicide result from temporary insanity caused by depression, we observe all the rites of mourning."

When it comes to Islam, as noted in the *Encyclopedia of Religion* (which is published by Macmillan), "Muhammad proclaimed that a person who commits suicide will be denied Paradise and will spend his time in Hell repeating the deed by which he has ended his life." But as with Christianity and Judaism, official Islamic doctrine has been softened over time by the understanding that those who take their lives are often suffering from a mental illness and are therefore not in full control of their senses. From my reading, it seems clear that determination of whether a person of the Islamic faith who takes his life goes to heaven or hell is a decision that is in the hands of God.

For anyone who has spiritual concerns about a loved one who has killed himself or herself, I strongly suggest consulting with a member of the clergy who is compassionate, understanding, and experienced in dealing with suicide.

If Muhammad said that Muslims who take their own lives go to hell, why do people who follow the Islamic faith who engage in suicidal terrorist acts believe they'll spend eternity in paradise?

The simplest explanation for what is an exceedingly complex issue is that this belief is a perversion of traditional Islamic teachings.

Does everyone have thoughts of suicide?

Most people have had casual thoughts of suicide at one time or another, especially when faced with life's inevitable frustrations, disappointments, and losses.

For people who have lost someone close to them through suicide—a family member, spouse, or close friend—having even casual thoughts of suicide can be very unsettling and even alarming. I recall fantasizing about suicide at various points in my life and wondering whether that meant I would wind up doing what my father did. And I can tell you that this idea was very upsetting to me, at least until I'd spent enough time in counseling to recognize that my passing thoughts about suicide were not an indication that I would feel compelled to follow through and actually kill myself.

As I've come to learn, casual thoughts of suicide are perfectly normal. If you are having thoughts of suicide that are more than casual, however, and those thoughts don't pass quickly, then there is reason to be concerned and to seek help immediately. Please see chapter 6 ("Prevention and Treatment") for a series of questions about what to do if you're feeling suicidal.

Do suicidal feelings pass?

In most cases, yes. People who have casual or even less than casual suicidal feelings eventually get over them. Again, please see chapter 6 ("Prevention and Treatment") for a more complete answer.

Is it possible to tell whether someone is feeling suicidal?

Most people who are feeling suicidal or planning a suicide give clues that something is wrong. Sometimes the clues are very subtle, like giving away prized possessions. And sometimes the clues are very direct, as Sandra discovered when her aunt telephoned her at work one Thursday afternoon and said, "Your father is going to kill himself, and you're the only one who can save him."

Sandra was twenty at the time she received the call from her aunt, and she was planning to leave the next day on a belated honeymoon. As she recalled in a conversation with me more than forty years after that shocking phone call, "It came out of the blue, although I knew my father was very depressed. He'd been moping around the house and started smoking for the first time in twenty years. But I didn't know until later that he'd made a previous suicide attempt, which had been hidden from me, so I had no way of knowing how dangerous the situation was. He'd been depressed in the past and gotten over it. I had no reason to think it would be different this time. So after work I went over to the house and said, 'What is this I hear about you wanting to kill yourself?' And I told him, 'You can't do this to Mom. It's not fair to her. You're retired now. This is the time in life she was waiting for. You can't do this!' "

Sandra extracted a promise from her father that he wouldn't kill himself and left the next day with her husband for a long honeymoon weekend in San Francisco with no expectation that her father would do exactly as he had threatened to do, but promised not to. Over the weekend, while Sandra and her husband enjoyed their time away, Sandra's father hanged himself. Sandra explained that she hadn't taken her father's threat seriously. "I believed his promise," she said, "because I hadn't been through anything like this before and just couldn't imagine that reality that he could actually kill himself. Looking back, this was the moment when some adult in my life should have stepped in to do some kind of intervention to bring in a professional to say to my father, you need help. This was not the time to lay that on a twenty-year-old."

My own father was not quite as explicit as Sandra's father had been about his wish to die, but as I learned just a few years ago from letters he wrote to his close friend Howard, there were very strong indications of his wishes. In several letters, beginning three years before his death, my father wrote about his desire to end his life, as well as his concerns about leaving his three young children without a father. (I would quote directly from the letters, but I put them away after reading them the first time, and it's too painful to consider reading them again.) And from what I've learned from conversations with my father's brother and my grandmother, the possibility of my father's suicide was very much a concern of many family members, but no one knew what to do.

For a more detailed answer to this question and a list of potential warning signs, please see chapter 6 ("Prevention and Treatment").

What are some of the most common myths about suicide?

There are many, and I've listed some of them here. I've drawn this list from several sources, including a list first prepared in 1961 by Dr. Edwin Shneidman, called "Facts and Fables on Suicide," and Rita Robinson's book *Survivors of Suicide*.

- *People who talk about killing themselves won't do it.*

  People who talk about wanting to die must be taken seriously because some people who talk about it do it.

- *There are no warning signs.*

  According to Edwin Shneidman, "Of any ten persons who kill themselves, eight have given definite warnings of their suicidal intentions."

- *Young people are more likely than old people to kill themselves.*

  People sixty-five and older kill themselves at a higher rate than those age fifteen to twenty-four.

- *Bad weather drives up suicide rates.*

  Contrary to what you might expect, spring and summer are the seasons when people take their lives in the greatest numbers. This phenomenon is discussed in more detail later in the chapter.

- *People who make one attempt will never try again.*

  Most people who attempt suicide will never try again. But 10 percent of those who attempt suicide once will eventually kill themselves.

- *Suicide is against the law.*

  It's not, but if you're caught assisting in a suicide, you can be charged with a criminal offense.

- *Most people who kill themselves leave suicide notes.*

  They don't. Only one in five or six people who die by suicide leaves a note.

- *People who are suicidal want to die.*

  Most people who are suicidal are in fact ambivalent.

- *Suicide is genetic.*

  Although there is no "suicide gene," or at least one hasn't yet been discovered, there are, as Rita Robinson notes in *Survivors of Suicide*, "sociological and biological factors in families that might seem to dispose them to suicide." Among these factors are inherited characteristics that increase the risk of suicide—such as some forms of mental illness (including clinical depression), dark temperament, and self-destructive tendencies—as well as the example set by the relative who takes his life. For these and other reasons, people who come from families with a member who died by suicide are more likely to die by suicide than those who don't. For a far more complete discussion about this subject, I highly recommend *Blue Genes*, a book by Christopher Lukas about the multiple suicides in his own family.

- *Rich people are more likely to kill themselves. Poor people are more likely to kill themselves.*

  As several experts have explained to me, "Suicide is an equal opportunity killer."

- *Once a suicidal crisis has passed, the person is out of danger.*

According to Edwin Shneidman, "Most suicides occur within about three months following the beginning of improvement, when the individual has the energy to put his morbid thoughts and feelings into effect." In other words, once a person begins to recover from the suicidal crisis, the first three months of the recovery are, contrary to what you might expect, a period during which he is at significant risk of completing a suicide because he now has the energy he lacked during the crisis to follow through on his "morbid thoughts and feelings." After the first three months, the risk diminishes.

Do people plan their suicides?

Many people who take their lives do it on impulse and make no significant plans in advance. This may be part of the reason only one in five or six people who die by suicide leaves a note. Others plan their suicides in advance, making preparations over a period of days, weeks, months, or longer.

For example, in my own family, both my father and sister-in-law (who took her life in 2008) planned their suicides. And so did Ruth, a once-vibrant woman in her early eighties who did not start thinking about suicide until after she was incapacitated by a fall. She said, "I've always been very organized, so I made a list of all the things I needed to do, from finding out exactly how I was going to do it, to saving up the right pills, to making sure all of my papers were in order, to giving away some things that I'd been saving for various people."

Ruth spent several months preparing for her suicide before actually following through with her plan. In chapters 4 ("Suicide and the Elderly") and 5 ("Attempted Suicide"), Ruth talks at greater length about her experience.

Do animals other than humans kill themselves?

Since it's impossible to interview animals other than humans about suicide, it's difficult to know for sure whether what appears to be suicidal behavior is in fact suicidal behavior. But there are cases that appear to be so. As explained by the reporter Natalie Angier in a *New York Times* article published in 1994, "Biologists have identified numerous examples of creatures that sacrifice themselves for their kin, from termites that explode their guts, releasing the slimy, foul contents over enemies that threaten their nest, to rodents that deliberately starve themselves to death rather than risk spreading an infection to others in their burrow."

Then there's the issue of depression, which apparently isn't restricted to humans. Kathy, the dolphin that played the title role in the 1960s television show *Flipper*, was moved to a small steel tank, where she had little contact with people, following the cancellation of her show. Her trainer, Richard O'Barry, related the story of her death in his arms in a January 1993 article in the *Smithsonian* magazine: "[She] committed suicide. I don't know what else to call it; it was deliberate. Every breath is a conscious effort for a dolphin, and she just stopped breathing. She died of a broken heart."

Another story, one that I found particularly compelling, was told in a *San Francisco Examiner* article from 1994. Octavia, a fifty-eight-pound octopus, lived in captivity in the Cabrillo Marine Museum in San Pedro, California. With tentacles measuring twelve feet in length, she didn't have a lot of room to stretch out in her four-foot-deep, six-foot-by-six-foot tank. On a Sunday night when no one was at the museum, she lifted a two-inch-wide drainpipe out of its fitting, allowing the water to drain out. She was found dead the next morning.

Perhaps lemmings are best known for what appears to be suicidal behavior. The lemming is a furry-footed, six-inch-long rodent that lives in northern climates. Every four years lemmings migrate en masse in search of adequate sources of food to feed their growing numbers. Apparently they go off in a random direction, one following the other, in a straight line. No matter what the obstacle—whether it's a mountain or the edge of a cliff—they don't alter their migratory course, even when it results in what one can only assume is accidental death.

Who dies by suicide?

No group of people is exempt from suicide, no matter how you slice the human family pie. That said, people from some groups kill themselves in greater numbers than do people from other groups. In the questions on this subject that follow, I'll take a look at some specific groups of people and how their risk of suicide differs from the norm. I'll also try to tell you why, but that's almost never as clear as the statistics.

Who is most likely to take his or her life?

White men, age sixty-five and older, are the most likely to die by suicide. In general, those who are more likely to take their lives are older and male, have become isolated from friends and family, suffer from some kind of mental illness such as depression or schizophrenia, and have drug or alcohol problems.

Why are white men age sixty-five and older the most susceptible to suicide?

After age sixty-five, white men on average experience considerable losses in terms of jobs, status, and health. All segments of the over-sixty-five population face similar challenges, but white men apparently have less experience coping with disappointments and setbacks, have further to fall in their status, and have fewer familial and community resources to call upon in comparison to other groups. For more information on suicide among those sixty-five and older, please see chapter 4 ("Suicide and the Elderly").

Is it true that more men than women take their lives?

Yes. Four times as many men as women take their lives. But if women completed suicides at the same rate as men, there would be a lot more female suicides every year than male suicides because three times as many women as men attempt to kill themselves.

If so many more women than men attempt suicide, why are there so many more completed suicides among men than women?

It's very tempting to launch into a discussion about the broad differences between men and women—for instance, men are more aggressive and impulsive, women are more emotionally expressive and less physically violent—and the impact of these differences on male versus female suicide rates. But I'll leave that to the gender experts.

Here's what we know. Women attempt suicide in far greater numbers than men, but typically choose less lethal methods (prescription medication versus guns) and therefore kill themselves at a far lower rate than men. Because men typically choose more lethal methods of suicide, they're more likely than women to complete a suicide.

These simple facts raise some complex questions for which I wasn't able to find satisfactory answers. For example, do women try to kill themselves more often than men because women want to die more often than men do? Or are women simply more likely to express their suicidal feelings than men (or to use a suicide attempt as a cry for help) but less determined than men to actually kill themselves?

Do men choose more lethal methods because they're more certain than women that they want to die? Or do they choose more lethal methods because they have easier access to them? (For instance, police have access to guns and more men than women are police.) Or because they're less afraid than women of being disfigured? Or because they're simply more violent than women? Finally, can the differences between male and female suicide rates and attempted suicide rates be explained by some combination of all of these reasons (and others I haven't cited)?

How is the suicide rate affected by age?

The suicide rate rises sharply with age, from a low of a little more than 1 per 100,000 for those between the ages of ten and fourteen to a peak of approximately 17 per 100,000 for people between the ages of forty-five and fifty-four. After that the rate falls to a low of approximately 12.5 per 100,000 for people between the ages of sixty-five and seventy-four, then peaks again at just over 16 per 100,000 for people age eighty to eighty-four.

What are the differences by race or ethnicity?

In the United States, non-Hispanic whites have the highest rate of suicide, followed by Native Americans, Hispanics, African Americans, and Asians.

What explains the differences between racial and ethnic groups?

There are no simple answers to this question, particularly because the differences and the reasons for them have not been thoroughly studied. But it's a given that all people are affected in different ways by cultural, social, and economic factors and that these factors have an impact on the number of people who kill themselves within each racial and ethnic group.

Are people who have lost a family member to suicide more likely to die by suicide themselves?

Yes, but there is no clear agreement on why this is the case.

There are probably several contributing factors, including the grief and, in some cases, depression that follow a suicide (or any death for that matter). Biology and genetics also come into play, since depression and schizophrenia, which are leading factors associated with suicide, can be passed on from one generation to the next. In addition, personality traits may be inherited, including self-destructive tendencies, as well as a greater or lesser ability to cope with life's challenges.

Finally, there is the example set by someone who dies by suicide, introducing into a family the idea of suicide as a realistic option for dealing with life. Over time I've come to believe that this is less a factor than the inherited family traits and that the suicide of a close relative may have the opposite effect. This was the case for several people I spoke with who said that following the suicide of a loved one they did everything they could to avoid the same fate. For example, they sought counseling in the wake of the suicide and, if necessary, treatment for depression.

For more information on this subject, see chapter 7 ("Surviving Suicide").

Do people who have had a close family member— a parent in particular—die by suicide worry that they will do the same? What can they do to lessen their concern and their risk?

Everyone's circumstances are different, but this is certainly a concern for some, if not many, people who have lived through the suicide of a close family member.

Victoria, a successful, ebullient, and sharp-witted forty-eight-year-old literary agent, witnessed her father's emotional collapse when she was thirteen. Victoria recalled: "My father was crying, and I remember him saying that he was now the age his father was when he killed himself, which was forty-four. That was the first I heard about it. He was very sad about it. That was also when my stepmother left him, so it was a bad year for him."

Beyond the fact of her grandfather's suicide, no one volunteered to provide Victoria with the details of what happened. So she asked. "I found out that my grandfather hung himself on the top floor of his townhouse. He had a new wife and a new baby when he killed himself. Subsequently, I learned through my grandmother—his first wife—that he suffered from terrible manic depression. He always felt like a failure and that he'd failed his family and his life. He had a lot of promise and was in fact very successful, but in terms of his expectations for himself he felt like a failure."

Victoria's father didn't exactly follow in his father's footsteps by abruptly taking his life, but Victoria recalled worrying that he would. She said, "He was very tortured by his father's death, and I attribute that to his father's suicide and to the biochemical component. Manic depression ran in the family. And while he didn't kill himself in one year, he did so over time. He drank a lot. He smoked a lot. He didn't exercise and was overweight. He ate very poorly. There were many nights when my father got so drunk at dinner that he'd fall asleep with his head halfway in the plate and I'd have to pull him out and put him to bed. He was a good guy, a good father to the best of his ability. But he was a tortured soul." Victoria's father was fifty-eight when he had a heart attack in his sleep and died.

When I asked Victoria whether she ever worried about killing herself, I was surprised by her answer because it seemed so contrary to her personality. She said, "I would say that certainly I worried about—and continue to worry about—doing it to myself, because I think that when something like that happens in your family, the stage has been set, so it's almost permissible. It's not unimaginable. So it's an option. I have to be more mindful of my moods. I endeavor to not get mired in things."

Victoria credits a loving and supportive relationship with her partner Diane and intensive psychotherapy for the stability she now enjoys. She explained, "Diane offered such a sense of ballast that as the years have progressed I've become more comfortable and secure. And for the five years after my father died I had a wonderful psychiatrist, and she saved me. She helped me see that none of your past is your fault. The future is of your own making."

Coincidentally, the magic number for me was also forty-four—the age my father was when he killed himself. It was also how old my father's younger brother was when he fell into a paralyzing depression. So, like Victoria, I worried. And like Victoria, I sought the help of a mental health professional to deal with my fears of following in the footsteps of either my father or uncle. (My maternal grandfather coincidentally died of a heart attack at forty-four, so I was more than a little obsessed with my mental and physical health in the years leading up to my forty-fourth birthday.)

Are people in certain professions more likely to kill themselves?

There are no reliable national statistics kept on suicide by profession, so this is not a question I feel comfortable answering in any definitive way. Nonetheless, from what I've read, there appears to be general agreement that police are more likely to take their lives than schoolteachers (which makes a lot of sense considering that most police are male, the majority of schoolteachers are female, and four times as many men as women take their lives), doctors are more likely than writers to die by suicide, and writers more likely than the average person.

It was once thought that police officers in general had a higher rate of suicide, and that's exactly what I wrote in the original edition of this book. So I was very surprised to read in the *New York Times* about a study by Dr. Peter M. Marzuk, a psychiatrist from Weill Cornell Medical College of Cornell University, who showed that the rate of suicide was no higher for New York City police officers than for other city residents (when adjusted for various factors). Apparently the suicide rate for police varies more because police suicide rates are based on a smaller group of people, but the rates are not higher over time.

Why are doctors more likely to kill themselves?

The suicide rate for doctors is higher than for any other profession in the United States, and interestingly, the rate of suicide for male and female doctors is the same: between three hundred and four hundred doctors die by suicide each year. The long list of reasons I've come across features stress combined with higher-than-average rates of alcohol abuse, a reluctance to seek help, and easy access to potentially deadly drugs. According to Dr. Charles F. Reynolds, professor of psychiatry, neurology, and neuroscience at the University of Pittsburgh School of Medicine and co-author of a 2003 paper on physician suicide (which was published in the *Journal of the American Medical Association*), the biggest contributing factor may be undiagnosed or untreated depression.

Is suicide more prevalent among U.S. military personnel?

Suicide is in fact more prevalent among people in the U.S. Army, the branch of the military that has been most actively engaged in the Iraq and Afghanistan wars. According to U.S. Army human resources data, the rate of suicide doubled between 2003—when the United States invaded Iraq—and 2008. In 2008 there were nearly

200 suicides. (This number includes 140 active-duty soldiers, 53 not on active duty, and 4 pending cases that had not yet been confirmed as suicides as of late 2009.) This alarming trend was not matched by the other branches of the military. And the full extent of the problem is not clear because there are no reliable figures for the rate of suicide among those who have left military service.

What accounts for the spike in U.S. Army suicides? Experts on this subject offer many reasons. The following list is drawn in part from a heartbreaking August 2, 2009, front-page story in the *New York Times* that focused on a series of suicides among members of the 1451st Transportation Company, which is part of the North Carolina National Guard: multiple deployments, relationship problems, financial pressures, drug or alcohol abuse, a history of emotional troubles (including depression), and post-traumatic stress disorder.

It was during my father's service in the Navy at the end of World War II that his emotional problems landed him in a military hospital. From his records, which I requested and received some years ago, it was clear that he was a deeply troubled teenager who had been suffering from a combination of depression, paranoia, and delusions. But it isn't clear whether there was a precipitating event beyond his work at a naval hospital in New York City, where he had been stationed. And with a history of mental illness in my family, I can only guess that his service in the military brought on or exacerbated whatever emotional problems he might have experienced even if he had never served.

During the years following my father's discharge from the military, he was treated at VA (Veterans Administration, now the Department of Veterans Affairs) hospitals several times for depression and was under the care of the VA in 1970 when he used his prescription medication to take his life. Because his death was deemed "war-related"—as my mother explained to me when I was a teenager—my brother, sister, and I qualified for GI survivor benefits. The education benefits, which were considerable, helped pay for my four years at a private college and my master's degree in journalism from Columbia University. So, in an odd way, the U.S. military helped finance the education that gave me the skills I needed to write this book. I like to think of that as one of the positive legacies of my father's suicide.

For information about what the military is doing to prevent suicide and for emergency resources for veterans, please see chapter 6 ("Prevention and Treatment") and the appendix.

Why do writers have a higher suicide rate?

As a writer from a family with a history of depression, I am especially interested in this question. Writers—as well as others who work in creative and artistic professions—are far more likely to have problems with depression than the average person, and that puts them at much greater risk of suicide.

Kay Jamison, a professor of psychiatry at Johns Hopkins University and the author of *Touched with Fire: Manic-Depressive Illness and the Artistic Temperament*, said in a *New York Times* article that writers are ten to twenty times as likely as the general population to suffer from manic-depressive or depressive illnesses, which lead to suicide more often than do any other mental disorders. She went on to say that "the cognitive style of manic-depression overlaps with the creative temperament. . . . When we think of creative writers, we think of boldness, sensitivity, restlessness, discontent; this is the manic-depressive temperament."

Who are some well-known writers who have killed themselves?

Sylvia Plath, Virginia Woolf, Ernest Hemingway, David Foster Wallace, the poet Anne Sexton, and the Japanese novelist Yukio Mishima are but a handful from a painfully long list of writers and other creative artists who have taken their own lives.

During which time of year are people most likely to die by suicide?

Contrary to what I might have guessed based on my own moods when the days are short, winter is not when people are most likely to kill themselves. According to A. Alvarez in his book *The Savage God: A Study of Suicide*, "The cycle of self-destruction follows precisely that of nature: it declines in autumn, reaches its low in midwinter and then begins to rise slowly with the sap; its climax is in early summer, May and June; in July it gradually begins once more to drop."

Alvarez suggests that the growing contrast between a suicidal depression and nature's annual rebirth makes life increasingly intolerable: "The richer, softer and more delectable nature becomes, the deeper that internal abyss which separates the inner world from the outer. Thus suicide becomes a natural reaction to an unnatural condition."

A more recent analysis of suicide data gathered over a five-year period from 2000 to 2004, conducted by two professors at the University of California–Riverside, found that July and August were the most common months for people to take their lives. April and May came in second. This analysis was published in 2009 in the journal *Social Psychiatry and Psychiatric Epidemiology*. I have no explanation for the discrepancy between this information and what Alvarez writes in *The Savage God*.

On which days of the week are people most likely to die by suicide?

Just about everything I've read says that people are most likely to kill themselves on Friday or Monday; the reason typically given is that those are the days when people seem to feel the loneliest. But according to the 2009 University of California–Riverside study I referred to in the previous question, Wednesday is the most likely day for a suicide (24.6 percent of the 132,000 U.S. suicides analyzed) and Thursdays the least likely (11.1 percent). The reason given by the sociology professor Augustine Kposowa, co-author of the study, is that Wednesday is in the middle of the workweek, which is when stress is the highest.

Where are people most likely to take their lives?

We may be most likely to hear about a suicide when it's a very public event—for example, when someone jumps from a bridge—but most people take their lives at home, or close to it.

Is the rate of suicide the same in every U.S. state?

No. The national average is about 11 suicides per 100,000 people. New Jersey has one of the lowest rates, at 6.52 per 100,000. Alaska and Montana are tied for the highest rate, at 19.57 per 100,000. The western states—excepting California, which has a suicide rate of 9.24—have traditionally had higher rates of suicide. The District of Columbia has the lowest rate of all at 5.01 per 100,000.

Why are suicide rates generally higher in the western states than in the eastern states?

No one has come up with a definitive answer to this question, but in my research I've come across some contributing factors that ring true. First, there's the traditional western frontier ethic of going it alone and not needing help, so people who are in trouble—suffering from depression, for example—don't seek the help they need and are therefore more vulnerable to suicide.

Second, the notion is still widespread that by moving west you can get a fresh start, but people who move west to get a fresh start are often disappointed to discover that no matter where they go to start over, most of the old problems go with them. And the old problems are then compounded by being in an unfamiliar place, where people are even less likely to have the support of family and community they need to deal with those problems.

What about the rates of suicide in countries outside the United States? Is it true that people are more likely to die by suicide in places like Sweden where winter days are short and the weather is gloomy?

According to the World Health Organization (WHO), about one million people around the world die by suicide every year, and the rates of suicide vary greatly from one country to another.

Suicide rates in the Nordic countries, with the exception of Finland (where the rate is 20 per 100,000), are not much higher than the suicide rate in the United States. The nations with the three highest rates are Lithuania (38.6), Belarus (35.1), and

Russia (32.2). Three countries at the other end of the statistics spectrum are the United Kingdom (6.8), Mexico (4.1), and the Dominican Republic (1.8).

Have people always killed themselves?

The first recorded reference to suicide appears in *The Dispute Between a Man and His Ba*, which was written four thousand years ago "in the first intermediate period of the Middle Kingdom in Egypt," according to George Howe Colt in *November of the Soul.* It was written by "a man who is tired of life and buffeted by ill fortune [and] considers killing himself."

It seems reasonable to assume that people took their lives prior to recorded history as well.

How have attitudes toward suicide changed over the centuries?

As George Howe Colt notes in *November of the Soul,* in contemporary Western society we generally consider suicide a psychiatric problem: "We study it, search for its causes, and struggle to prevent what we consider a tragic and sometimes shameful act." But that's not how it's always been. Different cultures have had different attitudes toward suicide depending on their spiritual beliefs and attitudes toward death in general, and those views have changed over the centuries.

For example, A. Alvarez writes in *The Savage God* that among the Vikings only those who died a violent death could enter paradise, or Valhalla: "The greatest honor and the greatest qualification was death in battle; next best was suicide. Those who died peacefully in their beds, of old age or disease, were excluded from Valhalla through all eternity."

Among the ancient Scythians, it was considered "the greatest honor to take their own lives when they became too old for their nomadic way of life; thereby saving the younger members of the tribe both the trouble and the guilt of killing them."

For the ancient Greeks, Alvarez notes, the act of suicide "passes more or less without comment, certainly without blame. . . . So far as the records go, the ancient Greeks took their lives only for the best possible reasons: grief, high patriotic principle, or to avoid dishonor." And whereas the Greeks tolerated suicide, the Romans, according to George Howe Colt, "made it a fashion, even a sport."

Early Christian teachings, according to Alvarez, were "at first a powerful incitement to suicide." He notes, "The more powerfully the Church instilled in believers the idea that this world was a vale of tears and sin and temptation, where they waited uneasily until death released them into eternal glory, the more irresistible the temptation to suicide became. . . . Why, then, live unredeemed when heavenly bliss is only a knife stroke away?" It wasn't until the sixth century AD, following countless suicides committed in the name of eternal glory, that Christian attitudes shifted and funeral rites were "refused to all suicides regardless of social position, reason or method."

In Japan today the attitude toward suicide—as well as the methods and reasons why people take their lives—generally mirror what prevails in the West. But historically, according to George Howe Colt, "suicide in Japan has enjoyed not only religious tolerance but state approval. The romantic aura that surrounds suicide grew out of the development of *seppuku*, a traditional form of suicide better known outside Japan as *harakiri*, or 'belly-cutting.' It was practiced by the samurai, or military class, who followed an ethical code known as *Bushido*—'the way of the knights.'" Colt notes that "*seppuku* originated about a thousand years ago during the beginning of Japanese feudalism as an honorable way for a soldier to avoid the humiliation of capture."

For an in-depth discussion of the history of suicide and differing attitudes across cultures, I recommend A. Alvarez's *The Savage God* and George Howe Colt's *November of the Soul*, both of which are listed in the bibliography.

In the United States, how was suicide dealt with in past centuries?

Prior to the twentieth century, suicide was generally viewed as both a crime and a sin. More than three centuries ago in colonial America, if you took your life, you could not count on a standard church burial.

In Massachusetts, for example, the "Self-Murther" act, which was passed in 1660, stipulated, "If any person Inhabitant or Stranger, shall at any time be found by any Jury to lay violent hands on themselves, or be willfully guilty of their own Death, every person shall be denied the privilege of being Buried in the Common Burying place of Christians, but shall be Buried in some Common High-way where the Select-men of the Town where such person did inhabit shall appoint, and a Cart-load of Stones laid upon the Grave as a Brand of Infamy, and as a warning to others to beware of the like Damnable practices."

In England during this same period of history, the deceased was tried posthumously in the coroner's court. If found guilty, as George Howe Colt explains in *November of the Soul*, the usual penalty was "property confiscation and burial at a crossroads with a wooden stake through the heart." The only way to avoid this fate was for a jury to rule that the deceased had acted from insanity. The last recorded burial at a crossroads as punishment for suicide took place in 1823.

Colt notes that the British colonies were far more lenient. For example, he cites William Penn's charter to Pennsylvania in 1700, in which he recommended "that if any person, through temptation or melancholy, shall destroy himself, his estate, real and personal, shall, notwithstanding, descend to his wife, children or relations, as if he had died a natural death."

Why do people kill themselves?

More than thirty years after my own father's suicide, I received a thick envelope from one of my father's best friends containing a few dozen letters that my father wrote to her in the last years of his life. Despite having long ago come to terms with the fact that I would never know why my father did what he did, I found myself reading through letter after letter looking for an answer— or answers—as to why he ended his life and, in the process, deprived me of a father.

Did I find clues? Yes, it's clear from his letters that suicide was very much on his mind. Did I find a satisfactory answer as to why he killed himself? No. And I've had to accept that there is no single answer. As Christopher "Kit" Lucas, my colleague and an author, put it perhaps better than anyone: it's the perfect storm at the worst possible time that leads someone to take his own life. No matter how many of my father's letters I read or how many times I read them, I can't know all the elements of the storm my father found himself in at the end of his life. And without talking to him, I can never really know what that moment in time was like for him.

More recently I received two more thick envelopes from friends of my father's who decided that I should have his letters. I read only a few before putting them on a high shelf in my office. Perhaps I was no longer as curious as I once was; more likely, I couldn't bear to read any more letters written by my father in his beautiful script about his ongoing despair and thoughts of suicide. But one thing I'm certain of is that no matter how many letters I read, I'll never find truly satisfying answers as to why he felt compelled to kill himself and leave behind his three children who very much needed him alive.

For those of us who have lived through the suicide of a loved one, the "Why?" question is just about guaranteed to haunt us for the rest of our lives. And even if we know some of the specific reasons why a loved one took his or her life, we're still left wondering why. Why did the person do it? Was it hopelessness? Was it the emotional pain of depression? What could it have been? And why didn't the person ask for help?

Even for people who really know why, like Patricia, whose mentally ill and severely depressed daughter had expressed a wish to die since the age of thirteen—and had indicated she'd had such thoughts since she was four—the search for answers after her daughter's suicide proved both compulsive and unsatisfying.

Patricia explained: "Even though you know she was depressed, your brain wants more information, more clues. My ex-husband and I almost sent her computer out to a computer forensic specialist hoping he could find something we missed. You look for clues everywhere. I talked to all her friends. I still go into her room looking for clues. She didn't leave a note, so to this day if I come across something I haven't looked at or gone through I look through it—like one of her books—to see if there's a note."

"We craved more clues," Patricia added. "We were insatiable. I don't think that craving will ever be satisfied. I want to have a conversation with my daughter: 'I know I can't have you back, but what was going through your mind in that moment?' I just want to know why?"

As you read through the following list of primary reasons why people take their own lives, keep in mind that although a reason may be listed here, its presence in a person's life is not necessarily sufficient reason for him or her to die by suicide. For example, most people who experience sudden loss, such as the death of a spouse, don't end their lives. Yet for other people who may already be struggling with depression, the death of a spouse could be the event that pushes them over the edge.

Also, if you're looking for an answer that will satisfy your desire to know why your loved one killed himself, I'm afraid you'll probably be disappointed, because for most people, including me, there is no satisfying answer.

Psychological and Physiological Reasons

Depression

It is not the everyday kind of depression we all have experienced that leads people to suicide. It is major, incapacitating depression—what the writer William Styron calls "the despair beyond the despair" in *Darkness Visible*, his remarkable book about his own suicidal depression. It's the kind of depression that is so painful that it leads some people to take their lives. Styron writes, "The pain of severe depression is quite unimaginable to those who have not suffered it, and it kills in many instances because its anguish can no longer be borne."

For more on this subject, see the question on depression later in this chapter. I also highly recommend Styron's eloquent and insightful book (listed in the bibliography), in which he describes his descent into and recovery from a suicidal depression.

Mental Disorders Such as Schizophrenia, Personality Disorder, Bipolar Disorder

People who suffer from a variety of mental disorders have a higher risk of suicide.

Revenge, Anger, Punishment

Some people use suicide or a suicide attempt or a threatened suicide as a way of getting back at a loved one over a grievance of some kind. For example, a young person might think to himself, *I'll kill myself and then you'll* really *be sorry.* Of course, if the person actually kills himself, he won't be around to witness the punishment he's inflicted on his loved ones.

Alcohol and Drug Abuse

People who abuse alcohol and other drugs, both prescription and illegal drugs, are at higher risk of suicide. Besides the personal and professional stresses associated with alcohol and drug abuse, drugs and alcohol can also impair judgment and allow people to act on self-destructive and impulsive feelings they might not otherwise respond to so drastically.

Illness and Physical Infirmity

Physical pain, infirmity brought on by old age or illness, and terminal disease can lead some people to take their lives. Some of these people take their lives because their pain is unbearable. Others are afraid of not being able to care for themselves, and still others are concerned about the financial cost and the burden on their families.

Sometimes a person's emotional state can be affected by a brain tumor or other brain disorder, and that is why it's key for someone who is experiencing a suicidal depression or is threatening to kill himself to have both physical and psychological evaluations to determine the source of the problems. In the case of my own mother, we didn't discover that her emotional distress and threatened suicide may have been related to her undiagnosed brain cancer until after she died from other causes and we read the autopsy report.

Prescription Drug Side Effects

Many medications—including some of the drugs prescribed to treat depression—have the potential side effects of depression, suicidal thinking, and impulsive or aggressive behavior, which can lead to suicide. For more information on the subject of prescription drug side effects, please see the question later in this chapter in which I address this issue at greater length.

Social Factors, Custom, for a Cause

Sacrificing for Others or the Community

A while back I heard a news story about an elderly couple in Florida. She had Alzheimer's disease. He had severe asthma. Money wasn't a problem; they had $10 million in the bank. In their note to their family, they explained that they knew they had enough money to be cared for but preferred that the money they'd saved be spent on young people who could make things better for everyone. The couple went into their garage, got in the car, turned on the ignition, and died.

This story reminds me of traditional Eskimo culture, where in lean times the sick and the elderly went off on their own to die in order to conserve the community's limited resources and ensure the community's survival. A more contemporary example is that of an unemployed parent who kills himself knowing that the insurance money will assure his family of the financial support he cannot provide in life.

Another example, which we may not think of as suicide, is that of a soldier who sacrifices his life in order to save his fellow soldiers, or a mother who throws her child out of harm's way knowing that she'll be sacrificing her own life in the process.

One more example is the story of a young man who killed himself at age twenty-seven. His mother wrote a letter to the editor of the *New York Times* in response to an article entitled "Quest for Evolutionary Meaning in the Persistence of Suicide." She wrote:

> Peter, who was brilliant, left us a sixty-minute tape, honestly describing his condition of pain, which began when he was seventeen. In the next ten years he managed to do a tour in the Army, finish college, teach math in a Roman Catholic school in

Guam and write three books for major publishers—while continually fighting the lure of death. He described his own condition for us, strikingly telling us he had "a missing part," he was "a Rolls-Royce—but without spark plugs." Yet underlying all of this in the last year of his life was his paralyzing fear that he would become violent. I have often wondered if my incredibly sensitive son killed himself to make sure this never happened.

Making a Political Statement

Individual acts of suicide (to be distinguished from suicide bombers and terrorists—see below) are used on rare occasion to make a political statement, as it was by two men in their twenties in Korea in 1987. Both men were apparently distraught over the failure of opposition leaders to unite behind a single presidential candidate and intended their acts of self-immolation as a protest.

Suicide Bombers and Suicide Terrorists

Suicide bombers and suicide terrorists are people who sacrifice their lives to accomplish an assassination or to wreak widespread destruction of life and property for a political or military goal. They typically do so by strapping bombs to their bodies or driving a vehicle laden with explosives and then detonating their deadly payloads when they have reached their target. Those who perform such acts typically do so in the belief that they will achieve honor and, depending on their religious beliefs, quick entry into heaven.

Decades before the September 11, 2001, terrorist attacks on the World Trade Center and the Pentagon in which terrorists commandeered commercial airliners and flew them into buildings—and long before suicide bombings became commonplace—Japanese "kamikaze" pilots made their deadly mark during the waning days of World War II. These pilots—who were named after the "divine wind" that twice thwarted Mongolian invasion fleets as they sailed toward Japan in the thirteenth century—crashed their planes into enemy ships, sacrificing their lives in order to disable or destroy their targets. These attacks resulted in the sinking of thirty-four American ships and the deaths of 4,907 sailors.

Social Custom

For hundreds of years in India, it was customary—or as George Howe Colt refers to it, a "blend of choice and coercion"—for a woman "to throw herself on her husband's funeral pyre to prove her devotion." The practice is called *suttee*, and although the British outlawed it in 1829, it still occurs on occasion to this day.

Sudden Loss, Trauma, Outside Threat

Loss of a Loved One

Whether it's the sudden death of a loved one or best friend or the breakup—or threatened breakup—of a marriage or relationship, some people are driven by loss to take their own lives.

For example, in 1993, when the Houston Oiler football player Jeff Alm accidentally crashed his car into a freeway guardrail and killed his best friend, he shot and killed himself only moments later. As reported by the Associated Press, "Alm, apparently distraught, . . . took a shotgun from the trunk of his car and shot himself."

Another example is that of a young woman in Queens, New York, who jumped from the sixteenth floor of her family's apartment house two days after her fiancé was murdered by a man who had been stalking her. Apparently shock and grief over her loss led to her suicide.

Loss of Job, Economic Distress

During hard economic times, when companies lay off employees or farms are threatened with foreclosure, some people, consumed by depression and a sense of hopelessness, see no way out of their predicament other than suicide.

For example, in the immediate aftermath of the economic crisis that unfolded in 2008–2009, there were a number of instances of high-profile businessmen who killed themselves as the companies they ran disintegrated underneath them.

There were stories as well of average people caught up in the crisis who felt compelled to take their own lives. One example that I found particularly heartbreaking was of an elderly woman who attempted suicide when her bank was foreclosing on her house.

Sexual Orientation, Gender Conflicts

Many of the problems experienced by gay, lesbian, bisexual, and transgender people result from the pressures and prejudices of society. These added pressures and prejudices can lead to psychological conflicts, depression, alcoholism, and drug abuse—all of which put members of these groups, especially adolescents, at greater risk of suicide.

Public Humiliation, Scandal

Sadly, on more than one occasion we've all seen news headlines about a leading businessman or public official caught up in a scandal who takes his life. For example, as reported in the *New York Times* in May 2009, the former president of South Korea, Roh Moo-hyun, "who had prided himself on being a clean politician during his term from 2003 to 2008," jumped to his death from a cliff in his native village. Three weeks prior to his suicide, Roh was questioned regarding $6 million in payments that he was believed to have solicited from a shoe manufacturer.

Most people who find themselves in such a situation don't take their lives, but there are those for whom the humiliation or the prospect of jail time proves unbearable. At the time of his questioning, Roh Moo-hyun spoke of his shame and apologized "for disappointing the people."

Of course, it's not only high-profile people who get caught in scandals or in humiliating circumstances, feel trapped by their circumstances, and see suicide as their only way out. We're just more likely to hear about it.

Outside Threats and Bullying

All kinds of outside threats—including genocide, war, blackmail, bullying, and extortion—have driven individuals as well as groups of people to take their lives.

Eve Meyer, executive director of San Francisco Suicide Prevention, a private, nonprofit organization that runs the nation's oldest volunteer, telephone suicide hotline service, told me the story of her parents' escape from a concentration camp during World War II. When they were prevented by a guard from crossing the border from France into Spain in their attempt to flee the Nazis, they decided they would kill themselves rather than risk being caught and returned to the camps and certain death.

Meyer explained: "I didn't learn this story until I was an adult. My brother told me how my father took my mother's hand, and the two of them turned to my brother and grandmother and took their hands and said, 'We're not going back. We're going to walk into the ocean.' My brother, who was eight or nine, fought them, but they dragged him across the beach to the water's edge. The guard caught up with them and told them it was a mistake and said they could go through. My parents never talked about it."

Nearly two thousand years earlier, 967 Jews killed themselves at Massada, in what is now Israel, rather than submit to the Roman forces that had encircled their mountaintop fortress.

Among the most poignant contemporary stories I came across in which an outside threat contributed to a suicide was that of Kiyoteru Okouchi, a thirteen-year-old Japanese boy who hanged himself from a tree in the family garden in 1994. Andrew Pollack of the *New York Times* wrote a compelling account of what led Kiyoteru to take his life: "For more than a year, four of his classmates had been demanding money from him, sometimes hundreds of dollars at a time. Once, when he would not comply, they held his head under water in a river. Another time they forced him to undress and left him in the gymnasium in his underwear." The young boy left behind a suicide note and a diary in which he gave a detailed account of the extortion and named his tormentors. Included along with the suicide note and his diary was a note to his mother promising to pay her back "the roughly $11,000 he had taken to give the bullies."

More recently I read the stories of two boys who were bullied because they were perceived to be gay and who killed themselves. One young man, Carl Walker-Hoover, was only eleven when he hanged himself in April 2009 after persistent name-calling left him so fearful of his fellow students that he ate lunch every day with a guidance counselor.

Please see chapter 6 ("Prevention and Treatment") for a question about how to deal with the situation of a child being bullied.

Do suicide notes offer any clues as to why people kill themselves?

Only about one in five or six people who kill themselves leaves behind a note. And even those who leave a note don't necessarily reveal anything that is helpful in understanding what led them to take their lives. As George Howe Colt writes in *November of the Soul*, "For many years researchers believed that notes held a key to understanding motivation for suicide, but several dozen studies have revealed little more than that suicide notes reflect the range of emotions of suicidal people."

That said, there are suicide notes that provide valuable insight regarding the motives or circumstances that led to a suicide. For example, the thirteen-year-old Japanese boy mentioned in the previous question left a note in which he explained that he had been subjected to the bullying and extortion of his classmates. In his note he said: "They took money from me, including 1,000 yen my grandmother had given me and the money I planned to use for having my hair cut. I had to cut my own hair. I should have committed suicide earlier but did not for the sake of my family."

It turns out that my own father left a suicide note, but I didn't learn about the note until my mother handed me a photocopy of it ten years after he died. She found the note tucked in a drawer and thought I'd be interested in seeing it. I was, although I was disappointed that there was no mention of my siblings or me.

In the handwritten note my father talked about being in a lot of pain and how we'd be better off without him. This was not an easy letter to read, although much of it covered practical matters like legal documents and money, of which there was very little. Unfortunately, I can't quote directly from the note because after reading it I promptly lost it. There are no other known copies, and the original was apparently misplaced shortly after my father's suicide.

Ten years after losing the copy of what I had thought was the entirety of my father's suicide note, I learned from my uncle that there was a second page, which was lost in the confusion immediately following my father's death. As my uncle recalled, in the letter my father spoke more personally about his motives for killing himself and his concerns about leaving behind his small children, but my uncle said that nothing he read provided a satisfying answer as to why my father took his life.

Not everyone who leaves a message behind leaves a written note. Some people leave recorded messages, as did Edgar Rosenberg—comedienne Joan Rivers's husband—when he took his life in 1987. According to an account in *People* magazine, he left two manila envelopes, one for Joan and one for his daughter, Melissa, in the Philadelphia hotel room where he took an overdose of Valium mixed with alcohol. "Each [envelope] was marked with three kisses—XXX. They found that in his meticulous way, Edgar was putting their affairs in order, sending them papers for estate planning, lists of the contents of the house, bank account numbers, his case of keys. . . . On tape cassettes were his personal messages."

Can you give some other examples of a suicide note that provided insight or comfort?

I first spoke with Karen two years after her father, a prominent scientist, ended his life at the age of eighty-two. He left behind very detailed notes for each of his two daughters. Karen explained, "Both notes had a personal part and a 'business' part. My note included contact information for his lawyer and accountant, bank account numbers, instructions about who should be notified about his death—everything I would need to know as executor of his estate. My sister's note told her what to do when she found his body." Karen's father lived in an in-law unit behind Karen's sister's house in Oregon, to which he had moved after his wife died a few years before.

"My sister woke up to find a note on her doorstep. There was another copy of the note in her mailbox. Dad informed her of what he had done and said that under no circumstances was she to touch him if he was still alive. He explained the law and how she would not be prosecuted if she simply let him die—but he was already dead when she found him." Karen's father died by suffocation.

Karen continued: "In his note he said that he had been conceal-
ing the extent of his memory loss, and that he didn't want to be
an expensive, useless, and unwanted burden to me and my sister.
He was very independent and there was no way he was going to
let anyone take care of him. He was also depressed, which is something we were aware of. He acknowledged in the note that he'd
never really gotten over his wife's death." (Karen and her sister
worked hard to help their father feel useful and needed, and he
had given them the impression that their efforts were paying off.)

Besides including practical information, like the telephone
number for the medical examiner and an explanation for his actions, Karen's father also thought to include words that were
meant to be comforting. Karen explained: "When I think about
the note I think about this wonderful line in which he wishes me
a long and happy life. That really meant a lot to me, and it always
makes me cry. It's clear he really wanted us to be happy and to
move on and to cherish our memories of him. But I have very
mixed feelings. He was eighty-two and had had a full life. But on
the other hand, I'm completely outraged. Most people feel it's a
perfectly reasonable thing for him to have done this in his situation, but to me it felt incredibly abrupt.

"If there was some way he could have confided in us it would
have made all the difference, but I can imagine he was afraid to
do that because he might have thought we would have tried to
prevent him from killing himself. I don't think we would have.
I imagine we both would have come around after our initial impulse to talk him out of it, but he never gave us the chance."

Karen asked that I include the contents of the first paragraph
of her father's note to her "in the hope that it will help someone
else through their nightmare."

Dear Karen,

*I'm very sorry for the shock I know my death will be for
you. But it is much better that you remember me as you last
saw me rather than some drooling idiot in an old people's
home. I really am beginning to lose my faculties at an alarming rate, so if I did not end things now, I'm afraid I would
become a costly, troublesome and unrecognizable burden. Be-*

*sides, I'm not getting much out of life since Barbara died—
I'm tired of my dreary life as it presently is; it's pretty empty;
I can't seem to get interested in all the activities you have so
kindly suggested. . . .*

Karen added that after rereading the entire letter, "it strikes
me as an absolutely lovely benediction and apology. I see that
he actually did apologize in his letter for not saying good-bye in
person and explained why. He said, 'I'm aware that you would
feel compelled to prevent my suicide.'"

How else can a suicide note be helpful?

In the wake of a suicide, the people left behind often feel guilty—
for not having done enough to prevent the suicide, for somehow
doing something to cause the suicide, for failing to recognize the
warning signs. A note that explains, "This decision was entirely
my own and you are in no way responsible for my actions," can
help assuage a surviving loved one's guilt.

John, whose younger brother killed himself at age forty-five,
asked the police whether they found a note when they got to
the scene of his brother's 1996 suicide. John said, "I was disappointed. Not a letter, not a note, not anything. I was blaming
myself for not recognizing how much trouble he was in, so I
always thought that a note would give me a handle, some insight
into what the hell was he thinking, where was he going."

John recognizes that he wasn't responsible for his brother's
death—something he's discussed with a psychologist—although
he still feels a residual sense of guilt. "I wanted exoneration from
any guilt or responsibility for my brother's death," he explained.
"I wanted a 'stamp of approval' that said it's not my fault that he
killed himself. Of course there's no such thing and I'm still so
unresolved about what happened."

When Kevin opened and read the two notes his partner of
thirty-four years left behind for him, he wasn't looking for anything in particular. He was still very much in shock from discovering Craig at the bottom of their pool after returning home
from a daylong trip to New York City.

Craig was a week shy of fifty-eight and had been struggling with health problems, but he had given no indication that he was in any danger of taking his own life. The first note, which was handwritten, offered some insight and explanation for why he killed himself and made clear that Kevin was in no way responsible for his death. Kevin recalled, "In the note he said that he was in such great pain that he wasn't able to do all the things that made life worth living, and he said that I was responsible for most of the good things in his life."

Craig's second note contained all his financial information and a check for $50,000. "He assumed I wouldn't have access to his money for a while, and he didn't want me to dip into my money," Kevin said. "He was thinking in very practical terms. He wasn't a person who had a lot of empathy, so I don't think he could have imagined what the terrible impact would be on all of us. I think he was focused on his pain and the life he wasn't going to be able to live."

Despite his intense grief in the aftermath of Craig's death, Kevin came to see that he wasn't responsible for Craig's actions. He said, "I didn't have great guilt. He knew I would never approve of what he did and kept his plans hidden from me, so there was no way I could have stopped him." Kevin said that he would not have left Craig alone for a minute if he'd known. He added, "It helped that he said that I was responsible for most of the good things in his life."

For more about Kevin's experience, as well as additional information about the guilt that people experience in the wake of a suicide, please see chapter 7 ("Surviving Suicide").

Why do young children kill themselves?

Many, if not most, children (ages five to fifteen) who attempt suicide or complete a suicide suffer from depression or another diagnosable mental illness. Some try to kill themselves to join a loved one who has died. Others, like the Japanese boy I mentioned earlier, are bullied or teased by their peers and see no other way out.

The Olympic diving champion Greg Louganis attempted suicide for the first time when he was twelve years old. Since early childhood, Louganis had suffered from undiagnosed clinical depression. At the time of the attempt he was feeling alienated from his adoptive parents and his classmates at school. What he says pushed him over the edge was the news from his doctor that he'd have to quit gymnastics because his already damaged knees couldn't take the continued pounding of his daily workouts.

Louganis told me, "I'd hoped to compete in gymnastics at the Olympics one day, but now that dream was gone. . . . I went into my parents' medicine cabinet and took a bunch of different pills, mostly aspirin and Ex-Lax. Then I took a razor blade out of the cabinet and started playing with it over my wrist. I started to bleed, but I didn't go deep enough to cut any veins or arteries. It also turned out that I didn't take enough of anything from the medicine cabinet to cause myself harm. . . . Afterward, I was even more angry and depressed, because I didn't see any way out."

Louganis's depression went undiagnosed for years and contributed to additional suicide attempts in his teens and early twenties.

What role does depression play in suicide?

Depression plays a tremendous role, but not run-of-the-mill depression. Everyone has experienced "normal" depression. You feel down. You lack energy. It's like having a bad cold, and like a cold, this kind of depression passes relatively quickly.

The depression that can lead someone to contemplate or attempt suicide is "major" depression or clinical depression, the kind that lasts two or more weeks. According to the National Institute of Mental Health, 15 percent of the people who suffer from this form of depression ultimately take their lives (although the actual percentage varies greatly depending on demographics—young versus old, male versus female, and so on).

Symptoms of major depression include a depressed or irritable mood, a loss of interest or pleasure in usual activities, changes in appetite and weight, disturbed sleep, motor retardation or agitation, fatigue and loss of energy, feelings of worthlessness, self-reproach, excessive guilt, difficulty in thinking or concentrating, and suicidal thinking or suicide attempts.

Barbara, who is a court reporter from New York, was a young

mother with two children when she experienced the kind of crushing depression that William Styron wrote about in his book *Darkness Visible*. She said, "It was like falling into this big black hole, and you're grasping and grasping, and it's so horrible so you just go to sleep. I slept all the time. I remember the absence of color too. Just this never-ending black hole. I always thought about the abyss and that I'd fall right through it and never be able to find my way back. It was so dark. Nothing. An empty void. It was pretty scary. I'll never forget that feeling. It was like it was happening to someone else. It was like looking at yourself from outside yourself. I couldn't imagine that this horrible pain would ever go away. I was in such turmoil and thought that suicide was the answer, but then I imagined what I would leave behind and that was too horrible to contemplate."

I asked Barbara what kept her from ending her life. She said there were two things: her children and the fact that she didn't have easy access to the means. She said, "I'm so glad I didn't have access to medication, because I think I might have succumbed to that feeling that I just couldn't take it anymore and needed to fade away. I never went to a doctor who prescribed anything. I never had access to pills." And Barbara added, "How could you do something like that to very young children? How do you say to your children, 'I don't love you enough to live'? But that's not what's really going on. It's about yourself and the pain. You just can't bear it."

Looking back to a time in her life when she couldn't get out of bed because she was so depressed, Barbara can hardly believe she's the same person. "I feel kind of divorced from it now because I no longer think in those terms," she said. "My life could always be improved, but it's a good place where I am now. But, boy, did I come close. I'm so glad I didn't because I have a really good life. I live with someone who loves me. And I have children and grandchildren and have friends I love and who love me. I have a life I love. I'm not rich, but I don't want for anything."

If you're experiencing the kind of depression Barbara described or someone you love is in the midst of a major depression, do not ignore it. Find a mental health professional who has experience treating major depression. Call your doctor or local community mental health center to get a referral. Or contact one of the resources I list in the appendix. Major depression can be treated, so there is every reason to get help for yourself or someone you care about.

In trying to help a loved one, you may find that he or she rejects your best efforts, so all you can do is try. In such a circumstance, I recommend seeking the advice of a mental health professional to figure out the best approach to getting help for your loved one. And if all else fails, a mental health professional can help you deal with your own feelings about being unable to assist a loved one who is clearly in trouble.

Is it true that people whose suicidal feelings result from clinical depression are at greater risk of suicide once they start treatment?

Yes. People who are severely depressed and suicidal may be so impaired by their depression that they don't have the energy or wherewithal to follow through on a desire to kill themselves. Once treatment begins and the patient starts coming back to life—but before the depression and suicidal feelings are gone—there's the danger that the person will have enough energy to act on his or her suicidal feelings. Mental health professionals who treat major depression know this and closely monitor their patients. This is one reason it's so important to seek the help of a mental health professional who is experienced in treating clinical depression. It's not enough to see your family physician for a prescription of antidepressants.

Is schizophrenia a cause of suicide?

Schizophrenia, which is a type of mental illness, does not cause suicide, but approximately 10 percent of those who suffer from the disease take their lives.

What role does alcohol play in suicide?

Alcohol does not cause someone to take his life, but as the psychologist Paul Quinnett points out in his book *Suicide: The Forever Decision*, alcohol removes fear and exaggerates moods—both good and bad moods.

One of the appealing aspects of alcohol is that it can take us out of ourselves and give us the freedom to think, do, and say things we might not otherwise think, do, and say. Unfortunately, when it comes to acting on bad feelings, including suicidal impulses, alcohol is a particularly deadly lubricant.

Approximately one-third of the adults who take their lives have been drinking prior to the suicide. And for alcoholics that number rises to 90 percent. Of course there are also people who use alcohol as a form of slow suicide by drinking too much and destroying their health over time.

Can you give a specific example of how alcohol can play a role in suicide?

Jeff Alm, the Houston Oiler football player whose death I mentioned previously, accidentally crashed his car on a Houston freeway, causing his best friend who was in the car with him to be thrown to his death. Alm then took a shotgun from his car and killed himself. A few weeks after the crash, medical officials reported that at his death Alm had had a blood alcohol level of 0.14 percent (the legal driving limit in most places is 0.10).

One can imagine that Alm's despair and guilt were intensified by the alcohol in his blood and that the alcohol reduced his fear and impaired his thinking. Both Alm and his friend were twenty-five years old.

Can the side effects of prescription medication lead someone to take his life?

When I researched this question, I was surprised by how frequently depression was listed as a potential side effect of prescription medications. Everything from sleeping pills and antidepressants to asthma medication and statins—which are prescribed to lower cholesterol—list among their potential side effects depression and "thoughts of suicide." Depending on the drug, the complete list of side effects often includes mood changes, aggression, impulsiveness, sense of hopelessness, and thoughts of hurting oneself.

(If you don't believe me, just do an online search. Type in the name of a popular prescription drug and the word "depression" or "suicide." You'll probably be as surprised as I was to see how many prescription drugs have these side effects. Or go to your medicine cabinet armed with a magnifying glass and read the microscopic print on the paper insert that comes with the medication detailing all of the potential side effects.)

So the short answer is, yes, the side effects of prescription medication can lead someone to take his life. Given how many people take prescription medications of all kinds, this is a comparatively rare occurrence. But if it's your loved one whose suicide is related to the side effects of a prescription medication, it's no comfort to know that such deaths don't happen very often. (There are no reliable statistics on suicides and prescription medications.)

Michelle finds no comfort in knowing that suicides resulting from the side effects of prescription medication are rare and hopes that by talking about what happened to her husband Paul she can help make it rarer still. As Michelle explained to me, five days after her forty-three-year-old husband began taking high doses of a drug used to lower cholesterol, she noticed that something wasn't right. "Paul was a screamingly funny, brilliant man, who was never depressed a day in his life," she recalled, "and suddenly he was different. I said to him over breakfast, 'You know, sweetheart, your affect is different.'"

Michelle, who teaches English at the University of California, had prior training in psychology, so she felt confident about her observations. Besides, after eighteen very happy years with Paul, she knew that his sudden moodiness was out of character. "We were incredibly close, so I knew something was wrong," Michelle said. "I told Paul that he seemed heavy, dark, but he just brushed it off."

Over the next several months, even as Paul's moods worsened, it never occurred to Michelle that the medication he was taking might have had anything to do with his sudden personality change. "Two months before he died," she explained, "I said to him, 'I've never seen you morose like this. Maybe you need to talk to somebody about what's going on.'" Much to Michelle's surprise, Paul agreed. "I just about fell off my chair," she said, "because Paul was the person everybody else went to for counsel."

Paul met with a social worker six times over the next two months. "He told the social worker he didn't like working at the law firm—he had been a university professor, but had worked as a corporate attorney for years—and wanted to sell our house," Michelle explained. "And I said, 'Okay, we'll sell our house, but it makes no financial sense.' Paul had always made sense, and I was watching him make no sense for the first time. I look back now and think, *Was I watching something I'd never seen before?* Yes, I was. But did it ever occur to me it was this drug? No. I'm not a wife who nags or monitors everything. I wasn't that kind of wife." In retrospect, Michelle wishes she *had* been, because nine months after Paul started taking the statin drug, and just a few hours after he kissed her good-bye as she left for jury duty—"he was laughing and talking about Valentine's Day"—he killed himself.

"Two days before he died," Michelle recalled, "we'd been talking in the kitchen, having coffee, and Paul held his head in his hands and he said, 'I can't think! I just can't think!' I was so confused by what he said, because the idea that he couldn't think, that this brilliant man couldn't think, made no sense."

Michelle continued: "Three weeks after Paul's death, one of our writer friends came to visit and said, 'Something does not make sense here.' Then, in the course of our conversation, I said to her that Paul was on this particular statin drug, and she said, 'You know, there's a connection between statins and suicide, and I'm familiar with the research.'"

Once Michelle was pointed in the right direction, she pursued every lead in the hope of unraveling the mystery of how her husband was transformed from a "screamingly funny, brilliant" guy into a "morose" and desperate man who could slice up his own neck with a razor blade, trash their house, go out into their backyard, and, as Michelle described it, "hold a twenty-two-caliber Remington to his head" and pull the trigger. She said, "I've since learned that there have been many cases around the world of suicide related to the particular statin drug that Paul was on."

For more about Michelle's experience, please see chapter 7 ("Surviving Suicide"). And for more information about the potential dangers of prescription medications, I highly recommend a book by Melody Petersen called *Our Daily Meds*.

What role does hopelessness play in suicide?

Almost all of us have experienced a feeling of hopelessness at one time or another, believing that whatever was troubling us would never get better, that there was no way out, that we had run out of options. But most of us who experience hopelessness recover relatively quickly from this feeling. Others don't, and these people are in significant danger of doing themselves harm.

In *Suicide: The Forever Decision*, Paul Quinnett says that hopelessness "is the one common thread among the majority of those who elect the suicide option. Despairing of any future solution to their problems, the utterly hopeless frequently find themselves thinking, 'What's the use? I might as well be dead.'"

If you're feeling hopeless, if you feel trapped, if you're thinking that you might as well be dead, you need help to get over these feelings. As my friend Posy often says, there are *always* options in life, even when you think there are none, and the first option you have is to get help. I realize that it's far easier for me to say you should take that option—to reach out for help—than it is to do so. Nonetheless, I encourage you to find a mental health professional (or to enlist a family member or friend in finding one). Perhaps if my father had reached out for help, my family and his friends would have been spared a lifetime of grappling with his suicide.

What role do genetics and biology play in suicide?

There is general agreement on the part of people who study suicide that genetics and biology play some role in suicide. Open to much debate is how large that role is and what exactly it is. The possibilities are intriguing, but nothing about this aspect of understanding suicide is set in stone.

What we know is that psychological disorders that increase the risk of suicide can be passed genetically from one generation to the next. And suicidal—or self-destructive—behavior may be inherited as well.

People who take their lives are more likely to have a brain chemical imbalance than those who don't. One brain chemical that has received special attention and is believed to be related to suicide is a neurotransmitter called serotonin, which is one of many neurotransmitters that control what brain cells do. Low levels of serotonin have been linked to depressed people who have taken their lives, but as George Howe Colt points out in *November of the Soul*, "it is not known whether the low levels are a cause or an effect of depression or impulsiveness."

What makes the biological/genetic issue so compelling is the possibility that if clearly identifiable biological or genetic factors are found for suicidal behavior, then corresponding treatments might be possible.

Can someone who dies by suicide be an organ donor?

Organ donation may not be something that occurs to a grieving family just absorbing the reality of a loved one's suicide, but they may be asked to consider it. That was Patricia's experience. Her twenty-year-old daughter survived a suicide attempt long enough to be taken to the hospital. When the neurosurgeon met with her to deliver the news that there was no chance her daughter would survive the gunshot wound to her head, he asked about organ donation.

Patricia recalled, "He was very direct. He said, 'Your daughter has a very severe brain injury, and no one recovers from this kind of injury. Would you consider donating her organs?'" The doctor explained that they would need to keep Elizabeth on life support until "her brain died," and then they would harvest her organs. And they would also need consent from both of Elizabeth's parents, which Patricia and her ex-husband didn't hesitate to grant. "So many people who lose someone to suicide don't have the opportunity to donate," Patricia said. "We were able to do that and feel that Elizabeth's life wasn't a total waste."

Patricia speaks at greater length in chapter 7 ("Surviving Suicide") about the impact that donating her daughter's organs had on her and on the lives of the organ recipients.

Chapter

2

HOW?

This chapter is *not* a "how-to" for people contemplating suicide. I've chosen to write about how people take their lives to help readers better understand suicide and perhaps gain some insight into the suicide of a loved one. It is not—absolutely not—my intention to give anyone ideas for how they might kill themselves.

If you are having strong suicidal feelings and are looking for the best way to do it, you've come to the wrong place. You need to get help, and I urge you to call the National Suicide Prevention Lifeline at 1-800-273-TALK (1-800-273-8255).

How do people take their lives?

In general, if it can cause harm, it has been tried at least once, but most people kill themselves using one of a handful of methods. These include firearms, hanging, drugs, motor vehicle exhaust, and jumping from high places.

What is the method most often used to complete a suicide?

In the United States, more people use firearms than any other means; guns account for more than half of all reported suicides.

Are there differences in countries that have strict gun control laws?

Yes, in nations where private gun ownership is highly restricted, guns are used far less frequently as a means of suicide than in the United States.

After guns, what are the most common means by which people take their lives in the United States?

After guns, the most common means by which people take their lives include asphyxiation (both hanging and suffocation by plastic bag), solid or liquid substances (including prescription medication), gases (other than domestic gas, but including motor vehicle exhaust), jumping from high places, cutting and piercing, drowning, jumping from or lying in front of moving objects, burns/fire, crashing motor vehicles, domestic gas (natural gas used for cooking and heating), and electrocution.

Don't a lot of people kill themselves using natural gas?

No. There's no knowing how many people *attempt* suicide by putting their heads in gas ovens, but only a relative handful of people actually die each year using this method, because the natural gas used in homes is not nearly as lethal as people think.

Where did people get the idea that cooking gas from a kitchen stove was an effective way to die by suicide?

As George Howe Colt explains in *November of the Soul*, "For many years the most popular method of suicide in Great Britain was asphyxiation—sticking one's head in the oven and turning on the gas. After the discovery of oil and natural gas deposits in the North Sea in the [1950s] and [1960s], most English homes converted from coke gas, whose high carbon monoxide content made it highly lethal, to less toxic natural gas. From 1963 to 1978 the number of English suicides by gas dropped from 2,368 to eleven."

Why do people choose the methods they do?

The methods people use to kill themselves depend on a number of things—from their gender, age, occupation, mental state, and degree of desperation to the availability of a particular method, as well as custom and politics. A desire to hurt oneself, to inflict pain on others, or to make a statement may also figure into the chosen method.

How do methods differ by gender?

The most common method of suicide for men is firearms, and men use guns more frequently than women. The most common method of suicide for women is poisoning.

How do methods differ by age?

The older people are, the more lethal the methods they choose. For example, elderly people are more likely to use guns to take their lives than people in their twenties.

Eve Meyer, the executive director of San Francisco Suicide Prevention quoted earlier, explained that elderly people choose more lethal means because they've had "plenty of time to think about what they're doing. They're not impulsive. They have greater access to the means. And they're deadly serious." For more information, see chapter 4 ("Suicide and the Elderly").

Young people, on the other hand, tend to be more impulsive and have less access to lethal means than do their elders. They're less likely to have carefully thought out what they're doing and more likely to use less lethal means to attempt suicide. The result is that they're not as likely as their elders to complete a suicide. For more information, see chapter 3 ("Teen/Youth Suicide").

How do methods differ by occupation?

Some occupations put the means of suicide within relatively easy reach. George Howe Colt cites several examples: Policemen have ready access to firearms, and not surprisingly, most policemen who kill themselves use guns. Among physicians, who are far more likely than policemen to have access to drugs, the majority of those who take their own lives use drugs, whereas dentists are more likely to use anesthetic gas.

How do methods differ by availability?

Beyond differing availability based on occupation, there are other factors that affect the availability of the means of self-destruction. In cities with tall buildings, like Chicago or Boston, or places that have spectacular ravines, such as the campus of Cornell University, more people jump to their deaths than in places with flat terrain and two-story buildings.

People who have easy access to prescription medication are more likely to choose drugs to end their lives than someone who does not. For example, my father was taking a sedative prescribed by a doctor at the VA hospital where he was being treated for mental illness. Over time, he set aside pills, and when he was ready, he took enough to end his life.

What does the impact of an individual's mental state— or psychological motivation—have on his or her choice of method?

I've thought about this a lot since my sister-in-law jumped off a building to her death in 2008. What must she have been thinking? About herself? About those she was leaving behind? Did she choose to die in such a seemingly terrifying way because she simply wanted to be certain that there was no turning back? Or was she mad at herself? Was she trying to send a message of some kind? Of course, only she could know what was on her mind and what drew her to the building from which she jumped. I can say with far more certainty what the psychological impact was on me. Her choice of method compounded the shock of her death, and I feel ill whenever I think about what she did. My father's death by overdose seems serene by comparison.

Over the years psychiatrists and psychologists have come up with all sorts of interpretations for the methods by which people choose to kill themselves. What seems more relevant to me is that the chosen method may reflect how much suicidal individuals want to die, how they feel about themselves, or how they feel about those they're leaving behind.

For example, some people choose a method of suicide, such as a drug overdose, that will spare their families the pain of discovering a body disfigured by a gunshot wound or a hanging. Others choose to use a gun because of its lethality and don't necessarily think about the impact on the person who discovers the body. On the other hand, someone who is very angry at himself may specifically choose a violent method to die. Or someone who is trying to punish, blame, or take revenge on those left behind may choose a method that sends a message. For example, nineteen-year-old William climbed into the back of his family's car one night and shot himself. He and his parents had been feuding for months over his choice of girlfriend, and he'd been forbidden to use the family car to visit her. William didn't leave a suicide note, but his message to his parents—whether intended or not—felt brutally clear.

How does method differ according to custom?

Custom has less bearing today than it did in centuries past. But in various cultures throughout history, as detailed by George Howe Colt in *November of the Soul*, different methods of suicide were customary, whether it was drinking hemlock in ancient Greece or belly-cutting in Japan.

What impact can politics have on a chosen method of suicide?

To make a political point or in an attempt to further a political cause, people have chosen to kill themselves in a variety of ways, from starvation and self-immolation to explosives.

One of the most famous images from the Vietnam War is that of a sixty-six-year-old Buddhist monk, Quang Duc, who took his life in 1963 by setting himself on fire in a busy intersection of what was then the South Vietnamese capital, Saigon (now Ho

Chi Minh City). He was protesting the treatment of Buddhists by the South Vietnamese president, Ngo Dinh Diem.

Suicide bombers and suicide terrorists, unlike Quang Duc, are intent on destroying other people or things along with themselves. Sometimes the goal is political gain, and other times these acts of violence seem designed simply to spread fear.

How does desperation contribute to the choice of method?

The sad fact is that if someone feels desperate enough to die, he will use just about anything he can get his hands on to kill himself. Sometimes desperate methods work, as in the case of a politician I used to work for who grabbed a steak knife from the kitchen silverware drawer and stabbed himself in the heart. Suffering from severe depression over a bribery scandal in which he'd been implicated, he'd already tried to kill himself once. He was in his kitchen on the phone to his psychiatrist when he tried the second time in what I can only imagine was a moment of desperation.

Desperation sometimes results from a poorly planned and unsuccessful suicide attempt by someone who is emotionally distraught. As the author Sherwin Nuland wrote in his landmark book *How We Die*, "In desperation, such people sometimes keep trying until they succeed, resulting in a body being discovered that has been lacerated, shot, and finally poisoned or hanged."

Why do people who want to end their lives jump off bridges?

People jump off bridges because they're there, just as people jump from tall buildings in places where there are tall buildings. But bridges apparently are different. While I find it hard to comprehend, some people see a mystical or romantic appeal in the act of jumping off a bridge.

As Eve Meyer at San Francisco Suicide Prevention explained to me, "They get into the newspaper. By jumping off a bridge, they're able to make a statement that they couldn't make when they were alive. Then somebody else reads it in the newspaper, and they think, 'I can make a statement too!'"

Are some bridges more likely to be chosen for suicide than others?

Yes, in large part because some bridges are easier to jump off of than others. Also, some bridges, like San Francisco's Golden Gate Bridge and the Brooklyn Bridge in New York, are thought to have a greater mystical, romantic, or aesthetic draw than others.

How many people have jumped from the Golden Gate Bridge? Has anyone survived?

Since the Golden Gate Bridge opened in 1937, more than 1,500 people are estimated to have jumped from the bridge, but Eve Meyer believes that the actual number is at least twice as high. She said, "They find a lot more shoes and briefcases than bodies, but they only count the bodies."

According to a 2009 study conducted by the nonprofit Bridge Rail Foundation, which used data from the Marin County coroner's office (the Golden Gate Bridge connects San Francisco with Marin County), the typical person who jumps off the Golden Gate Bridge is a forty-year-old, single, white man. The study covered a fifteen-year period during which 330 deaths were recorded. As reported in the *San Francisco Chronicle*, "the median age of victims was forty, 56.4 percent were never married, 19.4 percent were divorced, and 74.2 percent were male. A total of 80.3 percent were white. Of the 330 victims examined, twenty-seven were students and fifteen worked in sales. Nine were teachers."

Despite the more than 231-foot drop (from the highest point at low tide), cold water, and swift currents, approximately twenty people have survived, although almost all suffered significant injuries.

3

TEEN/YOUTH SUICIDE

When an adult takes his life, it's generally incomprehensible to those left behind. When a young person dies by suicide, the loss of life feels all the more heartbreaking, and we can't help but say, "She had her whole life ahead of her."

The questions in this chapter specifically address suicide and young people, including how to identify the warning signs of someone who may be in trouble and how to get help for those who need it. Some of the information I provide here concerning suicide applies to any age group. But much of the information is specific to people in their teens and early twenties.

Is youth suicide a big problem?

Suicide is the third leading cause of death among people fifteen to twenty-four. (Accidents and homicide are first and second.) Seen in the context of all people who take their lives, however, the rate of suicide among young people is actually slightly lower (10 per 100,000) than for the population in general, and that rate has declined by 30 percent since 1994.

However encouraging the declining suicide rate among young people may be for those who work to prevent suicides, there are still all too many families who find themselves confronted with the loss of a child. Carolyn, a mother of three whose seventeen-year-old son took his life, never imagined that one of her children would die by suicide. She said, "When I was growing up, I didn't know anyone who even *tried* to commit suicide. Maybe it happened and families called it an accident . . . but suicide?"

When Carolyn's son became deeply depressed, suicide was still something that never crossed her mind. "My son had been in a lot of trouble emotionally and into drugs," she explained. "He had also said things to me that should have caught my attention, but I didn't recognize that he was suicidal." Despite seeing a series of counselors, Carolyn's son apparently believed that there was only one solution to his problems and subsequently shot himself. To learn more about the impact on Carolyn of her son's death, please see chapter 7 ("Surviving Suicide").

What's the difference between teen and youth suicide?

It's all in the numbers. Statisticians and researchers divide people into different categories: when we talk about teen suicide, some people are referring to kids ages fifteen to nineteen, and others include those who are fifteen to twenty-four. Then there are also researchers who look specifically at twenty- to twenty-four-year-olds and researchers who study children between the ages of ten and fourteen.

In this chapter, I generally answer questions about "youth suicide," a term that covers people ages fifteen to twenty-four.

What about children ages ten to fourteen?

Suicide among ten- to fourteen-year-old children is comparatively rare: In 2006, 216 children in this age group took their lives. The rate of suicide for children ages ten to fourteen has been stable or declining in recent years.

I thought suicide among fifteen- to twenty-four-year-olds was a growing problem. Isn't it?

With all the headlines over the years about the "epidemic" of teen/youth suicide and about the doubling in the numbers of these suicides since the 1950s, you would think that this was a growing problem, with dramatic increases each year in the number of youth suicides. That's what I thought, but that's not what the statistics tell us. After leveling off between the late 1970s and mid-1990s, the rate of suicide in this age group has, in general, steadily declined.

What accounted for the big increase in the number of reported youth suicides between the 1950s and the late 1970s?

Not every expert on this subject can agree on the reasons for the increase. Here are some of the reasons I came across in my research:

- The increase was a result of the greater willingness of coroners to state the true cause of death. For example, coroners are less likely today to report a suicide from a gunshot wound as an accidental death than they were years ago.
- The rise was caused by a combination of family disintegration and the social and economic dislocation that goes along with it, greater competition for jobs, the increasing availability of guns, and the influence of movies, television programs, and rock music with violent and suicidal themes.
- The increase resulted from a decline in church attendance, coupled with high divorce rates and high unemployment. The theory here is that with fewer young people receiving religious instruction, they're less likely to view suicide as a sinful act, and that without religious faith, they are less able to get through difficult times.

I think all three of these explanations make good points, although to greater or lesser degrees. I'm willing to bet that the changing attitudes of coroners and the increasing availability of guns have been the biggest factors in the increase in reported youth suicides, followed by a combination of family disintegration, declining religious faith, and greater economic challenges. Given all of these very significant factors, I suspect that movies, television, and rock music played a negligible role, if any, in the increase in reported youth suicides.

What accounts for the decrease in recent years of the total number of reported youth suicides?

Without knowing for sure what caused the dramatic increase in the first place, it's difficult to say why the numbers of youth suicides remained stable for years and then declined (with the exception of 2004, when the rate jumped for a single year and then declined again). Certainly no one is going to argue that the decline in the number of reported youth suicides is the result of more stable family life. If anything, family life is more chaotic and unstable today than it was in the late 1970s. And guns are more available than ever.

Maybe the answer is that there's a greater willingness to talk about problems in general, so that clinically depressed and mentally ill young people have more freedom to discuss what's bothering them and are being treated more frequently with both talk therapy and medication. And perhaps targeted suicide prevention programs are making a difference. But whatever the reasons, the good news is that youth suicide is declining. The bad news, of course, is that thousands of young people still kill themselves each year and leave behind many thousands of distraught, grief-stricken, and guilt-ridden family members and friends.

How many young people attempt suicide each year?

For every completed suicide there are between 100 and 200 attempts.

Is there a difference in suicide rates between male and female youth?

Yes. Just like their adult counterparts, far more young men than young women take their lives. But far more young women attempt suicide than do young men.

Is there a difference in the rate of suicide between young people from affluent families and those from economically disadvantaged families?

No. Marsha Alterman, who is the former director of a crisis ho-tline for young people in Charleston, South Carolina, explained that, in this regard, suicide among young people is "an equal opportunity killer."

Why do young people attempt or complete a suicide?

There is generally no one reason why a young man or woman feels compelled to take his or her life. Sometimes you can point to a single event that appears to be the reason—like the breakup of a relationship or an argument with parents—but it's almost always more complicated. Even if there's a clear triggering event, in all likelihood the suicide, or suicide attempt, is something that's been contemplated for quite some time.

Virginia, who is a very attractive, petite, stylish fifty-year-old native Bostonian, tried to kill herself during her third year of college. It was something she had been thinking about for years. She explained, "I'd been depressed since even before college and always spent a lot of time alone in my room, lighting candles and reading a lot of Sylvia Plath and Virginia Woolf. I was sure I'd die before I was twenty-four, like Keats.

"I had this romantic image of myself as a poet and as a doomed person," Virginia said. "At some point [I] got carried away [with the image]. I decided to follow Sylvia Plath's example . . . she killed herself by putting her head in her oven and turning on the gas. No one told me that it was a different kind of gas in her day and that it was very difficult to kill yourself with the gas we use now."

Before her suicide attempt, Virginia found herself sinking into a deeper and deeper depression, and she spent increasing amounts of time alone. She continued her account of this time in her life: "I look back now and can see that I really withdrew from my friends. I had no one to talk to, except for my boyfriend, and when he decided to end our relationship because I didn't have the kind of background his parents would approve of, that just pushed me over the edge." Virginia further describes her suicide attempt and its aftermath in chapter 5 ("Attempted Suicide").

Everyone's experience is different, so trying to understand why a young person attempts or completes a suicide is almost impossible, especially when the attempt leads to death and the young person takes his reasons with him. But in the broadest sense, the young people who try to kill themselves are those who are unable to cope with life and become overwhelmed. They lose hope and, seeing no way out of their despair, feel that taking their lives is their only option.

For Colin, who was a senior at a midwestern university when I first spoke with him, his suicide attempt at fifteen had a lot to do with the pressure he felt from his parents to be a straight-A student. "I used to fantasize about killing myself as a way of getting back at them," he said. "But what finally made me do it for real was when I got a D on my math exam in tenth grade. I got home from school, and I went to my mother's medicine cabinet and swallowed a bunch of different pills."

Grades were a sore subject around Colin's house. "My parents never gave me any slack," he explained. "They're both really smart academically, but I always had to work extra hard just to keep a B average." A year before the attempt, Colin's parents had hired a tutor. "It didn't help raise much except their expectations of me," Colin recalled. "Whenever I came home with my report card, they yelled at me or punished me for every grade below a B. After a while, I felt like I was nothing. And then I got that D, and I thought my parents were going to kill me, so I figured I'd save them the trouble and do it myself."

The following is a list of general reasons why young people attempt to take their lives. Those who follow through on suicidal thoughts usually have several things going on in their lives at the same time. Again, it's the perfect storm at the worst possible time.

- Depression or some other mental illness, which may lead to feelings of helplessness and hopelessness and ultimately thoughts of suicide
- The breakup of a relationship or conflicts with parents
- Feeling isolated or feeling different

- An impulsive reaction to a short-term disappoint-
  ment—for example, a high-achieving student re-
  ceiving a low grade (Unlike adults, young people
  don't have the experience to know that not every
  crisis or defeat is permanent.)
- A sense of personal worthlessness
- Failure or fear of failure
- Problems with drug or alcohol abuse
- An unwanted pregnancy
- Parental divorce or family instability
- Sexual orientation conflicts and gender confusion
- Bullying
- Reports of other suicides
- A history of suicide in the family, which can lead
  a young person to think of suicide as a reasonable
  way of coping with problems (A history of suicide in
  the family may also indicate a history of depression,
  which can lead to suicide.)

Which young people are most at risk of taking their lives?

Odds are that an emotionally stable young woman from a happy
intact home who is doing reasonably well in school is unlikely to
have serious suicidal thoughts. However, a young man who suffers from depression or another mental illness, comes from a chaotic single-parent household, has few friends, and has attempted
suicide before is at great risk of completing a suicide.

Other major risk factors include everything from an inabil-
ity to discuss problems with parents to a prior history of abuse
(whether physical or emotional), the recent breakup of a relationship, problems with drugs, or the death of a family member.

Are there warning signs?

In retrospect, there are almost always warning signs that you can
identify. In advance of a suicide attempt or a suicide, it's much
harder to connect the dots than after, especially since so many of

the dots are the kinds of things that with most teens don't necessarily add up to a suicidal kid.

After her son's suicide, Carolyn read everything she could about suicide and discovered that there had been warning signs she missed. Determined that this would never happen to her other children, she kept a close eye on them for any signs of trouble. She explained, "I just about drove them crazy, because a lot of the signs are the kinds of things you might expect from any young person, suicidal or not—from problems with school to bad moods."

Not every moody or depressed young adult is suicidal. Nor is every high school student who suddenly starts getting bad grades necessarily thinking about ending his life. But it's important to pay close attention to moody or depressed young people and to watch out for these warning signs:

- Talking about wanting to die or making suicidal threats
- Problems in school, at work, or with the police
- Withdrawal from friends or family
- A sudden change in personality or behavior
- Giving things away, especially prized possessions
- A significant change in sleep patterns or eating habits
- A sudden lack of energy or enthusiasm for friends and activities
- More aggressive and impulsive behavior (such as violent outbursts)
- A history of physical or mental illness
- Running away
- An unwanted pregnancy
- Drug or alcohol abuse
- Rejection by a boyfriend or girlfriend
- The recent suicide of a friend or relative
- A sudden and extreme neglect of appearance
- An obsession with songs, poems, books, movies, or computer games with suicidal themes
- Previous suicide attempt(s)

This list is obviously very broad, and the vast majority of teenagers and young people who exhibit almost any of these behaviors—alone or in various combinations—don't attempt or complete a suicide. But some do, and because of that possibility it's prudent to pay attention, listen, and, if necessary, get help.

How much of a factor is drug and alcohol use?

Alcohol is an especially is a significant factor. More than half of all adolescent suicides and suicide attempts are associated with alcohol. In other words, more than half the young people who attempt or complete a suicide have been drinking immediately prior.

How much of a factor is prescription medication?

It's very important to be aware that many prescription medications have side effects that include depression, impulsive behavior, and suicidal thinking, as well as other side effects that can put a young person at risk of suicide. And some of these medications are the very drugs that are used to treat depression. So it's key to pay close attention to a child who is on prescription medication where there is the potential for such side effects and to consult a doctor immediately if you notice a negative change in your child's affect or your child complains of feeling depressed or talks about having suicidal feelings.

Does rock, heavy metal, or rap music lead teenagers to kill themselves?

No music of any kind leads teenagers to end their lives. But if your child or friend is obsessed with songs that deal with suicide and death, you have reason to be concerned, because this could mean that he or she is having thoughts of suicide.

How much of a factor is availability of firearms?

Readily available firearms can all too easily transform an adolescent cry for help into a final and fatal act of desperation. For young people especially, whose suicidal feelings may be sudden and short-lived, guns provide a very permanent solution to temporary problems.

A *Newsweek* article about teen suicide, that followed the 1994 death of the rock star Kurt Cobain (who was best known as the lead singer, guitarist, and songwriter for the grunge band Nirvana), made note of a study comparing adolescent suicide victims who had no apparent mental disorders with kids who didn't kill themselves. The study found only one difference between the two groups: a loaded gun in the house. If you keep a gun in the house, make sure that it is safely secured under lock and key.

Can conflicts concerning sexual orientation and gender identity contribute to a teen's suicide?

Young people who are wrestling with sexual orientation and gender identity issues face a range of problems that, combined with the usual challenges of growing up, increase their risk of suicide. Sometimes the conflict is over religious beliefs or societal condemnation. At other times the conflicts involve parents or other family members who reject or are hostile to their gay, lesbian, or transgender child or a child who does not meet their gender expectations.

These young people may experience bullying and physical abuse from classmates at school. And they may have no place to turn for help. So they suffer in relative isolation, unable to share with anyone what they're going through.

When Bonnie was fifteen, she told her parents that she was gay. Her parents had gay friends, and her mother was a psychologist, so Bonnie knew they weren't going to throw her out of the house and felt fairly certain that they would be accepting and even supportive. She said, "It was making me crazy, hiding it from them, because we talked about everything. I'm an only child, so I always got a lot of attention. What finally pushed me to tell them was that I had a crush on one of my classmates and I needed to talk to someone about it, so I decided to tell my parents about it one evening over dinner."

Bonnie's parents gave no hint of their shock as she described her crush on another girl and told them she was gay; dinner proceeded without anyone skipping a beat. She recalled, "My parents did a good job of listening and, I think, had pretty good advice about how to handle my crush. But as we were doing the dishes, my mother calmly explained to me how learning about the fact I was a lesbian was like experiencing a death for them and that they'd need some time to get used to it. I was totally stunned."

Looking back, Bonnie now knows that her mother was trying to explain her own feelings about what she'd just learned, but that wasn't the way Bonnie heard it at the time. She said, "I found out later that this was my mother's way of trying to let me know that they were having a hard time with this but that they still loved me. The way I heard it, they were telling me that I was dead to them. I was so upset and felt so rejected that I didn't know what to do."

That night, after her parents had gone to sleep, Bonnie decided to "punish" her parents. "I decided to teach them a lesson and show them what it would be like for me to be really dead," she said. "I felt like a robot as I went downstairs to the kitchen and got my mother's favorite paring knife, sat down at the kitchen table and started cutting. Thank God my mother heard me in the kitchen, because I hadn't cut very deep by the time she walked in. Still, I was bleeding and my parents rushed me off to the emergency room."

After a night in the hospital, Bonnie and her parents began family therapy, and after several sessions Bonnie was able to recognize that her parents did not wish her dead, loved her as much as they had loved her before, and would have been devastated if she had died. Now in her thirties and in a stable, long-term relationship, Bonnie finds it hard to believe that she ever wanted to end her life. She told me, "I've never come close to making an attempt again, and it's a little hard to imagine that I didn't want to live. At the time there were no resources, like the Trevor Project, for gay kids like me who were in crisis. I'm not sure I would have thought to call given the state I was in, but for a gay teenager today it's good to know that there's a place they can turn to for help."

For information about the toll-free Trevor Helpline, please see the appendix.

Is it true that one-third of all young people who die by suicide are gay or lesbian?

This is a number that's been tossed around so often that it's sometimes quoted as fact. But it's not. Various studies over the years have shown that gay and lesbian young people (as well as adults) are at a higher risk of suicide, but there is no conclusive evidence that as many as one-third of all the young people who take their lives or attempt suicide are gay or lesbian.

Two comparatively recent studies found the following: A 2006 Youth Risk Survey conducted by the state of Massachusetts found that lesbian, gay, bisexual, transgender, and questioning youth (LGBTQ) are up to four times more likely to attempt suicide than straight young people. And a San Francisco State University Chavez Center Institute report published in 2007 found that LGBTQ young people who come from a rejecting family are up to nine times more likely to attempt suicide than their straight peers.

Does publicity about a youth suicide—or suicides—lead others to do the same?

For some young people who are already depressed and inclined to be self-destructive, learning about the suicide of someone whose situation they perceive to be like their own may provoke them to do what they've already imagined doing.

This is not a new issue. Researchers on the subject often cite the case of an eighteenth-century romantic novel that was blamed for leading impressionable young people to kill themselves. The book, Johann Wolfgang von Goethe's *The Sorrows of Young Werther*, published in 1774, tells the story of an artistic young man who shoots himself. Various European governments responded by banning the sale of the book or forbidding its publication.

We can't pretend that youth suicide doesn't happen. And when it happens, the public needs to be made aware of it, along with information that can help prevent other suicides. Fortunately, many news organizations report these tragedies responsibly. But others don't, and screaming headlines and sensationalistic television news anchors don't help anyone and may just help push one more depressed and alienated teen to take his life.

What is a suicide cluster?

When one suicide triggers others over a period of days or weeks, this is called a suicide cluster. Sometimes the phrase "copycat suicide" is also used in these circumstances. Suicide clusters and copycat suicides most often, but not always, involve youth.

When the rock singer Kurt Cobain took his life in 1994, there was much speculation in the media as to whether his death would lead to a series of copycat suicides among young Cobain fans. It never happened. In writing about the fallout from Cobain's suicide, *Newsweek* noted that "while there was one apparent copycat suicide, by a twenty-eight-year-old man who attended the candlelight vigil and then went home and shot himself, most of Cobain's fans seem to have mourned him without endorsing his suicide."

What should you do if you think a young friend or your child is suicidal?

What you should do depends on the circumstances, but two things are key: listen and get help.

The first thing you need to do is listen carefully, because it's often not clear when someone is having suicidal feelings or thoughts. Even if your friend or child is in fact talking about feeling suicidal, he or she may express this in a way that's ambiguous, only hinting at suicide. For example, he may talk about wanting to "disappear" or not wanting to "go on" or feeling like "giving up." If you're not sure what you're hearing, you can ask, "Have you been thinking about hurting yourself?" Or you can be more direct and ask, "Have you been thinking about suicide?" If the answer is yes, ask why and then listen.

It may be tempting to dismiss your friend or child's thoughts and feelings by telling her that she's just being foolish or that things will be okay tomorrow. Don't do it, because that response will probably bring an end to the conversation and you won't have the chance to really find out what's going on. And if you don't know what's going on, you won't have the chance to help.

Helping may involve nothing more than offering to go with your friend or child to a school guidance counselor to talk about how he's feeling. If your friend or child won't go, you should take your concerns to someone you know who will show an interest in this person—a guidance counselor, clergy person, or family member.

Even if the suicidal young person has sworn you to secrecy, this is one case where it's okay to break your promise and get help. It's better to have a friend who is mad at you than one who is dead.

If your friend or child seems to be in imminent danger of hurting himself, call for emergency help *immediately*. It may feel like you're overreacting, or it may feel embarrassing, but it's the right thing to do.

What is being done to prevent teen/youth suicide?

Plenty, from high school programs designed specifically to reduce teen/youth suicide to special training for school counselors and teachers so that they can recognize students who are potentially suicidal.

For example, the American Foundation for Suicide Prevention helped fund a film about teen depression called *More Than Sad*, which is designed to help adolescents recognize the signs of depression—a major contributing factor to suicide—in themselves and others. For more information about this film, please see the appendix. And for more on the subject of suicide prevention, see chapter 6 ("Prevention and Treatment").

How do people react to the suicide of a teenager?

Suicide almost always leaves family and friends devastated and bewildered. When the person who takes his life is young, the devastation can be more extreme and the bewilderment more overwhelming. How, we wonder, could someone whose whole adult life was ahead of him end it before it had even begun?

For more on this subject, see chapter 7 ("Surviving Suicide").

4

SUICIDE AND THE ELDERLY

While it's perfectly natural for elderly people to speak about the end of life, it is not in the natural course of things for elderly people to kill themselves. Yet many elderly people, men in particular, find themselves on a path to self-destruction that proves ever more compelling as the years pass.

In this chapter, I've included all the basic questions about suicide and the elderly to give you a sense of who is most at risk, what warning signs to watch out for, and what you can do to help an elderly loved one or friend who appears to be in danger of taking his or her life.

What exactly do you consider elderly?

Although I personally don't consider age sixty-five to be the dividing line between those who are elderly and those who are not, that's how the statistics are calculated, and someone chose to call this group "elderly." So for the purposes of this chapter, when I refer to "the elderly," I'm referring to those people who are sixty-five years of age and older.

How big a problem is suicide among the elderly?

While 12.4 percent of the population is elderly, they account for about 16 percent of all people who take their lives.

How many elderly people attempt suicide each year?

Various experts estimate that among the elderly there are four attempts for every completed suicide. By comparison, for young people there are 100 to 200 attempts for every completion.

Why are elderly people more likely to complete a suicide than people from other age groups?

Elderly people are more likely to complete a suicide than those under sixty-five because when they decide to take their lives, they're very serious about it. Generally, these are not people making a cry for help or attempting to get back at a boyfriend or girlfriend, which is why they choose more lethal methods. Also, many older people live alone, so even if their suicide attempt is a cry for help, they're far less likely to be found in time to be saved.

What lethal methods are the elderly likely to use?

The elderly are more likely to use firearms, although, as with the general population, elderly men are more likely than elderly women to use guns. Elderly women are more likely to use pills or poisons. Elderly people are also more likely to use self-starvation as a method of ending their lives, or they may choose to ignore a doctor's advice or stop taking essential medication, knowing that this is likely to kill them.

When Jeanne's father was in his late sixties, he was told by his doctor that he absolutely had to quit smoking, lose weight, and restrict his intake of sugar. "If he didn't," Jeanne said, "the doctor warned him that he was in grave danger."

Jeanne's father, who never liked doing what anyone told him to do, did just the opposite of what his doctor instructed and even stopped taking his blood pressure medication. "We had screaming arguments over what he was doing," Jeanne recalled. "I told him he was committing suicide, but he said life wasn't worth living if he couldn't smoke and couldn't eat what he wanted. What got me was that he didn't care that he was robbing his daughter of her only surviving parent and his grandchildren of their only grandfather. I thought he was being incredibly selfish, but I couldn't get through to him. Nobody could."

Jeanne's father died eleven months later. "The death certificate said it was a stroke," she explained, "but I thought it should have said 'suicide.'"

Why do elderly people attempt or complete a suicide?

Elderly people take their lives for many of the same reasons younger people do, but their reasons more frequently also include ill health, chronic pain, fear of burdening children, economic problems, the death of a spouse, and loneliness. All of these factors can contribute to depression as well, or a loss of hope.

As with all people, when the elderly decide to take their own lives, most often there isn't one thing that you can point to as *the* reason. There may be one reason you can cite as the trigger, but once you take a closer look, you're likely to find other contributing factors.

For Ruth, a once vigorous and incredibly independent woman who was in her eighties at the time of her suicide attempt, a severe back injury was the final straw. "Since my husband died," she explained, "walking and ballroom dancing were the two things that saved me." Even during the deep depression that followed her husband's death, Ruth, who took great pride in her physical stamina, still walked three miles every day, and after a year of mourning she returned to ballroom dancing. "It wouldn't have been right to go any sooner," she told me.

Until her back injury, Ruth had always enjoyed good health. "I'd taken good care of myself, watched my diet, took vitamins, so I never expected to have problems," she said. Three crushed vertebrae, the result of a fall and advanced osteoporosis, left Ruth in great pain and unable to dance at all or walk more than a few blocks at a time. "I didn't want to see anyone or talk to anyone," Ruth said. "I stopped answering the phone. I had friends, but I shut them out. I was too embarrassed for them to see me in my condition. If I couldn't be myself anymore, I just wanted to die, and I would have if I'd gotten my way."

Ruth decided to take matters into her own hands. One evening, after straightening her apartment and putting on a fresh nightgown, she swallowed a bottle of painkillers and washed it all down with a half-bottle of scotch. "Since I never drank, I assumed it would help speed things up," she said. But Ruth's plan was thwarted when a neighbor became concerned after she knocked on Ruth's door and didn't get an answer. She called the building's superintendent, and they found Ruth on her sofa, unconscious, but still breathing.

"I was so angry when I woke up in the hospital," Ruth recalled. A week in the hospital followed by months of counseling, combined with antidepressant medication, got Ruth back on her feet. She did not attempt suicide again, although she remained reclusive until her death from natural causes three years later.

Are there differences in the suicide rate between the "young" elderly and the "old" elderly?

Yes. As the elderly grow older, their overall rate of suicide increases. But this number is misleading, because male suicide after age sixty-five increases steadily, while female suicide generally declines after peaking in middle age (forty-five to forty-nine).

Is suicide among the elderly a growing problem?

The rate of suicide for the elderly peaked in 1987 and has declined since, but at one time suicide among the elderly was a far greater problem. In 1933, for example, the suicide rate among the elderly was more than two times what it is today.

What accounts for the overall decrease since the 1930s?

No one really knows for sure, but among the possible reasons are the introduction since the 1930s of Social Security, Medicare, and various other government programs for the elderly. As difficult as life can be for the elderly, it is far better today than it was decades ago.

Is there a difference in suicide rates between male and female elderly people?

There's an enormous difference in the rate of suicide between men and women in general. It's even greater among the elderly, and that difference increases with age.

After age sixty-five, the rate of suicide for women decreases gradually to fewer than 5 per 100,000 for those eighty-five years of age and older. But for elderly men the rate of suicide increases significantly over the years, to nearly 45 per 100,000 for those eighty-five years of age and older.

Does marital status make a difference in the rates of elderly suicide?

Marital status among the elderly has an enormous impact. Married people have the lowest risk of suicide, and divorced and widowed people have the highest rates of suicide. Those who were never married fall in between the two groups.

When my Grandma Ethel died in 1973, I had firsthand experience with the impact that such a loss could have on a spouse. Within weeks of Grandma's death, Grandpa threatened to kill himself. Grandma and Grandpa had been deeply devoted to one another throughout their marriage, especially in their later years as Grandpa's memory began to fail. For much of their married life, they ran a gift shop in Brooklyn's Bay Ridge neighborhood and were rarely apart for more than a few minutes.

Because Grandpa needed twenty-four-hour care, after Grandma's death my mother moved him into a nursing home. The first three times we went to visit him, Grandpa asked where Grandma was, and my mother explained that she had died. Each time he greeted the news with shock, grief, and threats that he was going to kill himself. Although we felt confident that at the nursing home he wasn't a real danger to himself, his response was still heartbreaking.

After the third visit my mother decided to use Grandpa's compromised memory to spare him the news of Grandma's death. When he asked where Grandma was, she simply said that Ethel would be arriving shortly. He accepted that explanation and then promptly forgot that he had ever asked. Believing that his beloved wife was still alive, Grandpa never again threatened to kill himself.

Why do elderly white men have the highest rate of suicide?

In general, elderly white men have the furthest to fall both economically and socially as they age. They are also less likely to have a strong support network, and they are far less likely to ask for help.

Why do elderly African American women have a very low rate of suicide?

According to what I've read, elderly African American women have a very low rate of suicide, especially in comparison to white men, because they're more likely to have been tempered by a lifetime of coping with adversity. Their status in society does not decline with age. And they're far more likely to have a strong support network, including extensive family and community ties.

How can you tell if an elderly person is at risk for suicide? Are there warning signs?

For anyone with even a little experience with elderly suicide, it was obvious that Ruth, whom I wrote about in an earlier question, was in danger of killing herself in the months following her incapacitating accident. She withdrew from her friends. She met with an attorney to get her will updated. And she gave away favorite possessions to her niece and a couple of her young friends.

But for those close to her, everything Ruth did made perfect sense in the context of what was going on in her life and the kind of person she was. She had every reason to be depressed over her circumstances. And given how practical she'd always been, there was nothing really suspicious about her wanting to have her will in order. Giving away some of her favorite possessions should have been the tip-off, but even that didn't raise any eyebrows, because it seemed like a normal thing to do at her age. Of course, everything Ruth did also made perfect sense for someone who was planning to take her life.

In addition to the signs to watch out for in people of any age who may be suicidal, it is important to pay special attention to the following signs in the elderly:

- Talking of wanting to die
- A reduced interest in favorite activities and hobbies
- Depression
- Giving away treasured possessions
- Reworking or preparing a will
- Acquiring the means (for example, buying a gun or saving medication)

Is loneliness a big risk factor?

Yes. Loneliness and the lack of a social network are factors in suicide in general, but for older people, who often have a smaller or nonexistent social network because of the deaths of their peers, these are factors that contribute even more to suicidal feelings.

Which elderly people are most at risk of taking their lives?

Broadly speaking, elderly people who are most at risk are older white men who have debilitating medical conditions, who suffer from depression, who are widowed, divorced, or single, who lack strong religious faith, and who also lack a supportive social network. Of course, most people who fit this profile never attempt suicide, but those who do are most at risk.

John, a retired scientist, was in his early eighties when he took his life. In retrospect, his daughter Karen could see that her dad generally fit the profile of someone who was in danger. He was a widower, and he "never really found meaning in his life after his wife died," she explained. "They were exceptionally close and dependent on each other. But he was living in my sister's backyard—in an in-law house—so he wasn't completely isolated."

Karen's father was in almost perfect health, but what Karen wishes she had considered was how worried her father was about his failing memory. "After his wife died, he was concerned about his short-term memory loss," she said. "So at seventy-nine, being a scientist, he commissioned a battery of neurological tests. After he died, I found the report and read it, and the results were all over the map. He was in the ninety-ninth percentile in IQ and first percentile in his ability to navigate new situations. In the years before he died, he complained a lot that he was really concerned about his memory, didn't know what to do about it, and that there was no solution. I had personal experiences with this. He came to pick me up at the airport once and couldn't remember where he parked the car, and it was humiliating for him. We walked through the entire lot before he found the car."

Karen's father's suicide came as a complete shock. She recalled, "It was a really terrible moment. It never occurred to me in a million years that he would do this. It should have, given his kind of rationality. He wasn't going to go to a nursing home. And I hadn't considered that for my father losing his mind was every bit as terrible as terminal cancer, and he wanted to end his life before he was 'a drooling idiot,' as he put it in his suicide note."

Are family and friends more likely to ignore suicidal signs in an elderly person?

Yes. Most people don't think there's anything exceptional about an old person who talks about wanting to die, is depressed, or makes an effort to tie up loose ends. Depending on the circumstances, many of us just think of it as a normal response to old age.

Is it harder for doctors to detect when an elderly person is suicidal?

The elderly are less likely than younger people to talk about their problems, so unless the doctor is a gerontologist—specifically trained to work with the elderly—yes, it's more difficult for them to detect when an elderly person is suicidal. In addition, a doctor who is not trained to work with older people is more likely to dismiss an elderly patient's depression or talk of wanting to die as simply symptomatic of old age.

How common is it for elderly couples to kill themselves? Why do they do it?

It happens only a relatively few times each year, but these kinds of suicides—murder-suicides or dual suicides—are generally so heartbreaking that we're sure to hear about them.

Typically what happens is that an elderly couple faced with ill health decides to die together. Or a husband who has been taking care of his ailing wife (or vice versa) becomes ill himself and, fearing that he won't be able to take care of his wife, decides to kill her and himself.

One story I came across was reported by the Associated Press in 1983. Julia and Cecil Saunders of North Fort Myers, Florida, were eighty-one and eighty-five, respectively, and had been married for sixty years. Until Mrs. Saunders was placed in a nursing home in early 1983, they were rarely apart.

The AP reported: "Mrs. Saunders's dimming eyesight, heart congestion and a stroke had driven her husband to place her in a nursing home. . . . But she became hysterical over what she thought was poor care there, and Mr. Saunders took her home."

Three weeks later, they laid out the clothes they planned to be buried in, had lunch, and "drove to a rural corner of Lee County and parked. As cows grazed in the summer heat, Cecil Saunders shot his wife. . . . and turned the gun on himself."

The note they left read:

Dear children,

This we know will be a terrible shock and embarrassment. But as we see it, it is one solution to the problem of growing old. We greatly appreciate your willingness to try to take care of us.

After being married for sixty years, it only makes sense for us to leave this world together because we loved each other so much.

Don't grieve because we had a very good life and saw our two children turn out to be such fine persons.

Love,
Mother and
Father

What should you do if you think an elderly person is suicidal?

In a caring and concerned manner ask, "Have you been having suicidal thoughts?" Some people think that by asking a person if he or she is suicidal they will either encourage the act or plant the idea. This is a myth. According to Dr. Daniel Plotkin, a Los Angeles geriatric psychiatrist who helped me with several of the previous questions, "When it's brought up, it's a relief to the person contemplating suicide. It doesn't push them over the edge."

The next step after talking about it is to get help. If the danger doesn't appear imminent, then there's time to suggest that your friend or family member talk to his primary care physician. If he refuses, talk to the physician yourself and ask what you should do next.

You can also suggest that the person see a psychologist or psychiatrist, but then you may get into the problem of perceptions. Many older people have the idea that only crazy people go to psychologists or psychiatrists. Dr. Plotkin has run into this problem on more than one occasion when family members come to him asking how they can get their elderly relative to agree to see him. He explained, "I tell them to tell their relative that I'm a geriatric specialist. That way the relative won't think anyone is telling them they're crazy."

Unfortunately, there isn't always time to arrange for a visit with a doctor. If the danger seems imminent, call a crisis hotline or 911—and don't leave your friend or loved one alone.

What can be done to help an elderly person who is suicidal?

Elderly people who are suicidal benefit from the same standard treatments as those in any other age group, from antidepressant medication to group therapy. For more information on treatment, see chapter 6 ("Prevention and Treatment").

What can be done to reduce suicide among the elderly?

Some things are very practical and doable, like educating the public about the problem of elderly suicide. We should all know what to look out for. And without question, doctors and mental health professionals need to be better trained to recognize and treat elderly people who are suicidal.

Then there are those things that are less practical and more challenging, like changing our society so that older people feel more valued and have more opportunities to play a meaningful role in their communities. Changes like these would go a long way toward reducing the loneliness and hopelessness that contribute to the depression that so many older people experience.

Chapter

5

ATTEMPTED SUICIDE

An attempted suicide is a shocking experience for all concerned—including the person who makes the attempt and the family and friends who must try to make sense of what's happened. The hope, of course, is that the person who has made the attempt can be helped back from the brink so that he or she never tries again and goes on to live a full and satisfying life.

The questions and answers that I've included in this chapter are meant to help those who have attempted suicide better understand themselves. They are also meant to help those who have lived through the attempted suicide of a loved one understand what that person was experiencing and how they can be of assistance in the aftermath.

Who attempts suicide?

Hundreds of thousands of people attempt suicide each year. They come from all walks of life, all age groups, and all ethnic and racial groups. However, those who attempt suicide and live—as opposed to those who complete a suicide—are far more likely to be women than men. They're also far more likely to be young.

Much like the people who are more likely to complete a suicide, those who attempt suicide tend to be isolated, to suffer from some kind of mental illness such as depression or schizophrenia, and to have drug or alcohol problems. Widows and widowers are more likely to attempt suicide than coupled people, white people are more likely to do so than other racial groups, and soldiers are more likely than secretaries.

Are all suicide attempts the same?
Does everyone who attempts suicide want to die?

Not all attempts are the same. Some people who attempt suicide want very much to die and choose the most lethal means available. Plenty of other people aren't nearly so determined and choose methods that are less likely to result in death.

In his book *Suicide: The Forever Decision*, Paul Quinnett explains that counselors generally put suicide in three distinct categories: "First-degree suicide attempts are planned, deliberate, premeditated acts involving the most lethal means. Second-degree attempts are more impulsive, unplanned, and not as well thought out. Third-degree attempts are those in which the person deliberately puts himself in a dangerous situation in which he may die, but his intent is not so clear."

For example, someone walking through traffic on a busy street, hoping to be struck dead, would be making a third-degree attempt. Someone impulsively swallowing a bottle of sleeping pills after an argument with a girlfriend would be making a second-degree attempt. An elderly man shooting himself after getting all his affairs in order and writing farewell notes to each of his children would be making a first-degree attempt.

A first-degree attempt is more likely to result in death, but there are plenty of people who are very ambivalent about wanting to die, make a third-degree attempt, and wind up dead. And there are people who are very clear about wanting to die, make a first-degree attempt, and survive.

John had no idea what was going through his brother Brian's mind when Brian walked into his closed four-car garage, got into his truck, cranked up the Grateful Dead, and turned on the engine. John, who was fifty-three at the time of his brother's suicide and living in New York City, is the oldest of three brothers. Brian, who was eight years his junior, lived in California.

While Brian was the most financially successful of the three, John recalled that Brian had telephoned him "six weeks previously and asked for $2,000. It didn't register with me, 'Why is he asking for such a small amount?' I sent him the money but had no idea he was in such difficult circumstances."

Only after Brian's death did John learn that Brian had become a crack addict, that his house was in foreclosure, that three of his four cars had been repossessed, and that when Brian lost his job, "he went into a rage and went out to the parking lot and stomped on his boss's Mercedes."

It was also after Brian's death that John learned that his brother had had second thoughts about killing himself. John explained: "He changed his mind at the end, which is what the sheriff's office told me. He got out of the truck, fell, hit his head, and was bleeding. Somehow he got himself to the front door, turned the knob, but couldn't get into the house. They found his body on the ground, against the door. I really wish they hadn't told me any of that."

Why do people attempt suicide?

People attempt suicide for a variety of reasons, from extreme depression to misdirected anger.

Anger had a lot to do with Beverly's first suicide attempt. "I feel like it was a temper tantrum," she explained. "I had a friend named Renee who I was in love with, although I didn't know that at the time. We hung out together. She was gorgeous. We were both unhappy and neurotic. We seemed like a good fit for each other. She was probably the prettiest girl I ever knew, and the fact she was interested in me as a friend meant a lot. I was smitten with her."

Then one weekend when Beverly was staying overnight with her friend, something happened that changed the course of their friendship. Beverly recalled, "We were in bed together at her parents' place, and I woke up, and I might have tried to kiss her, and it freaked her out and it freaked me out. It was devastating, but we stayed friends. It was around this same time that I introduced her to my brother, and when she and my brother started becoming friendly, I was so jealous of their friendship that I took twenty pills, probably an over-the-counter thing. At the time I didn't think of it as wanting to get attention, but I was trying to get attention."

What are people thinking when they attempt suicide?

Some people have very clear thoughts, some are confused, irrational, or angry, and others are in a trancelike state in which they aren't thinking about anything other than doing what they have to do in order to end their lives.

Peter was in his midforties when he climbed over the railing of his Chicago high-rise apartment terrace. Following months during which he had sunk into a deeper and deeper depression, he found himself staring fourteen stories down to the street below. "To this day, I can't remember what happened in the days leading up to that moment," he said, "except that I was in such pain that I wanted my life to be over. I can't even say that I was thinking anything when I climbed back over the rail to safety. I was on total autopilot, with my self-destructive feelings doing battle with my will to live."

Ruth, who talked about her suicide attempt in chapter 4, had very clear thoughts as she swallowed the pills that she hoped would end her life. "I felt so relieved that it was going to be over," she recalled. "I'd lived long enough. I'd had a good life. And now I was miserable. I didn't see any reason why I should have to go on."

Beverly survived her first suicide attempt without getting her stomach pumped or anyone finding out. Beverly said, "I don't think I let anyone know what I did. I was in such agony. My whole life was agony at that time. I was a tortured soul: depressed, angry, very self-destructive. It's funny, I had this part of me that was very social. People always liked me. I was popular and pretty. But underneath, it didn't match. I was constantly beating myself up. I think a therapist at that point would have helped because I was sinking."

The feeling that Beverly vividly remembered having in the days and hours leading up to her second suicide attempt—again with pills—was extreme emotional pain and the sense that she was trapped and her only way out was death. "Killing myself was just to stop the pain," Beverly said. "I had just had enough. I felt like I was constantly beating myself up and that I was trapped in this world with my mom and there was no way to get away from her. Between her and me I didn't have any choice but to end my life."

Beverly survived her second attempt, but this time she wasn't able to keep secret what she'd done. Beverly's parents returned home early from an evening out after calling to check on her and deciding that something in her voice "wasn't right." She said, "My mother and I were so attached that she could sense anything wrong in my voice, so I'm pretty sure that I signaled to her in the tone of my voice that she should come home. I really believe that if I had absolutely positively wanted to die that night I would have."

Beverly has only a vague memory of talking to her parents by phone, but the next thing she recalls in any detail is "waking up for a minute while someone was banging on my chest—I guess they were pumping my stomach—and then falling back to sleep and then waking up in Coney Island Hospital. I remember the fluorescent lights. I was in a hallway. My hair was caked in vomit. I had thrown up at some point. They weren't supposed to let me out of the hospital without a psychiatric evaluation. I talked with the psychiatrist, and he asked if I was depressed. I said I was depressed. He asked if I would do this again. I said no. And that was it, and they sent me home." Beverly never tried to kill herself again, but she struggled with paralyzing depression for more than a decade before fully recovering. As Beverly explained to me, her recovery was the result of a combination of extensive psychiatric treatments and "also finding a spiritual connection and coming out to myself as a lesbian."

To meet Beverly today, now in her early sixties and with eyes that sparkle, you would never guess the struggle to live that she faced as a young woman. Like many of the people I interviewed who had attempted suicide, she seemed incredibly alive, even effervescent. Beverly has an infectious sense of humor and a life force that I find compelling. The fact that she was able to survive her early-life depression and suicide attempts should inspire anyone faced with self-destructive feelings; Beverly's experience shows that it's possible to recover and go on to a life filled with the full range of human emotions, including joyful enthusiasm for all of life's wonders. Beverly added, "You *can* survive and reclaim your life—you just have to fight like hell and never give up."

What should you do if you've just attempted suicide?

Get help. If you've injured yourself or taken an overdose, you need to get emergency medical attention. Even if you haven't physically harmed yourself, you still need to get help. You can start by calling a close friend, a relative, or your doctor and telling that person what you've done. If you're afraid to tell anyone you know, call a suicide/crisis helpline. If you think you're still in imminent danger of harming yourself, make sure you aren't alone or get yourself to a hospital emergency room.

Follow-up care with someone who has experience dealing with suicidal patients is critical. You and those around you may prefer to pretend that your suicide attempt never happened, which is a natural impulse, especially since all involved may feel embarrassed and confused. But ignoring the fact of your attempted suicide and not seeking help will just increase the risk that you'll try again. I can't say it often enough: get help!

What should you do if someone you know has just attempted suicide?

The immediate goal in the aftermath of a suicide attempt is to keep your friend or loved one alive and to make certain that he doesn't try to do it again.

What you do depends, of course, on the circumstances, but if the person has inflicted physical harm on himself, administer first aid and call for emergency help. For a more complete answer to this question, see chapter 6 ("Prevention and Treatment").

What is it like for someone to find a person who has attempted suicide?

Every circumstance is different, of course, but as you might imagine, finding a friend or loved one who has just attempted suicide can be a shocking and terrifying experience, especially for a young person. That was Luke's experience when he was fourteen years old. Now in his midfifties and retired from a career in the financial industry, Luke vividly recalls one of several suicide attempts made by his severely depressed mother. He told me: "I was getting ready to go to school, and I went to the bathroom, and my mother was bleeding over the sink. She'd slit her wrists. My father had just left to go to his job, but I was able to catch him, so he came back and took her to the hospital. I went to school."

I asked Luke if he could remember what emotions he experienced in the immediate aftermath of finding his mother, and without hesitating he said, "It was terror and fear. And anger too. I was angry that she had done that, but I didn't say anything to anyone when I got to school. I went to Catholic school, but I didn't tell any of the nuns because there was so much shame around suicide in the 1960s. I can't remember talking to anybody. You didn't even talk with the extended Italian family that lived throughout the neighborhood. Of course, everyone knew what was going on, but nobody talked about it. The first time I talked with anyone about what was going on with my mother's depression I was a freshman in college."

What should you do if you get a phone call from someone who has attempted suicide?

As I explain in detail in chapter 6 ("Prevention and Treatment"), the goal is to get help to that person as quickly as possible.

How do people react when they fail in a suicide attempt?

People react in a variety of ways, from anger and embarrassment to fear and relief. People who attempt suicide may be angry at themselves because, as the Olympic diving champion Greg Louganis says in his autobiography about his first suicide attempt when he was twelve, "I couldn't even get *that* right." They may also be angry at themselves for trying in the first place. Or they may be angry at others for preventing them from carrying out their plan.

Ruth was furious with her neighbor for calling the building superintendent after she didn't answer her neighbor's repeated and loud knocks at the door. She recalled, "I was so angry! I had everything planned. No one was supposed to come by until the next day, and I would have been gone by then. I know she meant well, but it took a long time for me to see it that way. I thought she ruined everything."

Ruth was also extremely embarrassed about what she had done. "The way I grew up, suicide was an awful thing," she said. "And now I had to face my family, and everyone knew. When they came to see me in the hospital, I couldn't look at them or talk to them. I thought I would die just from the embarrassment."

Following a suicide attempt, some people also experience great fear because they feel out of control. They may also be fearful of themselves for having tried in the first place.

For Peter, once he climbed back over the railing of his terrace and hurled himself into a corner in his living room, his terror over what he'd almost done was combined with a tremendous sense of relief. "I was totally relieved that I was still alive, that I hadn't gone through with it," he said. "But I couldn't move. I was afraid that if I got out of that corner that I might actually jump, so I stayed in the corner all night, just holding myself. When the sun finally came up, I managed to get to the phone and call one of my close friends to tell him what happened."

How do people react to someone who has attempted suicide?

People react in a variety of ways, but ideally with concern and understanding, as Peter's friends did. He told me: "My best friend flew out to stay with me for several weeks. She'd been through a severe depression herself, and she knew what I was going through. She never pushed me to talk. She was just there to take care of me. And once I was ready to talk, she was a great listener. My business partner was also amazing. He picked up the slack and encouraged me to take as much time as I needed to get better."

Not everyone is so fortunate. When Ruth tried to kill herself, she wasn't the only one who was embarrassed. Her sister was so ashamed that she didn't come to visit Ruth in the hospital. "I can't blame her, I was ashamed too," Ruth said, "but I wish she had come to visit. She was the one person that I wouldn't have turned away from."

After Ruth got out of the hospital, her sister was so afraid that she'd try again that she called Ruth several times a day. Ruth recalled, "After two days, I said, 'Enough!' I told her that I wasn't going to try again, but if she didn't stop calling me I'd start thinking about it. I thought that was funny—I still had my sense of humor—but she started to cry."

Shock is a typical response. Other people react with anger ("How could you do that!"), and not just family and friends. Sometimes people who have attempted suicide face hostile medical personnel and fellow patients who are filled with contempt for someone who would intentionally try to end his life.

Perhaps the worst response is no response. Some people simply go into denial and pretend that nothing ever happened. They may think this is the least painful way of handling things, but in the long run, pretending that everything is okay helps no one.

How can you help someone who has attempted suicide?

Much depends on your relationship to the person who has attempted suicide and the shape she's in following the attempt, but if you're a close friend or family member, you can be supportive of her recovery in both the short and long term. The key is to avoid making judgments and to listen.

If appropriate, talk to the mental health professionals who are involved in caring for the person who has attempted suicide and find out how you can help. Or ask your loved one or family member directly, "What can I do to help you?" You can also contact a suicide/crisis organization, explain your specific circumstances, and ask what you can do to help.

When Virginia, the college student who attempted to kill herself with cooking gas, called her parents following her suicide attempt, they came immediately to pick her up and bring her home. "I didn't wait for them to ask me if I wanted to see a psychiatrist," she recalled. "Before we even got home, I told them I needed to see a shrink and asked them to find me one. By that evening they had found a psychiatrist and made an appointment for first thing the next morning. They drove me to the doctor's office and waited to take me home. They were really great with practical things, but I wish they had been more comfortable talking about why I was so depressed in the first place. But my parents were never comfortable talking about those things."

Do people who attempt once try again?

Fortunately, most people who try to kill themselves once don't do it again. But according to George Howe Colt in *November of the Soul*, approximately 10 percent of those who make a first attempt will eventually take their own lives.

What happens to people who survive an attempt?

Someone who survives a suicide attempt may wind up in an emergency room, locked in a psychiatric hospital on a twenty-four-hour suicide watch, or at home in bed for a day or two with a very bad headache.

After initial treatment at the hospital for her suicide attempt, Ruth was transferred to the psychiatric unit of a private hospital. "Everyone was very nice to me," she said, "but I didn't like the idea of people watching me." After she left the hospital, Ruth made weekly visits to a psychiatrist who specialized in treating depression among older people.

Some people who attempt suicide are released following initial medical treatment. Others, like Ruth, are sent to psychiatric facilities where, depending on the case, they may stay for observation and treatment for a period of days or weeks. If you're believed to be in danger of making another suicide attempt, a judge can even place you in a hospital and force you to stay there against your wishes. Please see chapter 6 ("Prevention and Treatment") for a more detailed answer regarding forced hospitalization.

Do people who attempt suicide suffer from any permanent injuries?

Depending on the method of suicide chosen, people who attempt suicide and survive may suffer brain injuries, paralysis, nervc damage, scarred wrists, and disfigurement. Some people are left so impaired that even if they want to attempt suicide again, they can't.

Do people recover from an attempt?

Absolutely, although overcoming despair and hopelessness can take a long time. For some people, a close encounter with self-destruction can be a major—and ultimately positive—turning point in their lives.

For Peter, it was a slow road back to feeling normal again, but after the night he spent curled up in the corner of his living room, there was never any question that he wanted to live. In an interview ten years after he attempted suicide, he told me: "It was a tremendous shock to me that I'd reached the point where I was standing on the edge of my balcony, with nothing between me and a fourteen-story drop. When the sun came up the next morning, I was so glad to be alive—that I hadn't taken that final step. No matter how bad I've felt on occasion since that time, I've never regretted that I chose life over the abyss."

Chapter

6

PREVENTION AND TREATMENT

It's far easier to write about preventing a loved one from taking his or her life—or getting them into treatment—than it is to actually prevent a suicide when you find yourself in a situation where a loved one is in crisis. Unfortunately, I know from experience.

When my mother called from Denver (I live in New York) one fine summer day in July 2000 to tell me that she was going to kill herself, I wasn't sure what to do. In fact, I was dumbfounded. After announcing her intentions, my mother hung up the phone and I was left staring at the receiver in my hand. I thought to myself: *You wrote the book* (this book was first published in 1996). *You're supposed to know what to do. Do it!*

Of course I knew what to do, but I discovered that it is much easier to tell people what to do in a hypothetical circumstance than it proved to be when I had to follow through on my own advice. I probably should have immediately called one of the suicide hotlines to ask for advice or called emergency medical services (EMS) in Denver.

Instead, I called a friend who is a psychologist to ask her advice because I wasn't at all certain that my mother was serious about following through on her threat and I didn't want to make things worse by having emergency services show up at her door. So I discussed the situation with my friend, and we decided that all I could do was call emergency services in Denver. That's when I discovered that the police, not EMS, would be dispatched to my mother's apartment. I knew my mother would be furious, but I couldn't risk *not* taking her threat seriously.

Within a half-hour I had a call back from the Denver police that they'd found no one at home. And several hours later I had a call from my mother, who had gone out for a walk after hanging up on me and then went to dinner with friends (while I was having visions of her floating dead in her subdivision's picturesque lake). By the time she called, *I* was ready for treatment, and if I hadn't already been seeing a psychologist on a regular basis I would have sought one out. With the history of my father's suicide already under my belt, there was no way I could imagine dealing with my now-suicidal and incredibly erratic mother without the help and support of a mental health professional.

What follows in this chapter on prevention and treatment reflects my belief that we can only do the best we can under the circumstances—whatever they are. In my mother's case, that meant flying out to visit with her and making every effort to get her the care she needed (which proved to be very difficult since she herself was a mental health professional and feared that seeking assistance would compromise her ability to find work—she had only recently moved to Denver).

I firmly believe from everything I've read that we can indeed prevent many suicides through various methods—including education about depression, treatment through talk therapy, medication, knowing how to recognize the side effects of medications that can put people at risk for suicide, and so on. But I also think it helps to be realistic and concede that not all people who wish to destroy themselves can be prevented from doing so and that it's not in our power to single-handedly keep someone alive who doesn't want to live. We can't even force someone to get help if they don't want it, or force them to take the prescribed psychiatric medications they need to cope with depression or other mental illnesses. Sadly, I have experience with this as well: my sister-in-law attempted suicide in 2006 and went on to complete a suicide two years later after she stopped taking prescribed psychiatric medication.

Can people who have suicidal thoughts get over their self-destructive feelings?

Most people whose suicidal thoughts are casual and fleeting will in time stop feeling suicidal, and time may be all they need. For those whose thoughts are not casual and fleeting, particularly if the suicidal feelings are a result of clinical depression, schizophrenia, or alcoholism, for example, professional help is essential.

I first introduced Virginia in chapter 3 ("Teen/Youth Suicide"). She recovered from a suicidal depression through a combination of medication, talk therapy with a caring psychiatrist, and the passage of time. Virginia was frightened by her attempted suicide and knew she needed help. "Apparently I still wanted to live," she recalled, "because after the first time my parents took me to the psychiatrist, I continued seeing him."

That first visit with the psychiatrist was the beginning of Virginia's long climb out of depression and away from her feelings of hopelessness and despair. She explained, "My psychiatrist was a big man, full of life. After the initial visit, he prescribed an antidepressant, and then I met with him twice a week for the first few months. Most of the time we just talked about what was going on in my life. I liked his sense of humor, and one time, after telling him about some of the books I'd been reading, mostly depressing novels and books by people like Virginia Woolf, he told me to stay away from writers who killed themselves."

In time Virginia's depression began to lift. "It was such a relief, although I still wrestled with mild depression from time to time for years afterward. But I vowed it would never get that bad again. I decided I wasn't going to let myself get boxed in to the point where I felt there was no way out other than suicide."

Barbara, whom I wrote about in chapter 1 ("The Basics"), fell into a suicidal depression when she was a young woman and had two small children to care for at home. It was Barbara's husband at the time who "dragged" her to a psychiatrist. "He was a little worried," she said, adding, "Therapy helps a lot because you talk about these feelings that you can't talk about with friends and family because you feel ashamed. I thought that nobody else felt this way."

None of the several therapists Barbara saw over the years prescribed medication. "Maybe they didn't have the antidepressants they have now," she speculated. "What I did was I really fought it. When I would start to go into a depression, I would talk to myself and ask, 'Why are you feeling this way?' I fought it with any strength that I had and told myself how it wasn't good for me and the people around me to be depressed like that."

I asked Barbara if she had any advice for someone who is in a suicidal depression or for the friends and family of someone who is depressed. Here's what she told me: "I would say, get therapy real fast. I don't think you can battle depression alone. You're so turned inward and your thoughts are so focused on ending your pain, and that's all you can think about, and it overtakes you. I don't know that a friend can help you, and it's an awful big responsibility on somebody. Because if you wind up committing suicide, I don't think they could bear the aftermath. I don't know about the medication. I don't like to take medication, but if those thoughts had persisted I would have."

What kinds of treatments are available?

People who are experiencing suicidal feelings are treated in a variety of ways depending on the nature of their underlying problems and whether they're in imminent danger of hurting themselves. Treatment can range from a course of talk therapy with a mental health professional to antidepressant medication to mood-stabilizing drugs such as lithium to electroconvulsive therapy (ECT), which is a far more humane procedure than it was in the past. Treatment is most often conducted on an outpatient basis, but some people require hospitalization or a residential treatment program.

When Patricia's thirteen-year-old daughter became extremely depressed and began cutting herself, Patricia knew she had to do something. "I know with some parents there was no clue," she said. "But with me I got lots of warnings. Elizabeth didn't see life in color and never did from a very early age. She took no joy in life. We'd talk about that, and she'd say to me, 'Mom, I have no idea what you're talking about when you talk about taking joy in life.' She looked forward to books and movies, but she never joined anything—not a single sport, group, anything. She actually said she would like to die."

Patricia hoped that Elizabeth was "just trying to get attention, but I found a bottle of something in her room, which we removed. I found a rope in the garage that she'd fashioned into a noose. It was stunning, heartbreaking, frightening. You feel like a failure."

Patricia took her daughter to see "all kinds of psychologists and psychiatrists." Over time there were various diagnoses, including "borderline personality disorder, oppositional defiance disorder, severe depression, and I'm probably missing a couple," Patricia explained, adding, "she was also extremely intelligent and extremely funny. She was a real good pal to me."

During one of the meetings with her daughter's psychologist, he said that Patricia had to take Elizabeth "to a lockdown unit." Elizabeth went from the psychologist's office into a long-term residential treatment program for a total of eighteen months. To pay for Elizabeth's very expensive residential treatment program, Patricia and her ex-husband exhausted their savings because almost none of their daughter's care was covered by insurance.

Are there people who have suicidal feelings who do not benefit from treatment?

Yes, although a significant part of the problem is that people who are feeling suicidal don't always get proper treatment or the necessary combination of treatments, or they refuse treatment entirely.

But even among people who receive extensive treatment, some continue to feel suicidal. That was the case with Serena, a thirty-five-year-old professional who lives with her parents. She said, "I'd been struggling with depression and self-destructive feelings for quite a long time, and my psychiatrist tried two different anti-depressants. One seemed to do nothing, and the other made me feel even more suicidal. I tried suffocating myself, but I couldn't go through with it. I called my doctor to tell him what I'd done, and he recommended hospitalization."

Initially, Serena was very relieved to be in the hospital, but she quickly felt overwhelmed by her lack of freedom. She explained, "I was put in a locked ward, and I was on suicide watch for two weeks. I had constant supervision. I couldn't even pee alone. Still, I managed to get my hands on a pair of scissors, but fortunately they were discovered before I could hurt myself."

Serena was in the hospital for two months. She had individual and group therapy, and her psychiatrist prescribed lithium, but her depression didn't get any better and she became anorexic.

Finally her doctor recommended electroconvulsive therapy. "I was freaked out by even the idea of shock treatments," Serena recalled, "but I trusted my doctor, and I knew that it could be an effective method of treatment for people with severe depression. I went for six ECT treatments, and they weren't good for me. They made me horribly suicidal, and I was put on suicide watch. On Christmas Day I freaked out and had to be put in restraints because I'd tried to kill myself."

Despite this suicidal crisis, within several weeks of trying to kill herself Serena was stabilized, and her doctor recommended that she be transferred to a long-term care facility because she continued to have self-destructive feelings but was no longer in acute danger. Serena liked that idea, but her insurance had run out by then, so she returned home to her parents and began seeing a psychiatrist on an outpatient basis. "I'm on an antidepressant and mood stabilizer, and they've helped," Serena said, "but lately I've started feeling suicidal again. Fortunately, I have a very supportive network of people in my life, so I'm not isolated. That gives me hope that I'll make it. But I'm afraid this may be a lifetime struggle no matter what drugs I take or how long I'm hospitalized."

Are there people who can't be prevented from killing themselves?

I don't believe that everyone can be prevented from completing a suicide, especially those who are determined and secretive. John, an eighty-two-year-old scientist I first wrote about in chapter 4, carefully hid his intentions and plans from his daughters and went so far as to feign interest in the classes and activities his daughters arranged for him in the aftermath of his wife's death.

Patricia, who had known of her daughter's explicit wish to die since Elizabeth was thirteen, did everything a parent could do to keep her daughter from taking her life—from arranging therapy and extended residential treatment to supervising Elizabeth very closely—but her efforts proved to be not enough. As Patricia explained, "Summers were always the worst, because without the structure of school she could get horribly depressed. She should have been on all kinds of meds, but she refused to take any drugs other than one medication for anxiety. And after eighteen you can't force them. So I made sure she saw a psychiatrist that summer. I checked in with her throughout the day, three or four times a day."

On the day Elizabeth took her life, Patricia spoke with her several times. Patricia said, "At around noon I called and asked her if I could bring her lunch. She said no, but asked me to do some banking for her. At two she sent me an e-mail shopping list. At four she called and asked me what time I would be home, and that usually meant she was having a boy over. She had an off-and-on boyfriend. I said I'd be home at six."

As planned, Patricia came home at 6:00 PM and instantly realized that something was very wrong. She said, "The doors were unlocked, and we never leave the doors unlocked. Elizabeth's purse was on the floor. The TV was on, and the cats weren't fed. I thought something horrible had happened. I called for Elizabeth, and she didn't answer. I went to her door, and I heard a noise inside, but I didn't know what it was."

Patricia continued: "Elizabeth could be really hard-edged, so if I'd opened the door and a boy had been in there, she would have been furious. So I went and changed my clothes and came back, which probably took two minutes. I knocked on her door again, and finally I opened the door, and she was lying on the floor—very gracefully—and I thought she had fainted. Then I saw a lot of blood around her head and a gun about a foot from her hand. I realized then that the noise I'd heard was Elizabeth's breathing. She was still alive, but her eyes were dead."

With my sister-in-law, who had to be talked off the ledge of a high-rise building in 2006, I had a close-up view of how difficult it can be to intervene when someone you know is potentially suicidal. My sister-in-law was an adult in her late forties, nothing short of brilliant, fiercely independent, secretive, and sometimes hostile. She resisted any intervention by her family, and as we all learned after her death in November 2008, she also kept her psychiatrist in the dark about her state of mind and the fact that she'd stopped taking medication. As far as anyone could tell, she was not in imminent danger of harming herself. She had been in touch with several family members in the days before she chose to return to the same building she'd been talked down from two years earlier and jumped to her death. She left no note.

What should I do if I'm feeling suicidal?

Talk to someone about it—a friend, a parent, a teacher, your family physician. If your suicidal feelings have come on suddenly, you may simply be having a reaction to a new medication, and this is something to discuss with your doctor immediately. If these are long-standing feelings or feelings that have been growing over time, it's essential that you talk to a professional. You may feel embarrassed or ashamed of your feelings, but you will discover that you're not alone in having suicidal feelings and that help is available for those who need it.

If your suicidal thoughts are more than casual and don't pass quickly, it isn't enough to simply share your feelings with someone close to you. It's essential that you talk to a mental health professional who has experience helping people who have suicidal thoughts. Some people think it's enough to talk to their family physician and get a prescription for antidepressants, but many physicians aren't trained to deal with mental illness and patients who are having suicidal feelings, so it's important to get a referral to someone who has that experience. One way to find help is to call a crisis helpline, explain that you're having suicidal feelings, and ask for a referral.

Also, if you've reached the point where you've already acquired the means for killing yourself, like a gun or sleeping pills, get rid of them now and get help. If you keep these items around the house, you may be tempted to use them.

Serena explained to me that for the first two months she was out of the hospital, she avoided keeping plastic bags in her home. She said, "As long as they were there, I was afraid I'd use them to kill myself." Serena also strongly recommends not being alone when you're having suicidal feelings: "My friends have been wonderful over the years about having me stay over at their homes."

What should I say to someone who has told me she is suicidal?

Focus on listening and asking questions. The person who is talking to you about her self-destructive feelings has probably overcome a lot of fear and embarrassment to share these feelings, and one thing you can do is make her feel comfortable about opening up. You can also encourage her to talk to a professional, and you can offer your help in finding one. If you're not sure how to handle the situation, you can make a call to a mental health center or crisis telephone line and ask for advice on what to do.

If the person appears to be in imminent danger, then it's important to get help immediately. In that case, call a crisis center or local emergency services. Having been through this with my mother, I know how difficult or embarrassing it can be to make such a call. No one likes to feel as if he is overreacting or being an alarmist. But better to feel like an alarmist than to miss an opportunity to save a loved one from harming herself.

What should I avoid saying?

It doesn't help to say, "Cheer up! You have everything to live for." The person confiding in you is likely to feel dismissed by such a remark. Again, the key is listening and drawing the person out. Whatever you say should be offered in the spirit of making that person feel comfortable enough to keep talking. For example, depending on the circumstances, you can say, "It must be very hard for you to tell me about this," or, "I'm really glad you feel comfortable enough to confide in me."

What should I do if I find someone who has attempted suicide?

If you find someone who has attempted suicide, there are a number of things to do, depending on the circumstances. If the person has inflicted physical harm, administer first aid and call for emergency help. If he has attempted suicide using gas or carbon monoxide, get him into fresh air, administer CPR if necessary, and call for help. If the person has swallowed pills or taken some other poisonous substance and is unconscious, turn him on his side to prevent choking and call for emergency help to find out what to do next.

What should I do if I get a telephone call from someone who has just attempted suicide?

If you get such a phone call, make certain that emergency help can get to the person quickly. First, ask whether anyone is there with him. If so, ask the caller to put that person on the phone, then tell that person to call for emergency help. If no one is there, find out the caller's telephone number and address, including the apartment number, and ask him to unlock the door so that emergency help can get to him in the event that he loses consciousness. Then, armed with the information you have, call for emergency help.

How can suicide be prevented?

At first look, preventing suicide is simple. We have to identify those people who are at risk of taking their lives and then make certain they get proper treatment. That's far easier said than done, of course, for two primary reasons. First, it's not so easy to identify all those at risk. And second, even when those who are at risk are identified, not everyone gets appropriate treatment, treatment doesn't always work, and treatment is not always wanted. There's a third issue: the ability of our health care system to deliver the kind of targeted mental health care that's essential for those at risk of suicide. Right now such care is not always available or affordable to everyone who needs it.

How can I tell if someone is suicidal?

Contrary to what many people think, you *can* often tell when someone is contemplating suicide. Though people who are planning to kill themselves don't generally announce their intentions explicitly, there are usually warning signs.

As the suicidologist Edwin Shneidman explains in "At the Point of No Return," an article published in the March 1987 issue of *Psychology Today*, "about 80 percent of suicidal people give friends and family clear clues about their intention to kill themselves. They give indications of helplessness, make pleas for response and create opportunities for rescue."

Shneidman notes that there are three broad categories of clues: verbal, behavioral, and situational. Verbal clues include statements about not wanting to go on, about going away, or about not being able to stand the pain any longer. Several months before my father took his life, he told his brother on more than one occasion that if things kept going the way they were, he "didn't want to go on." He didn't say he planned to kill himself, but it was still a pretty good indicator of what he was thinking about. My uncle was alarmed, but uncertain what to do. My father also wrote to at least three of his friends that he was fearful that he might feel compelled to take his life.

In terms of behavior, according to Shneidman, the person who is planning to die may give away "prized possessions, such as a medical student giving away a valuable microscope." Or the suicidal person may suddenly prepare a will. He or she may also behave differently than normal, with noticeable changes to their usual eating, sleeping, work, and sexual patterns.

Situational clues are what Shneidman describes as "traumatic events in a person's life, such as illness, the breakup of a relationship or the death of a loved one."

Not everyone who expresses a desire to end their life does it verbally. Donna, a full-time mother of two young daughters, got a letter from her mother in which she talked about her wish to die. Donna told me: "Mom had been in and out of the hospital for drug and alcohol problems for years, so it's not as if I hadn't thought about the possibility of her accidentally overdosing. But until that letter, it really hadn't occurred to me that she would actually kill herself. Well, maybe it crossed my mind, but I didn't want to think about it. And it wasn't even that she said, 'I'm going to kill myself,' but she talked about being tired and how she would go to bed at night wishing she wouldn't wake up in the morning."

What are the warning signs that someone is at risk for suicide?

I've drawn the following list from several sources, particularly Rita Robinson's *Survivors of Suicide*. Keep in mind that most people exhibit some, or even many, of these warning signs at various points in their lives yet never go on to take their lives. However, others do, and that can make this all incredibly confusing and frustrating.

- Threats of suicide (for example, "I'm going to shoot myself" or "I don't want to go on")
- Preoccupation with death, including talk of hopelessness, helplessness, or worthlessness
- Previous suicide attempts
- Depression
- Trouble with school or work
- Alcohol or drug abuse
- Risk-taking
- Isolation: withdrawing from friends and family
- Personality changes or odd behavior
- Difficulty with sleeping or loss of appetite
- Moodiness, including anger and crying
- Giving away prized possessions
- Getting one's life in order, including the preparation or changing of a will
- The sudden appearance in the person of happiness and calm after a period during which some of the above characteristics were present

How does a mental health professional determine whether someone is at risk of suicide?

Mental health professionals assess risk by first interviewing the person who is believed to be suicidal. The mental health professional then uses the information from that interview to decide whether the person is suicidal and, if so, the severity of the danger.

All mental health professionals pay careful attention to what their patients tell them. Ona Lindquist, a psychotherapist in private practice in New York City, has had patients over the years who told her about their suicidal thoughts. She explained, "A fair number of my patients have expressed suicidal ideation—'I feel like killing myself.'"

Lindquist's challenge has been to assess whether the patient is actually in danger of following through on those thoughts. She said, "I have to consider a number of things: How long have I known this patient? How well do I know this patient? Is this circumstantial? Has it come up out of something that's going on in their life? Is it something that doesn't feel amenable to analysis? Is it something that I'm seeing as a progressive constriction of their emotional state? Or have they had a shitty weekend and they're really depressed, but they go to work and continue to see family and friends? Or they don't see family and friends and they're very lonely. I'm very concerned when someone is isolating themselves. You can't tell them to go out and make friends. When a patient expresses suicidal feelings, I'll ask them directly, 'What do you mean? Do you have a plan? Why now?'"

Current assessment techniques are more an art than an exact science, but they are an important way to begin identifying someone who is at risk of suicide. Lindquist concurred: "Some of the most important tools I have to work with are my clinical intuition, my clinical skill, and experience. That's not foolproof, but neither is medication, although if I think medication is called for I won't hesitate to ask—and sometimes insist—that a patient go for a consultation with a psychopharmacologist."

Do teenagers exhibit the same warning signs as the general population?

Teenagers and young people exhibit many of the same warning signs, but there are some differences. Please see chapter 3 ("Teen/Youth Suicide") for a more detailed answer.

Since bullying is now recognized as a reason why some young people take their lives, what can be done to stop bullying?

Parents who discover that their child is being bullied, whether physically, verbally, or online, have plenty of options.

The first challenge is finding out from your child what's going on. Because of their own fear that if their parents get involved it will only make things worse, children may resist talking about the abuse they've been subjected to. It may take the help of a counselor to reveal that bullying is behind a child's depression or acting out.

Once you know what's going on, and assuming the bullying is taking place at school, there are several things to do. As the *New York Times* columnist Dr. Perri Klass noted in a June 9, 2009, article, parents, teachers, the school principal, and the child's pediatrician all have a role to play in dealing with both the child being bullied and the bullies themselves.

Talking to the principal and teachers seems obvious, but you should also talk to your child's pediatrician. I learned from Dr. Klass's column that the American Academy of Pediatrics has an official policy statement on "the pediatrician's role in preventing youth violence." The statement was revised in 2009 to include a section on bullying, "including a recommendation that schools adopt a prevention model developed by" Dan Olweus, a research professor of psychology in Norway. The model, according to the professor, combines "preventive programs and directly addressing children who are involved or identified as bullies or victims or both."

So there's no need for parents to sit on the sidelines and watch their children being bullied (or doing the bullying). We know that bullying leads to unnecessary suffering and, in rare instances, suicide. If you're at a loss as to where to start, talk to your child's pediatrician, teacher, school counselor, or principal. Or call one of the crisis hotlines and ask for advice.

No child should feel compelled to end his life because of bullying, and it's our responsibility as adults to make certain that not a single child is ever bullied to death.

What about elderly people? Are the warning signs the same for them as for the general population?

Elderly people are not likely to be taken as seriously as younger people when they talk about wanting to die or being tired and not wanting to go on. Too often, we simply dismiss such statements as normal for someone in the later stages of life. Many of the other warning signs are the same as they are for people in general but are easy to overlook. Please see chapter 4 ("Suicide and the Elderly") for a more detailed answer.

What should you do if you think someone is suicidal?

Depending on the immediacy of the situation, you can call your doctor, a counselor, or a telephone crisis hotline (see the appendix) to get advice on what you can do to help a person you think is suicidal. If you're dealing with someone who is on the verge of taking his life, call the police or 911 and explain the situation. Every locality has experts with experience in dealing with this kind of emergency.

As soon as Donna, whom I wrote about earlier in the chapter, finished reading her mother's letter (in which her mother wrote of her wish to die), Donna called her family physician to ask her advice on what to do. After asking Donna several questions to assess whether her mother was in imminent danger of taking her life, the doctor suggested that Donna bring her mother in that afternoon to talk.

Donna's instinct to get professional help was absolutely on target. This is not something you can handle on your own, and you can't risk doing nothing, hoping the problem will go away.

Can you have a loved one forcibly hospitalized if you think she's in danger of killing herself?

Yes. A person who is deemed an imminent danger to herself can be forcibly hospitalized, but laws vary by state, so you'll need to check with your doctor or a mental health professional to find out what the requirements are where you live.

To provide an example of what's required to forcibly hospitalize a loved one, I spoke with Dr. Richard Hersh, associate clinical professor of psychiatry at Columbia University's College of Physicians and Surgeons in New York City, and Dr. Brett Blatter, assistant clinical professor of psychiatry at Columbia University's College of Physicians and Surgeons and director of Emergency Psychiatric Services at New York Presbyterian Hospital/Columbia.

Dr. Hersh outlined for me New York's requirements: "Three people need to fill out forms certifying imminent danger—either before a patient is admitted to the hospital or in the hospital emergency room. And by imminent danger I mean that there's information that the person has a plan and the intent to harm themselves in the near future. A person who says, 'I'm going to kill myself a year from Christmas,' would not be considered to be an imminent danger to themselves."

The three people required to forcibly hospitalize a patient include at least two licensed physicians (of any specialty) and an applicant. "The two licensed physicians," Dr. Blatter explained, "must 'certify' the patient, and an applicant must fill out a separate form. The applicant may be a family member, a hospital administrator, or an attending (board-eligible) psychiatrist."

I asked Dr. Blatter to elaborate on what he meant by "certify": "Certification means that the patient is imminently dangerous (to themselves or others), that the patient has a mental illness that can be treated in a psychiatric hospital, that a hospitalization is the least restrictive means of treatment appropriate for the patient (in other words, if it would be clinically appropriate and safe to treat the patient in an outpatient setting, the patient cannot be certified to an inpatient unit), and that the patient is incapable of or unwilling to sign into the hospital voluntarily."

Dr. Hersh added that when an emergency room doctor, for example, does an evaluation to determine whether a potentially suicidal patient is in imminent danger, the evaluation necessarily takes several factors into account, including whether the patient has acquired the means to take his life, his intent, and his history of suicidal behavior or mental illness.

Once a person has been forcibly admitted to a hospital, he may be kept for two or more weeks of treatment unless he objects. If the patient challenges the forced hospitalization, then a court hearing must be held within seventy-two hours to determine whether he can be kept beyond that point. According to Dr. Hersh, "Sometimes the court lets the patient go home, and sometimes they send them back to the hospital."

In 2003, when my mother found herself in an emotional state where she feared that she'd harm herself, she called me from a friend's house where she was living temporarily and asked me to take her to the hospital. My mother was at the end of a two-year period during which she had become increasingly volatile, depressed, and irrational. What we didn't know at the time was that she was suffering from brain cancer. What we *did* know was that our best hope was to get her checked into a psychiatric hospital, where she could be properly evaluated and stabilized before she harmed herself. In advance of picking up my mother, I researched the best inpatient psychiatric facility in the New York City area and called to make arrangements to bring her in.

The drive to the hospital was harrowing as my mother alternated between hysterical sobbing and irrational ramblings and accusations; for example, she was furious with me for taking her to the hospital even though she had asked me to take her. I was lucky to have my mother's favorite cousin, Jeannette, next to me in the front passenger seat to alternately calm my mother and place a reassuring hand on my arm when there was no calming her.

The plan had been for my mother to voluntarily admit herself to the hospital, but during the hour-long drive I began to worry that my mother wouldn't get out of the car, let alone check herself into the hospital. I hadn't thought to consider in advance what my legal options would be in that event, but I assumed that I could make a case once we got to the hospital that she was a danger to herself and had to be hospitalized against her will. In any event, there was no way I could take her home with me given the extreme state of distress she was in.

Fortunately, by the time we got to the hospital we were able to calm my mother sufficiently to help her out of the car and walk her into the building. And after the initial intake interview, I watched with an enormous sense of relief as my mother signed the admission forms. I had dreaded the thought of having to forcibly commit my own mother to a psychiatric hospital, although I would have done so if it had come to that. Still, as I left my mother standing in the corridor of the locked ward where she would be spending the next three weeks, I was filled with a mix of terribly painful emotions, including guilt and regret.

So when I suggest—as I'm about to do—that it's better to risk angering or upsetting a potentially suicidal loved one by forcing her to be hospitalized against her will rather than risking her self-destruction, I'm offering this advice with some sense of the wrenching emotions that go along with that decision. As Dr.

Hersh said to me during our conversation about forced hospitalization, "It's best to err on the side of caution."

What can you do if a suicidal patient refuses to take medication?

Only a judge can require a patient to take medication. Dr. Blatter (see the previous question for Dr. Blatter's credentials) explained that, "in general, we consider patients capable of making decisions about medication. Psychiatric medication can be administered to a patient over the patient's objection only in the case of emergency (immediate risk of injury to the patient or others). In a non-emergent situation (for example, a patient who is severely depressed and suicidal on an inpatient unit but not representing an immediate danger to themselves or others), a judge will hear evidence on behalf of the patient and the hospital, and the judge will make a determination about the medication."

Dr. Blatter added that it's rare for depressed patients to be taken to court for such hearings because, he said, "depressed patients are usually asking for help and are able to participate in treatment planning."

Not every depressed patient is immediately agreeable, however, to being treated with medication. As I discussed in the previous question, my mother admitted herself to a psychiatric hospital during a depressive episode. Once there, she was resistant to the idea of taking any kind of psychiatric medication, which led one of the social workers to call me and ask whether I could speak with my mother to persuade her to follow the psychiatrist's orders. My mother did indeed want to get better and after some gentle persuasion agreed to give the medication a try.

What is currently being done to prevent suicide?

All across the country and around the world, professionals and laypeople alike are involved in a variety of efforts to reduce the number of people who take their lives. These efforts include education programs about the problem of depression and suicide, the training of mental health professionals regarding suicide prevention efforts, volunteer crisis telephone hotlines, and the installation of barriers on bridges that attract people who wish to end their lives.

For example, the American Association of Suicidology sponsors the annual National Suicide Prevention Week (the week that precedes World Suicide Prevention Day, which is sponsored by the International Association for Suicide Prevention). The goal of National Suicide Prevention Week is to bring attention to the issue of suicide, to educate the public regarding the warning signs and risk factors, and to make people aware of the help that's available.

Typically, local groups run training sessions for mental health professionals, send public speakers to schools and community centers, and e-mail press releases and information kits about suicide prevention to local media. Organizations and institutions that participate in this annual event include crisis centers, schools, community mental health centers, hospitals, private treatment facilities, and churches, as well as major corporations and local businesses.

Are there specific resources for different age groups? For example, what kinds of resources are available for college students?

Yes, there are organizations that are dedicated to addressing the needs of different age groups and populations. For example, the Jed Foundation is focused specifically on working to reduce emotional distress and prevent suicide among college students. And the Trevor Project is focused on crisis and suicide prevention efforts among lesbian, gay, bisexual, transgender, and questioning youth (LGBTQ). For information about these organizations and other organizations that can provide you with the specific information and help you need, please see the appendix.

What can parents do to help a child who is heading off to college who has emotional problems and has attempted suicide in the past?

I find it hard to imagine how terrifying it would be to send a child off to college who suffers from a form of mental illness that puts her at risk for suicide (or who has made previous suicide attempts).

Sadly, I know parents for whom this doesn't require imagining. They were indeed terrified, but their child, who had previously been diagnosed with bipolar disorder and had attempted suicide once before, was on medication, she was stable, and she was not about to stay home for the rest of her life. So her parents did what they could to make certain the school she was attending had the capacity to deal with students who had mental health issues.

The parents of the young woman faced a significant challenge in getting their questions answered because they had committed to honoring their daughter's wish for privacy—she insisted that her parents not reveal her diagnosis to the student health representative they spoke with at her school. Their solution was to call the school's health services department and explain their need to remain anonymous before asking questions that ultimately reassured them that their daughter would be in good hands in an emergency.

How has the U.S. military responded to the dramatic increase in the number of suicides in the U.S. Army since the start of the wars in Afghanistan and Iraq?

Spurred on by the dramatic increase in the number of suicides in the U.S. Army since the wars in Afghanistan and Iraq began in 2001 and 2003, respectively, the Department of Defense and the Department of Veterans Affairs (VA) have stepped up their efforts to educate troops in all branches of the military about suicide risk. These departments have also hired more mental health workers and beefed up mental health programs. For example, one option available to some members of the military and their families is a Web-based service that provides face-to-face assessments, counseling sessions, psychotherapy, and medication management with psychologists and psychiatrists. Another example is the Army's new intensive training program in emotional resiliency, which was launched in 2009. The goal is to provide all 1.1 million soldiers and their families with better ways to cope with the stresses they are likely to face.

The VA has also contracted with the federally financed Suicide Prevention Lifeline (1-800-273-8255) to provide a telephone suicide hotline for U.S. military veterans (as well as for friends and family who are seeking advice about their loved ones). The service is free, confidential, and available 24/7. If you call this toll-free number and press "1" on your keypad, you will be routed automatically to the Veterans Suicide Prevention Hotline and a counselor who is trained to work with veterans who are experiencing an emotional crisis. Extensive information is also available to veterans on the Suicide Prevention Lifeline Web site (see the appendix for the links).

One very big challenge faced by those working to prevent suicides among members of the military is getting people who need help to make use of the available services. As noted in a *New York Times* article about a series of suicides among members of the 1451st Transportation Company, a unit of the North Carolina National Guard, "immersed in a culture of disciplined stoicism, they tend to see weakness in sharing their emotional distress. . . . [And] even veterans who seek formal counseling from the VA sometimes hide or play down their suffering."

All branches of the military provide extensive suicide prevention information and resources. Please see the appendix for a list of Web sites.

What can national governments do to mitigate the increase in suicides due to job loss during tough economic times?

As I discovered in a report in the medical journal *The Lancet*, some national governments responded to the economic crisis that began unfolding in 2008 by investing in programs to head off the expected increase in suicide rates because of job losses and economic hardship. For example, high investment in such programs in Sweden resulted in no increase in suicides. Low investment in Spain led to a suicide rate that rose in lockstep with the increase in the rate of unemployment. The *Lancet* report explains that social programs that deal with job loss—such as help with finding new jobs and support groups for the unemployed—are effective, but that cash payments alone, such as unemployment benefits, have little effect in preventing an increase in suicides.

What exactly is a suicide hotline?

Sometimes called a suicide prevention line or a crisis line, a suicide hotline is typically a telephone number that can be called at any hour of the day or night by people who are in a crisis of some sort or who are feeling suicidal. The telephones are staffed by volunteers who have been trained to provide an empathetic ear and to refer callers to the appropriate agencies for further help.

One of the first volunteer-staffed suicide prevention lines was founded in San Francisco in 1962 and is run by San Francisco Suicide Prevention. Eve Meyer, the executive director of the organization, explained how the suicide prevention line is run: "We provide very intensive training to ordinary community people to handle crisis telephone calls. They come in once a week for four hours to answer phones. We have ninety volunteers and get over two hundred telephone calls a day. When someone calls, we just listen, listen, listen like a vacuum cleaner. Most of them haven't had anyone to listen to them in a long time, which is why they're suicidal."

A twenty-four-hour free national telephone number—1-800-273-8255—is available to anyone in suicidal crisis or emotional distress. If you call, your call will be routed to the crisis center nearest to where you live. For more information, see National Suicide Prevention Lifeline in the appendix.

Who calls a hotline?

All kinds of people call hotlines, from distressed teenagers with relationship trouble to chronically depressed adults who need someone to talk to. However, as Dr. Herbert Hendin explains in his book *Suicide in America*, "the overwhelming number of calls and contacts do not come from the seriously suicidal segment of the population."

Karen Carlucci is assistant director of LifeNet, a New York City-based mental health information, referral, and crisis hotline that is one of the National Suicide Prevention Lifeline's approximately 140 crisis centers throughout the country. Calling Hendin's assessment "on target," she notes that "the people who call are not necessarily in a suicidal crisis, but they're feeling down or they're calling about someone they're worried about. Most of our callers are adults and young adults. Most are women. And during business hours we also get a lot of calls from health care providers asking for referrals to mental health providers—and of course we provide referrals for the general public as well."

Do suicide/crisis hotlines reduce the rate of suicide?

Suicide and crisis hotlines make a difference in the lives of some of the people who call, and they may reduce the number of people who attempt suicide. But studies have generally concluded that suicide and crisis hotlines do not have an impact on suicide rates—that is, they do not reduce the number of people who ultimately take their lives.

Karen Carlucci (see previous question) explained that the benefit of crisis hotlines is that "there's a phone number that's accessible to anyone who is feeling lost at the moment and needs to share with someone what they're feeling or what they're confused about regarding themselves or someone else. We offer some type of immediate response from a professional to help guide someone through their thought process. We help prioritize what action might be best to take first and we try to de-escalate their emotional distress."

Does restricting access to guns keep people from killing themselves? Don't people just find other ways to do it?

Common sense suggests that if someone wants to kill herself and a gun or other convenient method of self-destruction isn't readily available, she will find another way to do it. And for someone intent on suicide, that may be exactly what she does.

However, suicide is often an impulsive act, and if a loaded gun is not nearby when the impulse is strongest, by the time another means can be found the impulse may have passed. If alcohol is involved, the suicidal person may be more sober by the time he finds another method and therefore may be less inclined to follow through on a suicide attempt. It's also possible that whatever alternative method is chosen will not be as lethal.

This isn't just idle theory. As I mentioned in chapter 3, a *Newsweek* article about teen suicide that followed the suicide of 1980s rock star Kurt Cobain made note of a key finding of a study comparing adolescent suicide victims who had no apparent mental disorders with teens who did not take their lives: the only difference between the two groups was *a loaded gun in the house.*

Has anything been done to prevent people from jumping off San Francisco's Golden Gate Bridge?

The pedestrian walkway on the Golden Gate Bridge is closed at night in an effort to reduce the number of people who jump from the bridge. And television cameras on the span allow bridge employees to keep a watchful eye out for potential suicides. When a potential suicide is spotted, the California Highway Patrol can reach the person within one minute and restrain him or her. Emergency telephones have also been installed on the span so that people contemplating suicide (or witnessing a potential suicide) can call for help.

Why haven't protective barriers been erected on the Golden Gate Bridge to prevent people from jumping off?

This debate has raged for years, but until recently the pro-barrier advocates have always lost out to those who have opposed them. The argument against erecting a high fence or some other type of barrier has included the cost of construction, aesthetic concerns, and the erroneous belief that people who are prevented from jumping off the bridge by physical barriers will just find another way to kill themselves. (Suicidologists, according to George Howe Colt in *November of the Soul*, have long maintained that "suicidal people are apt to choose a highly personal method, and if that method is unavailable they may abandon their plans rather than switch to another.")

In 2008 the bridge directors finally approved a concept for a suicide deterrent: a safety net that projects from underneath the bridge and is designed to catch anyone who jumps from the walkway. However, the directors stipulated that only private and/or federal funds were to be used for the $40–50 million cost of construction, and there remain some not inconsiderable environmental hurdles to overcome. As of this writing, the environmental studies and efforts to secure federal funding were under way. When I checked in with Eve Meyer about progress on the safety net, she said, "My guess is that it will be a minimum of three more years and one hundred more suicides before it is built. It's possible that if a golden retriever were to jump accidentally, things might move much more quickly."

The barrier debate is not specific to the Golden Gate Bridge. At other bridges, river gorges, buildings, and highway overpasses in the United States and around the world that are a draw to potential suicides, the same arguments have been made both for and against constructing protective barriers.

Chapter

7

SURVIVING SUICIDE: COPING WITH THE SUICIDE OF SOMEONE YOU KNOW

The other day I was talking with a friend about another friend whose brother had just taken his life. She said, "Well, this is one club I bet he never wanted to be a member of!" We both laughed. And then she added, in a far more serious and sad tone of voice, "None of us did, but we didn't get the choice." Yet here we are, members of a club none of us ever wanted to join. At least we can take comfort in knowing we're not alone: tens of millions of people in the United States have been touched in some way by suicide, whether it was the suicide of a family member, a friend, or a colleague.

You only begin to discover just how many people have been affected by suicide when you start talking about your own experience and people feel free to share with you what they've been through. More often than not, when the subject of my work comes up in conversation and I disclose that I've written a book about suicide, the stories come pouring out. I never get used to it, and my first thought is always *I never would have guessed!*—as if you can tell who is a suicide survivor just by looking at them. Of course you can't tell, because we look just like everyone else, and the wounds we bear are for the most part invisible unless we decide to share them.

While we don't get to choose whether to be a member of the suicide survivors' "club," we definitely get to choose how we deal with the experience of living through the suicide of someone we know. And that's what this chapter is about: what to expect if someone you know has taken his life, what other people have experienced, how they feel about it, and how they picked up the pieces in the aftermath and went on living.

What is a suicide survivor or survivor of suicide?

Before I started work on this book, I thought a suicide survivor was someone who had survived a suicide attempt. But in fact it's the phrase I hear—and read—most often to describe someone who has lived through the suicide of a loved one.

That's only the first paragraph of the two-paragraph response I wrote to this question in the first edition of this book. After re-reading the original second paragraph, which seemed very angry to my eyes fourteen years after first writing it, my instinct was to cut it because I felt like I was reading someone else's words. Here's what I wrote:

> *I've never thought of myself as someone who "survived" a suicide. I feel I've coped with and learned to live with the reality of what my father did and how it affected my family and my life. And, of course, I did survive the experience. I'm still here all these years later, still wrestling with and talking about it. But to me being called a suicide survivor feels like I'm being condescended to, like a happy face is being pasted on a reality that isn't nearly so heroic or hopeful as the term* survivor *might suggest. I feel more like a victim of my father's suicide.*

Maybe it's the passage of time, in combination with many more years of counseling, that's helped change my perspective, because now I feel perfectly comfortable with thinking of myself as a suicide survivor. I no longer feel "more like a victim of my father's suicide." And while I continue to think about, talk about, and write about my experience, I don't feel like I'm still "wrestling" with my memories and feelings about my father's suicide.

To me that suggests I'm farther along the path of integrating the experience of being a suicide survivor than I was when I first wrote those words. Now I can look back at my experience with a sense of sadness about what happened, as well as with compassion for my father, rather than simply with anger, hurt, and confusion. That to me feels like progress.

How do people react to the suicide of someone close to them?

The sudden death of a loved one, whatever the cause, sets the survivor on a grief-stricken journey that in time ideally leads to an acceptance of the loss.

A death by suicide may bring to that already challenging journey an added dose of confusing, conflicting, and potentially devastating emotions, including shock, denial, guilt, blame, shame, anger, and even relief.

In the pages that follow I'll take you through each of the feelings that a suicide survivor is likely to experience. Please keep in mind that everyone's experience is different and that no one person is likely to experience all of these emotions in the aftermath of a suicide. Also, the order in which I've chosen to write about these emotions is not meant to suggest that this is the order in which suicide survivors experience them or that anyone experiences these emotions in such a compartmentalized way. Experiencing the suicide of a loved one is never so neat and orderly.

Shock

Virtually everyone is shocked by the news of a suicide, even if the suicide itself is not a surprise. That was my experience when I first learned of my sister-in-law's suicide in late 2008. She'd made an attempt two years before and had lately been increasingly isolating herself from others. While I didn't expect that she would kill herself, her decision to end her life wasn't a complete surprise because of her history of emotional problems and her previous attempt. Still, news of her suicide was breathtakingly shocking.

When John came home to a message on his answering machine in 1996 from the sheriff's office in Marin County, California, he knew that something bad had happened: "The sheriff said that my brother's body had been discovered by a thirteen-year-old girl who lived next door—whose mother had committed suicide two years before! Can you imagine how terrible this was for her? The sheriff then told me some of the details about Brian's death, said that this was a case of suicide—just like that—and that I needed to call the coroner's office."

John remembers feeling only numb when he hung up the phone. He said, "I just completely shut down. I was very detached. I didn't weep. I didn't cry. I remember thinking, *My brother could not have done this. He could* not *have* possibly *done this!*" Then John called his youngest brother, Gary, to explain what had happened. "My brother said, 'Brian couldn't do that! He couldn't possibly do that because he's not that big an asshole!' Gary was very angry, but I wasn't feeling anything."

When Kevin boarded a bus in New York City bound for the East Hampton house he shared with Craig, his partner of thirty-four years, he had no reason to believe that Craig would fail to be at the bus stop to pick him up as he always had been in the past.

The first clue Kevin had that something might be wrong was when he called to give Craig a heads-up about a half-hour out and got their voice mail. Kevin recalled, "Our system was that I'd call and let him know I was on the way. When I didn't reach him, I thought he was running errands and called his cell phone, but there was no answer. I tried not to panic and told myself that cell service was spotty out there, which it is, and hoped that Craig would be at the bus stop. But he wasn't."

Kevin had reason to worry, but suicide was not something that even fleetingly crossed his mind. Craig had been having health problems, including heart trouble—several years before, he'd had a stent put in to open a blocked artery—and more recently a clot in his optic nerve had cost him his sight in one eye. He'd also been suffering from a mysterious cerebral pain that several doctors couldn't explain. Given Craig's long list of health problems, Kevin said that he thought to himself, *Oh, my God, he's had a heart attack or a stroke and he's all alone.*

Kevin took a taxi from the bus stop and wasn't sure what he'd find when he got home. When he saw both of their cars in the driveway, "that's when I got really concerned," Kevin said. Their dog, Casey, was at the door to greet Kevin, but was agitated in a way that suggested something was very wrong. Kevin called out for Craig, but there was no answer. He then ran into their bedroom, which was empty, then went to his study, where he saw an envelope on the keyboard of his computer. Kevin continued: "That's when I knew he'd killed himself. I just knew and ran into the backyard, and there he was at the bottom of the pool."

I asked Kevin how in those first moments he could be certain that Craig hadn't simply had a heart attack while he was swimming in the pool. Kevin explained: "His clothes were all very neatly folded at the side of the pool, at the deep end. His shoes were lined up next to his clothes. He broke his watch at 1:35 PM and left that next to his shoes. There was an empty bottle of Valium at the side of the pool too. And he'd tied weights to a belt that he had around his waist."

At this point in the interview I had to pause and take a deep breath before continuing. I found it hard to imagine what a terrible moment of discovery that was for Kevin and felt bad asking him to recall what was clearly an incredibly painful memory.

When Kevin first saw his partner at the bottom of the pool, he screamed. "I was in total shock," he said. "Then I called 911, and the woman who answered asked, 'How long has he been in the pool?' I was out of my mind and said, 'I just got here, how would I know, you nitwit!' and hung up. Next I called my sister and told her what happened and she said, 'Stop talking like that! It's not possible!' so I hung up on her too." Within just a couple of minutes the police arrived, having been alerted by the 911 operator. They pulled Craig's body out of the water and laid him by the side of the pool. Then they questioned Kevin to make certain that Craig's death wasn't a homicide.

The days that followed Craig's death were a blur as Kevin's friends and family stepped in to look after him and to make the funeral arrangements. "I didn't do much of anything," Kevin said. "I was in shock."

My father's brother—my Uncle Richie—was stunned when the call came from the police that my father was in the hospital following an overdose of medication, but not entirely surprised. Given my father's history of depression, his overdose didn't come out of the blue. My uncle explained, "If it had come six months earlier, I wouldn't have been shocked." (My father had been hospitalized for depression a half-year before he overdosed.) "But we thought the real crisis had passed. Irwin was being treated with psychiatric medication and seemed to be improving. He'd found a place to live and went back to work. But I can't say we weren't forewarned that my brother was a potential suicide. He had a history as a young man of mental illness. Then he had a long period of being functional, but he was not a stable human being even in the days when he was going to work and raising a family. Still, it was a shock when we got the call from the police. Of course, at that point I didn't accept that he was going to die."

The second shock for my uncle came when my father's initial hopeful prognosis turned out to have been overly optimistic. My uncle said, "The day after he was admitted to the hospital, the doctor called and told me that my brother had opened his eyes. He said he thought he was going to be all right. The doctor was a nice guy and very reassuring. But the next day it was a different doctor, and by then my brother was motionless. The pneumonia was worse, and he had a fever. This second doctor was very cool and abrupt and told me, 'Your brother doesn't stand much of a chance.' It was a roller coaster." My father died the next morning.

Four decades after my father's suicide, I can still picture the moment when I learned that he was dead—and even after all this time, when I conjure that picture, I get a sick feeling in the pit of my stomach. I came home from school and knew right away that something was wrong. My mother was unexpectedly home from work, and she seemed grim. I asked my younger brother, who was nine years old and had gotten home from school before me, if Dad was dead. He wouldn't answer. So I had a pretty good idea what was coming when my mother asked me to come into her bedroom and sat me down on her bed and told me my father was dead. Even so, it was a crushing, shocking, primal agony unlike anything I had ever known. When my mother broke the news to me, I yelled, "No!" and ran from her bedroom and locked myself in the bathroom—the only place in our small apartment where locked privacy was possible. I grabbed on to the towels hanging from the back of the bathroom door and pulled them down as I collapsed in a heap on the floor. I buried my head in the mound of soft cotton and screamed and screamed and screamed.

For me the immediate period after my father's death was characterized by a sense of unreality. I felt numb. I was dazed. I hardly cried. I was disoriented. I couldn't sleep. I could hardly eat. I now know that what I experienced was shock and that what I felt is not at all uncommon for those who experience the sudden loss of a loved one.

Denial and Disbelief

Confronted with the suicide of a loved one, some people can't accept what has happened. They simply can't believe their loved one "could do that to me. It couldn't be. It's a mistake." They convince themselves that it was an accident that their mother drove under a truck, that their son overdosed on sleeping pills, that their grandfather jumped from an office building. All accidents. "She must have fallen asleep at the wheel." "He must have forgotten how many pills he'd taken." "He fell out the window." "He was just playing around with the rope and must have slipped."

No matter how obvious the facts are to someone on the outside looking in, people who are coping with the twin shock of a sudden death and the likelihood that their loved one took his or her life may find it impossible to cope with what's happened. In such a case, denial and disbelief are perfectly understandable responses.

Sandra is a high-energy sixty-year-old freelance theater director who lives in northern California. Her exuberance, sense of humor, and positive outlook on life give no hint of the two suicides she's lived through. In 1969 her father, who suffered from undiagnosed and untreated bipolar disorder, hanged himself. Fifteen years later her mentally ill brother, whom Sandra characterized as a "crisis factory," also hanged himself.

In chapter 1, we heard Sandra speak about getting a call from her aunt a few days before her father's suicide telling her that her father was going to kill himself and that she was the only one who could "save him." Before leaving on a belated honeymoon weekend, Sandra, who was twenty at the time, extracted a promise from her father that he wouldn't do anything to harm himself.

Shortly after Sandra returned home that Monday, her mother telephoned her. Sandra recalled: "She said that something had

happened and could I come over right away. I didn't really want
to because I was exhausted. And finally she said, 'Your dad is
dead.' I said, 'What happened?' She said that he'd had a heart
attack. I wanted to believe it. For one thing at this point I still
. . . it was easier to believe that something took him rather than
him taking himself."

Immediately after her father's death, there were clues that
Sandra's father didn't have a heart attack (aside from the fact that
he'd threatened to kill himself just the week before). For one
thing, Sandra overheard a conversation between her mother and
the mortician. Sandra said, "I heard him say, 'We made him look
as good as we could.' I didn't know what he meant. Why would
someone who had a heart attack not look okay in the coffin? There
was an implication that something was being hidden. There was
also an aura of secrecy between my mother and her sister."

Over the weeks that followed, Sandra and her mother would
test the waters with each other regarding the truth, but Sandra
didn't really want to know and her mother didn't really want to
tell. As Sandra remembered, "I would ask her if he really died
from a heart attack, and for a while my mother lied. You have
to remember that after my father killed himself my mother went
into an infantile state of incapacity. She couldn't eat, she couldn't
sleep. So while I don't think I really wanted to know what happened, I also didn't want to push my mother, who was already
having a terrible time. But after a few weeks my mother would
say in response to my asking, 'Do you really want to know?' But
before the conversation went any further, one or the other of us
would run to the bathroom and vomit."

Then one evening a few months after the suicide, while sitting
at the dinette table in her mother's kitchen, Sandra asked again.
"I'd been getting braver, and that evening I asked her, 'Did he
slit his wrists?' And she said, 'No, he hung himself.' "

Sandra was shocked by what her mother told her. She said,
"I think the world goes black. I felt like fainting. That's what
caused me to vomit all those other times, just anticipating that
this was what might have happened. So now it made sense that
they would need to fix him up. But I didn't want to believe it,
didn't want to know, but by then I wanted to know. So when you
hear something like that, you go into a sort of swoon. Hanging
yourself is so premeditated. You can't hang yourself quickly. You

have to choose the spot, buy the rope. You have to really think that out. I asked my mother where, because I didn't know. Then she told me he did it in the basement of their apartment building while she was asleep upstairs. She remained in that building for twenty-something years. I don't know how. I would have moved away very quickly."

Michelle, whose account of her husband Paul's suicide following nine months on a prescription cholesterol-lowering medication appears in Chapter 1, wasn't sure what to think when she returned home from jury duty to find their house surrounded by the police. Michelle recalled, "I had tried to call Paul at noon to see if I could have lunch with him, but he wasn't at the office. That was unusual, but I wasn't worried." When she'd left the house that morning, Michelle recalled, Paul had been laughing and joking about Valentine's Day, which was a month away, as he kissed her good-bye.

After parking her car, Michelle started to cross the street when a plainclothes detective spotted her and held up his hand. She said, "He knew immediately who I was and brought me over to the police car that was right in front of the house. They asked me if I was Paul's wife, and then I knew. So I asked, 'Is my husband dead?' And they said, 'Yes.'"

Michelle thought her husband had been murdered. She said, "They started grilling me and asked whether we'd had a fight. I explained that I never raised a hand in anger at Paul, and he had never raised a hand to me. That's when they told me he had scratches on his neck. They thought I had done that. I said, 'No, he was murdered, he must have been murdered, because I didn't do that.'" (It was only after the autopsy report came back a month later that Michelle learned that the scratches were self-inflicted wounds made with a razor. Death was the result of a single gunshot to the head.)

Over the next couple of hours, as Michelle was questioned outside her house, the police began sharing details of what they had found. She said, "They were telling me bits and pieces, like the house was torn up. I told them that Paul was this incredibly civilized man, not someone who would tear up a house. So at that point I knew that something was really amiss, but they kept saying they were pretty sure it was a suicide."

It wasn't until the police told her there was a suicide note that she let go of the idea that he'd been murdered. Michelle continued: "It was four or five hours after I first got home, and they still had not allowed me to see Paul or go into the house, and they tell me there's a suicide note and asked for my help with it." The police handed Michelle the note, on one side of which was a drawing of Paul, Michelle, and their dog, with the sun shining above. Michelle recalled, "My husband used to draw these hysterical little stick figure drawings of us and our dog, Damned Spot." This drawing was no different than the others, except that beneath the stick figures Paul had written: "I have loved you so much and you have loved me so well. Your Paul."

Michelle said that the police were far more interested in what was on the other side of the page. "There was tricky light in the alley," she said, "and it was hard to read, but what we thought Paul had written was, 'I could explain why, but everybody will have to figure it out on their own.' Almost everyone I showed that letter to said Paul's suicide was impulsive, but at that moment I just didn't know what to think."

Shortly before midnight Michelle was allowed to see her husband's body—"I kissed him," she recalled. And then she was taken inside the house. What she found shocked her. She described the scene: "It was just wild. The closets and cupboards are thrown open and emptied out. There was blood everywhere. (And I'm still finding it. Just the other day I found a book covered in blood.) It didn't make sense, but I'd had enough training in psychology to know that this was a psychotic break. No way that Paul did this in any sort of mind that was his own."

A little later in this chapter Michelle discusses the research she did in an effort to figure out what led her husband to take his life.

Denial or disbelief that a suicide has occurred can last for a moment or for hours, as it did for Michelle. It can last for days, or at least until a medical examiner confirms the awful truth. Or it can last for months—as it did for Sandra—or it can last forever, no matter what the coroner says or what is clearly demonstrated to the contrary. There is no getting around the fact of a loved one's death, but there is no end to the possibilities when it comes to the ways in which you can convince yourself that death occurred from natural causes.

In addition to the kind of denial I've just described, there's also something I call "official" denial. That's when the doctor or medical authorities conspire with family members to hide the truth. This is done—as it was in my father's case—with the best of intentions, to spare everyone the shame of a suicide and the judgment or condemnation of society. Unfortunately, official denial can keep suicide survivors from learning to live with the truth about what really happened.

With my father's death, it was easy to achieve official denial. By the time he died, four days after he'd overdosed on tranquilizers, there wasn't a trace of the drug in his body. The official cause of death was pneumonia. I always got a chuckle out of that explanation. A forty-four-year-old man who was as strong as an ox, who was loading sacks of mail onto trucks only days before he died, who just the week before was playing football with me and my brother, who was rarely if ever sick with even a cold, and who'd suffered for years with mental illness—died of natural causes? The amazing thing was that virtually everyone seemed to accept that explanation—or at least they didn't openly reject it.

Even at twelve, I thought the whole thing was such a charade that I couldn't bear to tell anyone the official version of my father's death. For one thing, I didn't think I could be convincing. But I didn't want to tell the *real* truth because from everything everyone *wasn't* saying I was convinced that suicide was so awful that it was unspeakable. So I generally avoided telling anyone that my father was dead. I just pretended that nothing had happened.

Charlie, who worked for years as a big-city newspaper reporter, discovered just how complicated the issue of denial can be when he wrote an obituary for a young friend, Scott, who had hanged himself. Charlie recalled: "Scott was an intern at the paper the previous summer. He did really well and later landed a job at one of the top twenty newspapers." Charlie heard from Scott that the job was great, but that he hated living in the city where the newspaper was located and, as Charlie recalled from his conversation with Scott, "a simmering depression blossomed."

Charlie explained: "Scott told me that he had told his brother that he was afraid he might hurt himself. And his brother told him that he needed to drop everything and get himself to a place where he could get his life in order, which he did. Scott and I spoke maybe every couple of months. On one of those calls I said, 'You *are* getting help, aren't you?' And he said, 'Don't worry, I'm taking care of it.' I was satisfied with his answer. I wasn't concerned, especially since he didn't say anything about still being unhappy. I know in retrospect that I should have been concerned, but he seemed to be taking care of the problem."

When it came time for Charlie's newspaper to publish Scott's obituary, Charlie felt that writing it himself was the least he could do for his friend. "I knew Scott best of anyone in the newsroom. And I just wanted to flow into this thing that had happened and deal with it that way."

Because of Scott's history of depression and the circumstances of his death, Charlie didn't think to question whether his death was a suicide until the obituary ran and he got a call from Scott's sister-in-law. Charlie said, "She told me that she was familiar with depression and that Scott had mentioned depression, but she didn't think it was suicide. I think they wanted the newspaper to publish a correction or a clarification." In response to the call, Charlie's editor sent for the coroner's report, which had concluded that Scott's death was a suicide.

Charlie reviewed the coroner's report and didn't find anything to dispute that conclusion. Still, he was sympathetic. "Look, I was trained in the reality business, but I also saw my mom when my dad had lung cancer, and my mom reached for whatever she could to soften the whole thing. Here he's a frail old man, and the doctor said that chemo would give him a five percent chance of better results. And my mom says, 'He definitely has to get chemo.' I think the chemo killed him, but that's the route my mom took."

I asked Charlie if he would have handled the obituary differently if he had known before it was published that the family would object to his characterization of Scott's death as a suicide. I was surprised by his answer because I'm not sure I would have expected a reporter to consider anything but the facts. Charlie said, "Looking back, I'd make the same choices, but I think we could have found a middle ground. As I later learned, the family wanted the obituary to say, 'by his own hand,' and I said 'suicide.' If they had been lobbying me, I would have said sure, we can go with that. I don't think the readers would have been compromised in any way. The family's contention was that it was by his own hand *accidentally*, and that's how they would have read it. For me it still would have meant by his own hand *intentionally*."

Grief

Intense grief is a perfectly normal reaction to the loss of a loved one. And for some people, the grief experience can be very physical. They lack energy, have trouble sleeping and eating, and may develop headaches and stomach problems.

Daniel was so overwhelmed by the grief he experienced over his older brother's suicide that he turned to drugs to kill the pain. When I spoke with him, it had been only six months since his brother's death at age thirty. "We were best buddies from just about the day I was born," Daniel told me. "He was three years older than I am, and we did everything together. At first, I was just numb, bumping into walls. The first night, I fell asleep crying, and I woke up crying hard. I cried so much that my vision was blurry."

During the first seven days following Daniel's brother's suicide, a period that included arranging and attending the funeral and visiting the house where his brother shot himself, Daniel was overwhelmed with grief. "It was so painful that I couldn't imagine how I'd get through it. So I bought a ton of dope, and whenever I was on the verge of feeling pain or crying, I'd smoke some. I've pretty much done that on and off since then, but I've quit for a while so I can start dealing with my emotions."

Daniel thought he was past the worst of his feelings of grief, but while reading the newspaper on the morning of the day we spoke he came across the brand name of the gun his brother had used, and it all came rushing back. "It was just one word that brought it all back. The feelings were as intense as they were on day six or day seven, and it's a half-year later. How much longer do I have to do this? I feel like I didn't get a good deal in life. I want my money back. It's six months and a day, and I want to get going."

Despite his frustration, Daniel knows that it will be a while longer—months, or perhaps years—before he is finished grieving the loss of his brother. "I know it will take me even longer if I keep doing dope," he said, "but there are times I just can't take the pain. I wish I were stronger."

Not everyone grieves the loss of a loved one right away, and it may be some time before shock gives way to grief. For children especially, grieving may be unconsciously set aside. That was my experience. After the initial shock of my father's death,

I went on with life, almost as if nothing had happened. Nearly a decade later I was so deeply unhappy—and really had no idea why I was so unhappy—that I felt compelled to seek professional help. Much to my surprise, soon after starting once-a-week sessions with a psychologist, I found myself propelled back into the painful period of my life following my father's suicide and began grieving his death for the first time.

For more on this subject, please see the question "How long does it take to get over the suicide of a loved one?" later in this chapter.

Rejection and Abandonment

The suicide of a loved one can feel like the ultimate rejection. The person has gone forever, and those left behind, whether parents, children, spouses, or friends, can't help but feel as if they've been rejected and abandoned.

When Kevin's partner Craig took his life, Kevin was left alone for the first time in thirty-four years. He said, "I felt very abandoned and angry too. Craig and I had been together since law school. We had developed a whole life together and had a whole life ahead of us. And then all of a sudden this person who had been with me through every major event in my life, left. I remember thinking, *As bad as he was feeling, wasn't our life worth living for? What about our dog? Our families? The going gets tough, and you go?* What he did said to me that our life together wasn't worth living."

Four weeks after Craig's death, their beloved dog Casey developed a rash. Kevin recalled, "I had to give him oral medication with a syringe. It's a four-hand job, but I tried to do it myself. Casey struggled, and the medication went everywhere. I just sat down on the floor and cried and said to myself, *Look what you did to me! Look what you did to* us!"

The first nine months for Kevin were the most difficult. After a lifetime shared with another person, he worried about being alone. "What if I died or something happened to me? There would be no one to find me," he said. "Then after nine months something happened— nothing in particular—and I realized I could handle being alone."

Anger

Last year I attended the American Foundation for Suicide Prevention's National Survivors of Suicide Day annual program in New York City and was struck by something a man about my age said regarding his struggle to deal with his anger in the wake of his teenage son's suicide. In the years since the suicide, he said, he'd worked hard to get past the anger he felt toward his wife, his son, and himself and had largely succeeded. Then he paused and said he wasn't so sure he'd gotten past his anger at his son for what he'd done to the family.

Following a suicide, those left behind may find themselves feeling angry about a lot of things. I was angry for a long time and still felt quite angry when I first wrote this book in the mid-1990s, twenty-five years after my father died. While I no longer feel angry, I thought it would be useful to include the original list of the targets of my anger:

- The Veterans Administration hospital where my father was treated, for not properly diagnosing his depression and for supplying him with the pills he used to kill himself;
- My uncle and grandparents, for not having my father committed when they knew he was suicidal;
- My mother, for not recognizing that my brother, sister, and I all needed counseling;
- My father, for killing himself, for abandoning me, for destroying my family, for ruining my childhood, for leaving me with the legacy of suicide, for not giving me a chance to say good-bye;
- My entire family, for pretending that my father didn't kill himself, for making me feel ashamed of the truth.

Other people direct their anger at God or the mental health profession. They may also be angry at their dead loved one for:

- Leaving them with unanswered questions
- Not giving them a chance to help
- Making them feel guilty

- Making them feel responsible for the suicide
- Making them feel ashamed and embarrassed
- Doing such a selfish thing
- Leaving them behind to deal with the police, the medical examiner, the morgue, the funeral home, and the mess—both physical and emotional

If their relationship with the person who died was a troubled one, those left behind may also be angry at their loved one for robbing them of the chance to reconcile. Or they may be angry at themselves for not recognizing that there was a problem. They may even be angry at themselves for being angry.

Not everyone faced with a suicide experiences anger. In an interview in the magazine *Entertainment Weekly*, Wendy O'Conner, the mother of Kurt Cobain, the popular rock musician who killed himself in 1994, said, "People have asked me, aren't you angry at Kurt for taking such a cheap way out, for leaving Frances [his daughter] and you, and I said, no, not at all. People don't understand what depression is. . . . He was a wonderful person, but he just couldn't stand the pain anymore. That's why I'm not angry at Kurt."

Guilt

The primary reasons why people feel guilty is because they weren't able to do anything to prevent the suicide or they fear that they did something to contribute to it. For example, they didn't get home in time . . . they had a fight with their spouse just before the suicide . . . they were too strict . . . they were too lenient . . . they weren't loving enough . . . they didn't help their friend get the right help . . . they failed to recognize that there was a problem . . . they wished their parent was dead and told him or her so . . . they inadvertently provided the gun or medication with which their loved one took his life. The sense of guilt can be crushing, and it can last a lifetime.

I'm lucky because I knew I wasn't responsible for my father's suicide, so I didn't feel guilty about that. I also knew that, given my age, I could not have been responsible for what he did, nor could I have done anything to prevent it.

Nonetheless, there was plenty for me to feel guilty about, just as there is for most people who have lived through a suicide. For example, I felt guilty for feeling relieved that my father was dead (more on that later in this chapter). I felt guilty for being angry with my father for killing himself. He was dead, so how could I have been angry with him? And I felt guilty for having been angry with my father's brother (my Uncle Richie, whom I adored) for not doing more to prevent my father's death.

Feelings of guilt were multifaceted and overwhelming for my Uncle Richie, who was twelve years younger than my father. He told me, "My immediate feelings were, of course, terrible sorrow, but then there was a creeping in of some relief, which was at the base of what was bugging me. How could I be the kind of person who would feel relief at the loss of someone who was beloved by me? But in the preceding months I had been so frightened of what he might do, especially since he had access to you and your brother every weekend." (My parents were separated, and my brother and I spent every Saturday with our father.)

My uncle continued: "I thought he might harm you. He was so heavily medicated that I thought he might accidentally drive off the road. I also thought he might use that method to kill himself, maybe even with the two of you in the car. And I didn't know what to do about it. So it was a relief not to have that worry anymore, but I felt terrible for feeling relieved."

My uncle also felt guilty because he didn't believe he'd done enough to try to head off his brother's suicide. He explained, "I absolutely felt guilt that I couldn't save him. He'd given me signals. I wasn't aware those signals should be taken seriously. Of course, now it seems completely unworldly and naive that I didn't take those signs seriously. He had spoken to me about the possibility of suicide. He said, 'If this pain doesn't stop, I'd rather not live.' He didn't say, 'I'm going to kill myself and take the boys with me,' but I no longer trusted his ability to reason, and I was nervous about it. We all were."

I asked my uncle what more he thought he could have done. He said, "At the time, I was paralyzed with inaction. When he told me that he didn't want to live, I'm sure I said, 'It's always worth living,' but I didn't ask, 'What do you mean? What are you talking about?' I was afraid to hear the answers. And I could not get up the courage to say to him, 'Irwin, you're seriously ill, and you need to be hospitalized.' I could not visualize myself having him committed. He trusted me, and I felt that it would be a terrible betrayal. I was afraid of alienating him. I had a discussion with my mother about committing him, but she said she could never do it. I more or less followed her wishes, and I didn't seek professional help to find out what we should do, but I should have."

What further complicated my uncle's experience of his brother's suicide and contributed to the guilt he felt over not being able to do something to help him was the special relationship the two of them had had from the beginning. My uncle recalled, "He was everything to me, and he adored me. He waited twelve years for a brother and showered me with a tremendous amount of love and attention. I saved him from being an only child, and he was very unhappy before I came along."

My grandmother loved to tell the story of how she came to have a second child twelve years after she had my father. When my dad was ten, he started agitating for "a brother or a puppy." My grandfather was dead set against a second child because he wanted to devote their limited resources to their one child. So with my father's promise that he would look after a dog, they got one. The puppy lasted through only a few accidents before my grandfather insisted it go back to the pound, and so my grandparents went to plan B and came through with the baby brother.

My uncle told me: "Irwin was a very unusual big brother. With a twelve-year age difference, brothers usually don't have much going for them, but he took me everywhere. Taught me how to play ball. He was as much father as brother. So I feel I failed my brother, particularly since he was there for me when I was growing up. I give myself a lot of heat for not coming through for him. I count it as the great failure of my life."

As if my uncle didn't already have a full plate of guilt, there was more. "I let you guys down when you needed support the most," he recalled. "That was a special time when someone really needed to stand up for the three of you [my brother, sister, and me]. Your sister in particular needed a surrogate father, but I couldn't do it because I was ashamed of myself and felt guilty for allowing her father to die. Several years later, when Heidi asked me to walk her down the aisle at her wedding, I said no because I didn't feel worthy. I hadn't been there to save her father and hadn't been there for her in the aftermath. That engendered a lot of guilty feelings."

Kevin, whose partner Craig drowned himself, first addressed the issue of guilt earlier in this book in a question about suicide notes. In the handwritten note Craig left behind, he stated that Kevin was "responsible for most of the good things in my life," which Kevin thinks was Craig's effort to let him know that he had no reason to believe he was in any way responsible for Craig's decision to end his life.

When I met with Kevin three years after Craig died, he explained that Craig had been a perfectionist and not someone who could imagine life as a "semi-invalid," but that he never gave any indication that ending his life by his own hand was in the cards. Consequently, Kevin, who is a compact, rugged-looking sixty-two-year-old with an expressive smile, said he didn't struggle with overwhelming guilt—in no small part because Craig was so careful to keep his plans hidden. Kevin had no clue what Craig was planning, so there was no opportunity to intervene.

Still, after a lifetime as a hardworking and successful executive—who now devotes his time to assisting nonprofit organizations—Kevin wasn't going to let it go at that. Like many of us faced with questions after a suicide—and hoping to uncover what role, if any, we might have played in our loved one's death—he dug deep, looking for evidence, trying to come to some sort of understanding about what happened. In the process, Kevin was able to confirm that he had nothing to feel guilty about.

Kevin recalled, "I've gone over the transcript of our lives from the weeks and months before Craig died and examined everything. The day before he killed himself he bought six really nice bottles of wine to take with us the following weekend on a planned visit to see friends in upstate New York. But the week before that he filled the Valium prescription that he took before drowning himself. My therapist explained to me that Craig was probably operating on two planes."

The day Craig died, Kevin said, there had been nothing to indicate that he shouldn't make his planned trip to New York City. It was only in retrospect that Craig's behavior seemed odd. "It was just one thing," Kevin said. "Every night for thirty-four years he would set places at the table for the two of us for breakfast the next morning. And the morning I left there was only one place setting and I asked him, 'Why didn't you set a place for yourself?' He said he would have breakfast later. It was strange, but I didn't think anything of it. I called him at 11:00 A.M. to say I'd gotten to the city, and he sounded tired, and I told him not to worry about making dinner. He said he'd be talking to his therapist by phone later in the afternoon, and that was the last time we spoke."

There was one other memory that stood out. "The night before he died," Kevin said, "Craig made a really nice dinner for us. And afterwards we went out for ice cream. The service was terrible, and Craig said, 'That's the last time I'm going to get ice cream here.' But other than these little things, there was no indication he was going to do this. He was very smart. He knew if he discussed this with me I would have stayed with him the whole time."

Kevin also discovered clues that suggested Craig had been thinking about suicide for some time. In preparing for Craig's funeral, Kevin asked his niece to go into Craig's library to find some poetry by Jorge Luis Borges, one of Craig's favorite writers. "My niece comes back with the book, and she's white. And she said that in the book there was a piece of paper marking a short poem about suicide that had the line: 'I will die and, with me, the weight of the intolerable universe.' Reading that made me mad because Borges made it sound like suicide lets you give up all your burdens, that it's the most wonderful thing. Borges had gone blind, but he didn't give up on life. Clearly Craig read that poem more than once, because he had marked it. I don't know if he intended to leave a clue by marking it. I don't know if he left it there for us to find, but it was some indication that suicide was something he'd been thinking about."

One other mystery that Kevin was left to sort out was the broken watch that Craig had placed beside the pool. It was stopped at 1:35 P.M. Kevin wondered, "Did he break his watch to let me know that I couldn't have saved him if I'd come home five minutes earlier? He knew I wouldn't be home until late afternoon, so was this some kind of message to keep me from feeling guilty? I don't know. But after thinking through everything, I came to the honest conclusion that Craig was going to kill himself and went to great lengths to hide his plans."

Kevin had some final thoughts on the issue of guilt: "You

can't get away from thinking 'what if?' But the way Craig did it, there aren't a lot of what-ifs. And with everything else I've had to deal with in the aftermath, I don't want to be burdened by guilt. I've spent so much time going over the transcript of our life together in the final six months, looking for things to beat myself up over. I didn't find anything. I've come to believe that what he did wasn't a cry for help. And given what I know now, I couldn't have intervened." Kevin added that it was conversations with his therapist over a period of many months that helped him "get to this point."

Blame and Self-Recrimination

When it comes to blame after a suicide, there's more than enough to go around. Blame can come from every direction and go in every direction. If you're the parent or spouse of the person who died, there will inevitably be people who blame you for being a bad parent or a lousy spouse—no matter what the circumstances.

If you're the psychiatrist who was treating the person who took his life, you may be blamed for not doing your job right, and sometimes that blame will come from your own colleagues. If you're the sibling and you didn't take in your mentally ill brother when he had no place to live, there will be family and friends who can't help but blame you for not doing more to prevent his death. If you were the colleague who sat at the adjacent desk, your other colleagues may wonder why you didn't intervene. And of course, people who have lost a friend or loved one to suicide blame themselves, directing what may be their harshest condemnations inward at their already wounded hearts.

Rightly or wrongly, suicide inspires blame. It's normal. It's natural. We all do it—how can we not?—and it's awful and destructive for everyone.

"For a long time, I blamed the psychologists," Carolyn told me, explaining her feelings over the suicide of her seventeen-year-old son more than a decade ago. "He had drug problems, he was depressed, he was angry, we couldn't control him. So we sent him to all kinds of counselors, and not one of them ever told us he was suicidal. I know all about the patient-client confidentiality business, but someone should have warned us what to look out for."

Carolyn saved plenty of blame for herself. "I really tortured myself, thinking I should have known," she said, "but it was something I wasn't familiar with. I didn't know anything about suicide, so I couldn't have known what symptoms to watch for. It wasn't until I walked in on him with the gun in his hand that I realized he was suicidal. I had only a split second to say, 'Please, don't!'"

John, who was fifty-three when his forty-five-year-old brother Brian killed himself, blames their mother: "Throughout our childhood our mother attempted six times, so it was a pattern we were familiar with. My mother's first attempt at suicide was when I was eight years old. She threw herself down the steps when she was pregnant with Brian. Later she rammed her car up against an overpass. She cut her wrists. She ran a hose into her car. Mother would have been on a pretty strong medication now, but in those days they'd check her into the 'booby hatch' for a few weeks and then send her home. I think we all learned to be depressed at Mummy's knee."

John didn't save all of the blame for his mother. He said, "I blame the whole family. I said, 'Let's just blame *all* of them!' And over time I've removed all of the family pictures from our apartment. I was cleaning house. I didn't want any images of Brian around either. I don't recommend that necessarily for everyone, but that's worked for me. I think there will always be dark clouds in the background because of Brian's suicide, and removing any reminders has helped me keep them at bay."

My Uncle Richie blamed my mother for his brother's suicide, which contributed to my uncle's absence from my life in the years following my father's death. "I was very angry with your mom," he recalled. "I blamed her for throwing your father out of the house at his most vulnerable time. He'd just been in the hospital, so I thought the timing was awful, even though she had just cause to want a separation. I also felt she didn't treat my mother right in the aftermath. Your mother told Grandma that Irwin had to be watched, implying that she was responsible for what happened. For those reasons, I resented your mother and didn't want to have anything to do with her, and you guys lived in the same house. I should have been above my antipathy for your mother. It called for a bigger person than that. There are tragedies and things in life that call for you to put aside those kinds of feelings, but I couldn't do it."

As the years passed following my father's death and I became more aware of the circumstances around his suicide, I found it very easy to place blame. It was my uncle's fault that my father killed himself: he should have done *something* to stop him. It was my grandfather's fault: he was always very critical of my father. It was my mother's fault: she should never have asked him for a separation. It was the fault of the doctors who were treating him: they were negligent and gave him enough drugs to overdose. They were all to blame.

For a long time I never thought to blame my father for his own suicide. It was, after all, his actions that led to his death, but I didn't think to make him responsible for what he did, and when those thoughts crept into my head, I felt guilty for thinking them and pushed them away. After all, my father was the victim of the neglect of others, of their failure to see what was going on, of their failure to intervene. If only they'd done the right thing, he'd still be alive. Wouldn't he?

Whenever my grandmother and I talked about my father's death, there was always one thing I could count on her to say: "If only I hadn't gone to Florida." "If only . . .": it's the start of a phrase that's thought and spoken by almost everyone who has felt responsible for not preventing the suicide of a loved one. "If only I'd come home earlier" . . . "If only I'd known there was a problem" . . . "If only I hadn't yelled at him" . . . "If only I'd told her I loved her" . . . "If only I'd been more understanding" . . . "If only I'd dragged him to a psychiatrist."

When my father swallowed a fatal dose of pills, his parents were in Florida visiting with my grandmother's brother, who was gravely ill. My grandmother had been torn between staying home and keeping in close contact with my father and spending time with her brother. While she was away, her worst fear came true.

No matter what I said, and no matter how many times I said it, my grandmother went to her grave blaming herself, believing that if only she'd stayed home my father would not have taken his life. There's no way to know exactly what would have happened if my grandmother hadn't gone to Florida, but I feel certain that my father would have killed himself anyway—if not on that particular weekend, then another time. I wish my grandmother could have believed that.

Sandra didn't see how she *couldn't* blame herself. "Don't

forget," she told me, "my aunt said, 'You're the only one who can save him.' I bought it. I blamed myself. I wasn't experienced or old enough to know better. All I could think about was what I could have done: stayed around, talked to him more, intervened, not just left town, taken it more seriously. But you don't know it's an actual possibility until something like that happens. Two years earlier my father was seriously depressed, and he got over it. So why wouldn't he get over it this time? It was really unimaginable that he would kill himself."

Over the many years since her father's death, Sandra said, she has worked hard to "disabuse myself of the belief that I could have saved him." She continued, "Eventually I came to recognize that I couldn't save him and that it wasn't my fault. But you never get over blaming yourself. For the rest of your life you wish it was something that didn't happen, so you keep going back to it and thinking, *How could I have seen it coming? How could I have stopped it?* It's impossible not to replay that in your head. I don't know how you could *not*, because you just never get over it." Sandra said she knows that she wasn't to blame, but added, "It's still hard not to blame myself." Maybe that's the best any of us can do: try not to blame ourselves and try not to assign responsibility to anyone else—except, perhaps, the person who died by his own hand.

Michelle, whose husband Paul shot himself after nine months on a prescription drug that left him in an increasingly "morose" state of mind, doesn't blame her husband, but she still blames herself for not figuring things out until well after it was too late. She said, "The what-ifs proliferate. Five years later I still ask myself, *What if I'd asked in those first days after he started taking the statin drug* [which can cause depression and suicidal thinking] *if his change in affect could be related to the drug?* I see an affect that's different in my guy, and I don't even do a quick search on the Internet? Even though I know I'm not the one who prescribed the drug, I'm going to die with this. The what-ifs can really kill you."

Confusion

The suicide of a loved one leaves in its wake painful confusion that's expressed with a one-word question: *Why?* Embedded in that question are three other questions that begin the same way:

Why didn't we see it coming? Why didn't she come to us for help? And above all else, why did she do it?

Daniel is still asking himself why his brother took his life. Daniel's brother had recently bought a new house following a painful separation from his wife. Daniel said, "He seemed real excited about the house and was getting it ready for his two kids to visit. It wasn't like he was unemployed or anything; he had a good job. I thought he had everything to live for. Sure, his wife was getting remarried to someone he didn't like, but that's no reason to kill yourself. I want to know why he did it. Why would he do this to his kids? To *me*? I have this sinking feeling that I'll never know the answer. I'm not even sure *he* knew why."

In their search for answers, Daniel and his parents went to the house where his brother died. "We took the place apart," he said, "trying to find a clue, a reason, an answer—something. But there was nothing, except for the bloodstained carpet in the room where he shot himself."

Relief

Feeling relieved following the suicide of a loved one is not un-common and is especially likely when the person who died was in some way a burden in life. For example, if a loved one had struggled with chronic depression or schizophrenia, had been in and out of hospitals, or had been abusing drugs or alcohol, his or her death is likely to be something of a relief.

Relief is a troubling emotion in the context of the suicide of a loved one. But whether we're at peace with that feeling or experiencing tremendous guilt, there's no getting around the fact that sometimes we feel relieved that our loved one is dead.

Patricia had struggled with severe back pain from around the time her mentally ill daughter first expressed her wish to die at age thirteen. For the next seven years, Patricia had scans, visited chiropractors, took painkillers, but nothing seemed to help. However, as Patricia recalled, "on the day she died my back pain went away and has never come back. I also stopped grinding my teeth. It was a sign of the horrible stress I was under. If I could trade, I'd have my daughter back in a second, because it was worth it to have her in my life—I miss her so much, we were very good friends. But not to worry every day about her cutting herself, whether she was eating, and whether or not she was going to kill herself, that was a relief. Of course, it was also hard to get used to not having to worry about that constantly."

Sandra, whose brother hanged himself fifteen years after her father did the same, would not trade anything to have her brother back. Other than how "devastated" she felt for her mother having "to experience such a terrible loss again," Sandra felt only relief. She explained: "I called him a crisis factory. He turned out crisis after crisis, whether it was getting arrested or being put in jail or overdosing, from his teen years on until he killed himself."

For most of the years between her father's death and her brother's death, Sandra was able to keep her distance from her brother, and she did what she could to protect her mother as well. But Sandra's mother had a hard time saying no to her son. Sandra recalled, "He was living with my mother on and off, and I was saving those articles about mothers who were hacked up by their sons and stuffed into the upholstery. I was sure he would eventually kill my mother, so when he killed himself I was relieved."

When Sandra returned home after her brother's funeral, she found herself in the middle of an unexpected—and as she recalled it—bizarrely appropriate celebration. "I was working at a restaurant, and my first day back was a Sunday," she said. "There was this little vagabond guy named Brucie—he was a regular customer who had no money and was mentally challenged—and he was sitting there when one of my colleagues came over to me with a piece of pie with a candle in it like it was my birthday, but it was out of sympathy for my loss. And Brucie saw it, so he yells out loudly to me across the restaurant, 'Is it your birthday?' What am I going to yell back, 'No, my brother committed suicide!' So I said, 'Yeah, it's my birthday.' The next thing I know, everyone in the restaurant starts singing "Happy Birthday." I was stunned, too stunned to cry. And really, it was ironic, so I laughed. Of course I laughed. I couldn't have written that! If you put that in a play, the critics would say, 'What, are you crazy?'"

After the singing ended, Brucie left the restaurant and returned a half-hour later. "He comes back with a little box with a ribbon around it," Sandra said, "and inside is a jar of potpourri. What could I say? In a sense it *was* my birthday. My brother's death was a form of release. A form of newness. I was also so relieved *not* to have a threat to my mother anymore. As sad as it was for my mother and for me, I was very relieved. You know, they say suicide is a permanent solution to a temporary problem. But in my case it was a permanent solution to a permanent problem. I know that sounds harsh, but it's honest. For me that little weird birthday celebration, if you want to get new-age-y about it, was a celebration of my being released. How could I *not* be relieved?"

I used to be embarrassed about the fact that one of the first emotions I experienced once I got over the initial shock of my father's suicide was relief. Part of me thought his death was a good thing. I was certain that God—or someone—would punish me for feeling that way, so I never told anyone. But there were a couple of good reasons for feeling as I did.

The primary reason had to do with the relationship between my parents. They had been through a bitter and stormy separation two years before my father died. The welcome calm that settled over our once-tense household after Dad moved out was threatened by my father's clandestine visits to the apartment when my brother, sister, and I were at school and my mother was at work.

In the weeks before my father's death, my mother talked to me about changing the locks on the door to our apartment. I was terrified of the confrontation that I knew would follow. My father's temper was legendarily explosive. Dad's death meant that the confrontation would never take place.

There was another reason I was relieved. Because my dad had emotional problems, I feared he'd wind up institutionalized. I imagined how terrible it would be to visit him after he was locked up in a state mental hospital; my twelve-year-old imagination conjured up a Dickensian scene. I also didn't know how I'd explain to friends that my dad was in a mental hospital. His death meant I'd never have to deal with that either.

Compassion

On some level it's hard *not* to feel at least a little compassion for a loved one who takes his life. It may not be the first thing you feel, but it's often in the mix. For Leslie, whose sixty-three-year-old father killed himself, the strongest emotion she experienced—at least once the initial shock had passed—was compassion. Leslie's father had been depressed all his life, and no treatment seemed to help him out of his despair. Leslie told me, "Nothing worked, and he tried everything, from shock treatment to the latest antidepressants. You can't imagine how many doctors he went to see and how frustrating it was for him. He really suffered."

Leslie always thought her father would wind up killing himself. Still, it was a shock. "No matter how much you prepare for something like that, it always comes as a surprise," she said. "But I wasn't angry. How could I be? He was in pain, and he'd had enough. I think it would be selfish of me to feel angry or abandoned or any of those things people usually feel. I was sad, but more than anything I felt compassion for a man who I loved and who I'd watched suffer for as long as I can remember. He's at peace now. And I don't care what other people think, because other people don't know how hellish his life was."

Betrayal and Deception

It didn't occur to Karen and her sister that their eighty-two-year-old father, a retired scientist, might be planning his suicide, but they were concerned enough about his isolation following his wife's death—and in light of his failing memory—that they worked hard to help him feel connected and useful. Karen enrolled her dad in cooking classes at the local food co-op, which he had expressed interest in and said he enjoyed. And Karen's sister worked with their father on a plan to help other elderly people with tasks that were beyond them but were easy for him, like purchasing and installing a new television.

Karen explained, "My sister's goal was to help him find a way that there could be more to his life than reading the *New York Times* and eating lunch. They were going to make up flyers and investigate social service groups he could volunteer for. He pretended to go along with this."

After his death, Karen discovered from her father's computer records that he'd been planning his suicide for eight months. And all during that time he'd feigned interest in the things his daughters had thought would help him feel less depressed, more connected, and purposeful. "I don't think we ever diverted him from his intentions," Karen said. "I really felt duped." Karen also added that she felt angry and overwhelmed with grief. It didn't help that her father had taken his life on Karen's birthday, although she's fairly certain he wasn't aware of the date, especially since his memory had been failing. "I'm sure he forgot about it," she said.

Shame and Embarrassment

From the way my family dealt with the facts of my father's death, it was clear to me that they were embarrassed over what he did and that what he did was shameful. What other reasons could there be for all the whispers, the closed doors, and the invented cause of death?

The shame and embarrassment that people experience over suicide is complex. Some of it has to do with how Western society viewed suicide in centuries past—when suicide was considered a criminal offense and the surviving relatives could be punished for the suicide of a family member. And it wasn't just the families who were punished. The person who died by suicide was forbidden a proper burial because taking one's life was considered sinful.

Today we no longer punish the families of suicide victims, suicide is generally not considered sinful by mainstream religions, and suicide victims are buried in cemeteries like everyone else. Yet plenty of people make hurtful judgments about those who kill themselves and look down on the family members they leave behind. The person who died is seen as defective, the parents as incompetent, or the spouse as awful. How, people ask, could a suicide happen in a good family? There must be something wrong with the family. The parents had to have been terrible parents for their child to do such a thing.

No one said anything to Kevin to indicate that they blamed him for Craig's suicide, but that didn't keep him from feeling embarrassed over what they might think of him. "My embarrassment," he said, "stemmed from my own ego. Would people think that I hadn't taken care of Craig? Would they wonder if our life together wasn't worth living? Intellectually, I know I shouldn't worry about that sort of thing, but even three years after Craig's death it's something I think about."

Wherever the judgments come from, those of us who have lived through the suicide of a loved one are often left feeling ashamed, embarrassed, and highly motivated to keep the suicide a secret. Unfortunately, keeping the secret leaves us feeling all the more alone and isolated.

I like what Victoria said to me when I asked whether she tells people about her grandfather's suicide. (Victoria's grandfather was forty-four years old when he killed himself, and his death had a dramatically negative impact on Victoria's father, whose self-destructive behavior she attributed in part to his own father's suicide.) Victoria said, "Of course I tell people. I'm not ashamed. People who commit suicide have suffered. It's sad, not shameful."

Isolation

Many people who live through the suicide of a loved one feel all alone in the world, as if they're the only ones who have had this experience. Part of the reason they feel this way is because they're too embarrassed, ashamed, grief-stricken, or guilt-ridden over the suicide to share their story with anyone. Or they simply don't know anyone who has had a similar experience.

It doesn't help much to know that tens of thousands of people every year experience the suicide of a loved one. Those are just numbers. Unless you actually talk to someone who has been through the same thing, it's easy to feel entirely alone, as if no one has any idea what you're going through. This is why I recommend that anyone who is experiencing this sense of isolation talk with other people who have been through the suicide of a loved one. Please see the appendix for information on how to find such a support group.

Depression and Sadness

Sandra, the theater director whose father hanged himself when she was twenty years old (and whose brother subsequently hanged himself as well), read the original edition of this book and took issue with my failure to distinguish between depression and sadness. She said, "We use the term 'depression' too liberally. When we are temporarily dismayed about something, it's sadness. It signifies temporary. You're depressed if you can't get out of bed for two weeks. I've seen depressed, I've been depressed, and sadness is a different thing."

It is perfectly normal to experience sadness (and grief) when a loved one dies, whatever the cause. And some people who lose a loved one may also become depressed in addition to feeling sad. They may even have suicidal thoughts.

Sandra's wish that I distinguish between sadness and depression was based on her own experience after her father died. She was definitely sad, but she also fell into a deep depression. And while she was able to get out of bed in the morning, she found it a struggle to get through each day. Sandra said, "I remember for a year or so afterwards I'd go to work, come home, eat, and go to sleep. I'd care for my mom as much as I could, but I was confused and depressed."

Sandra knew she needed help. She recalled, "When I couldn't get it together emotionally, I went to see the rabbi at the temple in Los Angeles where I'd gotten married. He was a youngish rabbi." Sandra explained to him what had happened and described the depression she was experiencing. And the rabbi's response? "He said that I should take up tennis. Really! And then he said he wasn't quite sure where to direct me because he didn't have experience with what I'd been through. He said he would call me back. That was 1969, and I'm *still* waiting for the call. What an unconscionable thing not to call me back! That put me off Judaism big-time after that."

Because she knew she still needed help, Sandra didn't simply go home and pull the covers over her head. Instead, she said, "I got into group therapy. That was the most intense thing. I was in group therapy for years. I talked about what happened, and that helped. I don't know why it helped, but it did. What was good about it was the people I was telling about my experience weren't involved in what happened, so they could anchor me. Everybody else in my family was affected by the suicide. Both of my brothers literally went crazy after my father killed himself. My family was shattered. To be with a group of people who weren't part of it and could give you perspective on it was helpful."

The key with depression is to get help, because it's generally not something you can get over on your own. And if you're having suicidal thoughts, it's dangerous *not* to reach out for help. For Sandra, group therapy was effective. For others, one-on-one talk therapy is the answer. And for still others, a combination of talk therapy and antidepressant medication may be required to recover from a period of depression.

For anyone experiencing persistent and incapacitating depression, it's important to seek *professional* help. I know there are plenty of regular doctors who are happy to prescribe antidepressant medications for patients they think are depressed. But I don't believe that most regular doctors are qualified to assess someone who is experiencing depression following the suicide of a loved one. Nor do I think that most primary care physicians are qualified to prescribe antidepressant medication *and* provide proper follow-up care.

From everything I've read, and according to the professionals I've consulted, the best course of action is to meet with a qualified mental health professional. Then, if antidepressant medication is recommended, you should be referred to a psychopharmacologist, who can work with you to decide which is the best medication for you and who carefully monitors your progress on the medication. Often a depressed individual needs only a short period of time on medication to recover. But deciding whether or not to go on medication, determining the length of time you need to be on it, and knowing when to go off it are all decisions that need to be made in consultation with a mental health professional who knows what she or he is doing.

Suicidal Feelings

Over the years I've thought about suicide a lot. From an early age, I wondered if I would wind up just like my father. Would life ever become so intolerable that I too would want to take my life? When I learned that I was at greater risk of suicide because my father killed himself, I really started to worry that I was destined to follow in his footsteps. (For a long time I didn't understand that the fact that the surviving children of a person who dies by suicide take their own lives in greater numbers than the general population doesn't mean there's a causational relationship between these deaths by suicide.) These feelings contributed to my decision to see a mental health professional; I was determined not to do what my father had done.

Some people who experience the suicide of a loved one have thoughts of suicide in the immediate aftermath. Their thoughts have to do with a desire to end the pain of their grief or a desire to be reunited with their loved one. For others, like me, these feelings—or just the fear of having these feelings—are the result of suicide being introduced as an option. In other words, if your parent, sibling, or friend could turn to suicide to manage pain, then you could too.

With the passage of time—and professional help—I've grown more comfortable with my fleeting thoughts about suicide and am no longer frightened by them. I know these are feelings that many people have, especially those who have lived through the suicide of a parent. I also know that despite the fact that I'm at a greater statistical risk for suicide because my father killed himself, I am not compelled to do as he did.

Kevin says that he never seriously considered killing himself in the aftermath of his partner's suicide. But, he explained, "at various times over the first year I remember thinking, *What's the point of all of this?* Given all the hurt and grief, I felt like this was no way to live. My sister and doctor suggested I take an antidepressant, but I didn't want to. Instead, I started back at the gym and did more running, and the natural endorphins helped." Kevin also saw a therapist on a weekly basis.

When Kevin thought about suicide and what it would be like to end his life, he also thought about the impact it would have on those he left behind. He explained, "What always stopped me from killing myself was thinking about my dog and what Craig's suicide did to me and his family and how I can't do this to my sister and her kids. I don't think I ever seriously thought about it, but I wondered what it would be like to jump from the balcony of my high-rise apartment. And I came to think, *I don't want to leave quite yet.*"

Kevin also found that fantasizing about his own suicide gave him the opportunity to imagine what was going through Craig's mind when he "made the decision to die." Kevin said, "I wondered if what I was feeling was what he was feeling. Was I as depressed as he was? I seriously thought about suicide, but I don't think I ever thought I would do it or that it would be a solution."

Fear

Besides fearing for oneself because of suicidal feelings, as I did, people are bound to worry about other family members killing themselves once a parent, sibling, child, or friend has done it.

After Carolyn's son took his life, one of the things she feared most was that one of her other four children might do the same. She said, "I had no reason to believe that any of them was suicidal, but then, I never thought my son would kill himself. So I watched my other children like a hawk. If they were suicidal, I didn't want to miss any clues. I know I made them crazy with the way I worried and questioned them, but for the first couple of years I couldn't help it."

The suicide of a loved one—of a parent in particular—can inspire fear in survivors that they will follow in their footsteps. For other people, however, their fear is not for themselves. They are fearful that their dead loved one will not go to heaven because they've killed themselves. I like to think that of the many reasons people don't go to heaven (assuming that heaven exists), suicide is not among them.

Wish to Forget

Some people want to forget. They want to put the circumstances of their loved one's death behind them and in the process erase any trace of their existence: photos come off the walls, belongings are given away, even prized mementos are put in the back of a closet or donated to charity.

One woman I spoke with even asked not to be told how her sister died and demanded that family members not discuss anything in front of her. She knew her sister's death was a suicide, and she strongly suspected that her sister chose a method that left her too disfigured for an open casket at the funeral. But she preferred to imagine a peaceful death for her sister—pills perhaps. She felt certain that she would be unable to cope with any more pain than she had already experienced and was eager to put the experience behind her without knowing any more than she did.

My family chose a different course by pretending my father's death was from natural causes. And while his disappearance from our lives wasn't total—my uncle kept my father's 1964 white Buick LeSabre (with the powder-blue interior) for years, and my grandmother didn't remove a single framed photo of my dad from the walls of her den—once the funeral was over no one said a word about him. Ever.

Years later I learned that my grandparents never discussed with each other the nature of my father's death during the decades they lived beyond him. My grandmother even wrote a note to her surviving son and his wife shortly after the suicide in which she said, "I will never bring sadness into your home." By which she meant that she would never talk about my father's death in their house. And she never did.

Need to Know

At the other end of the spectrum are people who don't want to forget and want to know what happened. That was part of the motivation for the filmmaker Dana Perry when she chose to do a documentary about her son Evan, who was bipolar and jumped to his death in 2005 when he was fifteen. The resulting film, *Boy Interrupted*, debuted at the Sundance Film Festival in January 2009 and was broadcast on HBO in August of the same year.

Perry explained, "There are many choices people can make. One is to build a wall and never face this. I took out the pictures of Evan and pored over them and every scrap of media we had and everything I could find and tried to absorb it, to keep alive the experience of our lives together. That life was full of beauty and growth and poetry and fun mixed with a lot of despair and fear."

In contrast to people who decide to remain silent about their deceased loved one, Perry and her family did the opposite. "We think it's healthy to talk about it," she said. "We talk about Evan, and we talk about him in a positive way. For one thing, I don't want Evan's younger brother to go through life saying 'I didn't have a brother.' It is so important to me to acknowledge that Evan was here, which was another reason to make the film, to say that he was here." Later in this chapter, Perry discusses how making *Boy Interrupted* helped her deal with her grief over Evan's death.

Michelle also had an intense need to know what happened, especially because her husband Paul's suicide "made no sense." Paul had an ebullient personality and "had never been depressed a day in his life" until he started taking a prescription medication.

But it was only in retrospect that Michelle discovered that the drug Paul was on—one of the popular statin drugs prescribed to reduce high cholesterol—could have been the cause of the confusing mood changes she'd observed over the nine months he took it. It was a friend who tipped Michelle off to the possibility that there was a connection between the drug and Paul's suicide.

Once Michelle made the connection, she used her experience as a university professor to pursue every lead. She said, "I had an assistant I was very close to, and when she found out what happened, she said she would go to the biomedical library to do the research. It was a couple of months before I could go myself. But even in the days right after Paul died I started having conversations with doctors who were experts on the subject of statins and suicide. I also started writing, just pouring out onto the page everything that was going on in those months leading up to Paul's death. I had three pretty miserable weeks going over everything I'd said to Paul, everything I'd observed, everything I hadn't done but might have that could have saved Paul's life. But after spending hours in the biomedical library, I knew that what I'd watched happen over the course of nine months wasn't just my imagination, because there were other documented cases just like Paul's."

In her effort to unravel the mystery of Paul's suicide, Michelle also made an appointment to speak with the social worker Paul had seen six times in the weeks before his death. Michelle said, "Paul had already scheduled an appointment with the social worker, and I kept the appointment and said to the social worker, 'You need to tell me everything. I'm his wife, and I have a legal right to know.' But the social worker was defensive and wouldn't tell me a thing. I asked to speak with representatives of the health care company, but they wouldn't speak to me without legal representation and treated me like I was a crazy widow. In the end I had to subpoena Paul's medical records, which they took months to produce."

After all of her research efforts, and with the encouragement of the medical experts she consulted and the assistance of her attorney, Michelle decided to pursue a legal case against the manufacturer of the drug that Paul had been prescribed by his doctor. But Michelle knew she had to proceed with caution. She explained, "Everyone wants to say, 'That's the crazy widow who just wants to come up with an alternate story.' So I was keeping close tabs on myself to make sure I didn't come off as the crazy widow and really had to get my ducks in a row before going ahead with the legal case."

Four years after Michelle first went to court, the manufacturer of the drug Paul took for the nine months prior to his suicide won on summary judgment. (Based on the information provided by both sides, the judge decided in favor of the manufacturer without a trial.) Still, Michelle doesn't regret making the effort. She said, "Going into this, people warned me that I wasn't a sympathetic plaintiff because I had a good job and no children. But I said to myself, *I may not have children, but there are a lot of young men who are put on these drugs who do*, so I felt compelled to try." Michelle, who is a published novelist, is now writing a book about her experience in the hopes that she can focus attention on the potentially deadly side effects of one of the most widely prescribed classes of medication in the world.

Does the method by which a loved one dies affect the impact of a suicide?

Theoretically no—the method does not affect the impact of a suicide, at least not over the long term. But for the person who discovers the injured loved one or the body of the loved one, the method can very well have a major impact, especially in the case of a violent death, which can be more difficult to cope with than a death that is not.

Patricia, whose daughter Elizabeth used a gun to shoot herself, found her daughter on the floor of her bedroom, with a gun a short distance away. "I was beyond shocked," she recalled. "I was as stunned as if it were a thermonuclear warhead. It was such a horrible, violent thing to do. She knew how completely anti-gun I was. I don't think I'd ever touched a gun in my whole life."

After Elizabeth's death, Patricia tracked down her daughter's friends and learned from them that her daughter had bought the gun two years before while she was still in high school. "She told some of her friends that it was for self-defense," Patricia said. "She told others that it was probably how she would kill herself. None of them said a word to me."

Patricia also learned from one of her daughter's friends that Elizabeth had said "she wouldn't shoot herself at home because

she wouldn't want her mom to find her." Of course, it was Patricia who found her, and she held Elizabeth while she waited for
the ambulance to arrive. Patricia recalled, "I was afraid Elizabeth
would choke, so the 911 lady said I should take her in my arms.
I had flashbacks like I was holding my baby when she was born."

After Elizabeth died, Patricia filled out papers with the police
department to ensure that the gun would be destroyed.

What is the impact of a suicide on families?
How do families react?

Just as a suicide can devastate individuals, its impact on a family—
the complex web of relationships among brothers, sisters, parents, friends, uncles, aunts, and cousins—can be monumental.
Some families are blown apart by the guilt and blame that can
follow a suicide. Some are drawn together, rallying to support
one another as they struggle through their individual and collec-
tive grief and confusion. Other families continue on in silence,
pretending as best they can that nothing has happened or that
the suicide was an accidental death.

In my own family, my father's suicide blew apart already
strained and fragile familial ties. I think of my father's suicide as
an emotional bomb that he set off in our living room. No one
else was killed, but people were scattered in all directions, and
the emotional wreckage was everywhere.

In the immediate aftermath, my older sister, who was seventeen, retreated emotionally and physically from the family. My
favorite (and only) uncle, my father's brother, virtually vanished
despite the fact that he lived only a half-hour from us by car. My
father's closest friend, who was made to feel unwelcome, disap-
peared from our lives. My father's parents endeavored to go on
as if nothing had happened, believing that they could best help
their loved ones by sparing us the grief that threatened to engulf
them. My mother, busy supporting three children and struggling with her own emotional turmoil, was a blur. My younger
brother and I shared the same tiny bedroom but lived in virtual
isolation from each other. It wasn't until years after I'd left home
that my brother and I talked about the nature of our father's
death for the first time. And for my brother at that time the news
of our father's suicide was a revelation. He'd had no idea.

Shattered, scattered, angry, bewildered, guilt-ridden, ashamed, we all went about nursing our wounds in different ways. On our own, some of us eventually came to terms with my father's death and reached out painfully on rare occasions through the years to share our experiences of that struggle, but never as a family.

Fortunately, my family's experience is not everyone's experience. In contrast, the death of Daniel's brother brought together a badly fractured family. Daniel's parents, who were both divorced and remarried, had for years communicated only through their children. Daniel and his mother hadn't talked in two years over the fact that he was gay. "She wanted nothing to do with me," he said. "So when I got the news from my father that my brother had shot himself, I didn't exactly volunteer to call her."

Daniel's father offered him the choice of calling his other brother or his mother. Daniel was even more estranged from his brother, so he agreed to call his mother. His friend Joan held his hand while he made the call. Daniel recalled, "I told my mom to sit down, to take a deep breath. I told her point-blank that my brother had killed himself. She screamed, and I told her I'd call her back. I let three minutes pass and called again to tell her that I'd pick her up at the airport that night."

Daniel was very anxious and nervous as he drove to the airport, but seeing his mother again wasn't as bad as he'd anticipated. He said, "Given what had just happened, I think it was of some comfort for both of us to see each other again, and there was so much to arrange that we didn't have much of a chance to focus on the fact we hadn't talked to each other in two years."

In the six months after the suicide, Daniel's mother visited him twice, and they now speak frequently by phone. "She now accepts that she has a gay son, and we've started sharing things," he said. "She'll call up just to talk about what happened during the day or to talk about my brother and how she's feeling about it. And I call her."

Daniel also has more contact with both his father and his surviving brother: "I'm more likely to tell my father what I think now, and we talk about what happened to my brother. My other brother, who never called me in the past, calls up and just bursts into tears. He's having a real hard time with this, and it turns out that I'm the one he feels most comfortable talking to."

Almost everyone in Daniel's family has sought professional counseling, and they've even talked about going to counseling together as a family. "We've talked about it," he said, "but there's so much other stuff that we haven't dealt with as a family that we're all a little reluctant. I know it would do a lot of good, but we're not there yet."

How do people react to the suicide of a spouse?

How a surviving spouse reacts depends a lot on the condition of the relationship and the circumstances of the suicide. But most often a surviving spouse feels guilty for not having prevented the suicide, as well as rejected or abandoned. Even if their relationship was a good one, the surviving spouse is likely to interpret the suicide as a statement about their married life. He or she may also feel shame and be fearful that others will look on him or her as having been so awful to live with that the spouse was driven to suicide.

For Michael, his wife's suicide on her birthday sent a message, whether or not it was intended. Michael recalled, "She didn't leave a note, but one of our running arguments had been that I never remembered her birthday." Relationship problems weren't the only thing that Michael's wife had on her mind when she killed herself. She had recently been fired from her job because of a drinking problem. "They warned her," Michael said. "I begged her to get help. But she didn't think she had a problem. She was quite drunk when she shot herself, so if I can take any comfort in this it's that she wasn't thinking clearly when she did it."

Alison's husband Allen was also under the influence when he drowned himself in the swimming pool of his apartment complex. Alison recalled, "He'd swallowed a couple of different over-the-counter medications. Apparently they didn't work fast enough, and after filling three legal pads with his thoughts, he threw himself in the pool." But unlike Michael, Alison didn't feel rejected, and she was certain that her husband's suicide was not a comment on their marriage. She said, "He was a very depressed young man when I met him, and I guess I figured I could save him. I couldn't."

During the time they were married, Alison's husband had been unable to work and Alison was the primary wage earner. Allen spent much of his time caring for their daughter, Rachel, who was born a year after he and Alison were married. After five ycars of marriage, Alison and Allen decided it would be best to separate.

The breaking point for Allen came on the day he and Alison were supposed to sign formal separation papers. "He completely wigged out," Alison recalled. "That night he came over to the house and apologized for all the horrible things he'd said to me earlier in the day and told me what a wonderful mother I was and how proud he was of Rachel. It sounded to me like he was giving a farewell speech, but I put that out of my head. I didn't want to think about it."

As Allen was leaving Alison's house to go back to his apartment, he asked her if he could spend the night. "I told him I didn't think it was a good idea, and he left," she said. "The next morning I went to work, and soon after I got to the office his mother called me to ask if I knew where he was. My heart dropped. I think in that moment I knew he'd done something crazy. I got in my car and drove to his apartment. The police were already there. They'd just pulled him out of the pool, and he was lying on the deck. I became hysterical—just to see him there completely lifeless. I felt guilt, tremendous guilt. I believe I did the right thing by not letting him stay over that night, but it's been seven years since his death, and I still feel a twinge of guilt that I was responsible—even though I know I wasn't."

It was only recently that Alison started feeling that her late husband had abandoned her. "Now that Rachel is getting older and is involved in various activities at school, it's hard for me being the only parent," she said. "It makes me angry. And it also makes me angry that he's left such a burden for Rachel. This is something she's going to have to deal with for the rest of her life."

For Michelle, whose forty-three-year-old husband took his life after nine months on a prescription drug that transformed him from "a screamingly funny man" into someone capable of shooting himself, the big adjustment was going on without the most important person in her life. In the first hours after returning home from work and finding her house surrounded by police cars, Michelle was asked repeatedly by a detective, "Don't you need to call somebody?" Michelle said, "For eighteen years I was with this incredible human being, and he was the one person I wanted to call, but he was in the coroner's van parked next to the house." Eventually Michelle decided to call her husband's sister.

Michelle continued: "When Paul died, I felt that half of my mind had gone. We were incredibly close. He was the most brilliant man I'd ever met, a big reader, and incredibly funny. We had an intellectual life that was very emotional in the best ways and fun, and we loved to cook. When he died, that emotional and intellectual fabric was gone. Your life is just destroyed. You don't have anything that is recognizable as your life. You have to find another reason to live because love is the reason to live. So you look around your house and ask, what does this mean without the other person? It doesn't mean a fucking thing. You reach the point where you have to say, 'I have to find meaning again.'"

In the five years since Michelle's husband died, she has worked hard to find meaning in her life, but it remains a struggle. She said, "My life is easy with respect to creature comforts and devastated in every other way. Paul and I were two peas in a pod, and now I'm the pea in the pod without him."

How do parents react to a child's suicide?

Parents are left wondering what they did wrong. Were they too strict? Were they not strict enough? Were they too attentive? Were they not attentive enough? Even parents of children who were well into adulthood are left wondering: Was I a bad parent?

When my grandmother and I talked about my father's suicide, she reviewed my father's childhood, recalling disagreements between mother and son that she thought might have contributed to the emotional problems that eventually led a forty-four-year-old man to take his life. How could she not wonder? How could she not feel that his death was a reflection on her abilities as a mother? It seems like the most natural thing in the world for a parent to do.

For parents, the suicide of a child has the potential to bring extra doses of guilt and self-recrimination. A parent is supposed to know and protect his or her child. How could a parent let that happen? And as if the self-recrimination weren't enough, there are the fears about how others will view them as parents. What must people think of them? What terrible things do people think the parents did that led their child to take his or her life?

Patricia, whose twenty-year-old daughter Elizabeth killed herself after years of struggling with mental illness and a feeling that "she didn't belong in this world," knew she had done everything she could to keep her daughter alive. As she explained in chapter 6 ("Prevention and Treatment"), the enormous effort she made with Elizabeth seemed to be paying off. So in addition to the shock and grief caused by her daughter's suicide, Patricia was left feeling that her effort and Elizabeth's life itself had all been a waste.

For Patricia there was one other issue to contend with as a parent: Elizabeth was Patricia's only child. She explained, "I've lost my identity as a parent. I feel jealous of other people's kids going back to school. And then there are all the dreams I can't have now. I assumed I'd have grandchildren, that I'd have someone to put me in a nursing home. With Elizabeth's passing, that's all gone now."

How does the suicide of a child affect the ability of parents to be good parents to their surviving children?

Parents who have lost one child to suicide may react to their other children in a number of different and conflicting ways that can make it difficult to be good parents. Fearing that their other children will kill themselves or that something bad will happen to them, they may become overly protective. Or their confidence in their parenting abilities may be so shaken that they're unable to be as strong and supportive as their children need them to be in a time of crisis. They may also be so absorbed in their own grief that they withdraw from their children, becoming neglectful just when their children need them most.

Parents who are incapacitated by grief may also find themselves swapping roles with their surviving children. The children take on the role of parent, offering comfort, taking care of the funeral and other necessary arrangements following the suicide, and managing everyday tasks until the grieving parents are back on their feet.

How do couples react to the suicide of a child?

It is not uncommon for marriages to be strained to the breaking point over the suicide of a child. The grief, guilt, and blame can quickly tear at the fibers that hold a marriage together. Some couples are ultimately destroyed by the experience, others weather it, supporting each other through the ordeal, and still others retreat into silence, enduring the pain of their loss in isolation.

For Carolyn, whose seventeen-year-old-son shot himself, the suicide was almost the end of her thirty-three-year marriage. She told me: "Our marriage barely survived it. The reason the marriage ultimately survived was that I read every book on grief. I went to a counselor. I had to make it survive. My husband did not read. He did not talk. He kept everything inside."

Shortly after the suicide, Carolyn's husband began to drink heavily. She recalled, "He couldn't deal with the pain. I told him a month or two after he began drinking, 'I understand why you're drinking, but I have to tell you I can't handle my grief and your drinking at the same time. Either you quit or we'll have to separate.' And he quit. I know he did his work in his own way, but he couldn't verbalize anything."

Over the years I wondered how my grandparents dealt with my father's suicide. Despite the difficulties they had with my father because of his radical politics and severe depression, he was still their first and much-loved son. I asked my grandmother about this when she was in her early nineties, and she said that in the two decades between my father's suicide and my grandfather's death, they never talked about it. I know I must have had a shocked look on my face, because my grandmother elaborated, explaining that they talked about my father, but that each respected the other's feelings and never raised the subject of his suicide.

How do young children react to the suicide of a parent?

Young children who have been through the suicide of a parent can experience a whole range of emotions and express them in different ways. They may feel rejected by the parent who has died. They may blame the surviving parent for causing the suicide. If they ever secretly wished that parent dead, they are likely to feel guilty for having somehow caused the death by the very act of wishing. Or they may blame themselves, thinking that if they hadn't been so bad, if they had been better children, then Mommy or Daddy wouldn't have chosen to leave. They may cling to the surviving parent, fearing the loss of that parent too. Or they may cling to a favorite doll or pet.

Some children begin to have nightmares. Others withdraw from their friends, spending increasing amounts of time alone. They may also act out in all kinds of ways, from cutting classes and failing at school to taking drugs. Other children react in quite the opposite way and become hyper-responsible, taking care of their grieving mother or father in the immediate aftermath of the suicide.

Alison's daughter Rachel had more of a problem with other people's reactions to how she dealt with her father's suicide than with how she reacted herself. Alison recalled, "Rachel was only four, but she seemed to accept pretty well what happened. She seemed sad, but other than that, she really was herself. I feel awkward saying it, but I feel lucky that my husband killed himself when he did. If Rachel had been older, I think she would have taken the loss much harder, and she would have also had an understanding of the stigma of suicide. I also think that what helped her was my honesty about the whole thing. She knew from the very beginning exactly what happened to her father."

The first hint of trouble, however, came when Rachel's kindergarten teacher called Alison to tell her "that the other children were getting scared when Rachel said her father committed suicide. And that got the kids asking the teacher questions about suicide, and she didn't know what to say. I told her she'd have to deal with it, because I didn't want Rachel to feel there was any reason to hide the truth."

I used to be proud of the way I reacted to my father's suicide. After the initial shock wore off, I went back to my life as if nothing had happened. I missed only one day of school. I didn't have outbursts or cry uncontrollably. I was stoic and mature about the whole thing. As several of my relatives reminded me at the funeral, I was the man of the family now. I took my job seriously.

There were only a couple of clues that there was anything really wrong, and it wasn't until years later that I figured this out. I had always done well in school, but in the months after my father died I had trouble with some of my classes and almost failed math and science, which were normally my two strongest subjects. Also, within a few months of my dad's death I developed a skin disorder that required weekly visits to the dermatologist for years.

I know now that I did what kids generally do when faced with the death of a parent, whether or not it's from suicide. The whole experience was so overwhelming that I put off grieving until I was older and capable of handling it. I did this unconsciously—my only conscious effort was to "be a man" about the whole thing—because my natural defense mechanisms were taking care of me.

I finally sought the help of a psychologist for the first time in my early twenties because I was deeply unhappy and didn't want to live an unhappy life. Remarkably, I didn't imagine that my unhappiness had anything to do with my father's death until I started talking and found myself discussing his suicide.

No matter how a child reacts to the suicide of a mother or father, keep in mind that to a child the loss of a parent is enormously traumatic no matter what the cause of death. And as the child grows up, he or she will have to come to terms with that death. In the case of a parent's suicide, it's an awful legacy to leave behind for any child.

Following the suicide of a parent, children need consistent love and support, which is exactly what Alison gave to Rachel. Ironically, the immediate aftermath of a suicide is just the time when a child is likely to be ignored by the surviving parent and the other adults in that child's life. Often these key people are so preoccupied with their own grief that they overlook the needs of the child. Or they may assume that the child is not affected in the same way they are and therefore doesn't need special attention.

Children are unlikely to react in the same way that adults do. They may not do anything more than shed a few tears and remain quiet. But don't let that fool you: children are almost always acutely aware of everything that has happened and no less affected by the suicide than the adult survivors.

How do adult children react to the suicide of a parent? Do they react differently than young children?

No matter how awful it is to have a parent take his or her life, the experience of an adult whose parent does so is fundamentally different from that of a young child. Besides having both a level of understanding and coping skills that young children don't, grown children are not wholly dependent on their parents in the way young children are. Adult children are just as likely to be devastated, but their day-to-day home life is not shattered by the sudden absence of a parent who has killed himself or herself. And although their sense of loss and abandonment in the aftermath of the suicide may be profound, it is likely to pale in comparison to what is experienced by a child.

Not every adult child is devastated or left bewildered by the suicide of a parent. A year before we spoke, Evelyn's eighty-five-year-old father took his life by locking himself in his garage and turning on his car. She recalled, "It was a real blow, especially since my mother had died just a few months before, but I was more sad than anything. It was clear to me that Father was simply at sea without my mother. He'd said a number of times how he didn't want to go on without her, but I didn't take that to mean he would kill himself. It seemed perfectly rational for him to say that he didn't want to go on without her. I guess I feel more than a little guilty too, because I didn't listen clearly to what he was saying."

How do you explain a suicide to a child?

Whether the person who died is a parent, sibling, grandparent, close family friend, or some other important person in a child's life, the parents (or surviving parent) need to tell the truth about what has happened. Of course you wouldn't explain the suicide in the kind of detail you might go into when talking to a close adult friend, but it's important to explain what happened in clear terms that a child can understand. And you need to be prepared to answer in a direct way the questions that will inevitably follow.

If you're thinking of hiding the truth from your child, here are a few things to consider. First, even if you haven't said anything, your child may already know the truth. That was my experience, and I know I'm not alone. No one told me that my father killed himself. I overheard my mother's conversation with my Aunt Mynette (my father's brother's wife) the day my father was found unconscious at the rooming house where he lived. My mother closed the door to the kitchen, which was where we had our one phone, but I listened through the keyhole. From what my mother said in response to my aunt, I learned that my father was in the hospital. Then after a long pause, I heard my mother say the word "pills" in a way that made it clear she was unconsciously repeating something my aunt had said to her. I had no trouble drawing my own conclusions.

When my father died three days later, the official word was that he died of pneumonia. What that lie suggested to me was that suicide was a terrible and embarrassing thing. Since my father's death was something that had to be lied about, it must have been something to be ashamed of. At least that's the assumption I made. I also learned that adults weren't to be trusted: they lie. I know these weren't the messages my family wanted to convey to me, but they were the messages I received.

Children take the lead from the adults around them. If you indicate by your actions that suicide is something so awful and shameful that you have to lie about it, your child will respond accordingly, and you will rob him or her of the chance to deal with the loss in a constructive way. If, on the other hand, you are direct, honest, and supportive, you will help your child begin to cope with a range of inevitably complex emotions.

Knowing what I know now about suicide, and given my experience, this is how I wish my mother had explained things to me (and ideally she would have been supported in this by my father's family): "Your father loved you very much, but you know that he was very unhappy and that he had emotional problems. [My father's emotional problems were no secret to me; I had observed his depressions and bouts of paranoia firsthand.] The pain had become so great for him that he decided he couldn't go on any longer. He swallowed a lot of pills. The doctors tried everything they could to save him, but there was nothing they could do, and he died."

These simple sentences would have been all the opening I needed to ask the many other things I wanted to know, from whether or not my father had left a note (he did, but I didn't learn about it until ten years later) to why the doctors couldn't save him. Ideally, I would have been able to ask any question with nothing off limits. But without that opening, there was no way for me to ask anything. And from the way the adults were acting, I knew that I shouldn't.

When Alison's husband Allen drowned himself, there was never any doubt in Alison's mind that she was going to tell her daughter the truth. She recalled, "After they took away Allen's body, all I could think about was getting Rachel out of school before word filtered out that Allen had killed himself. I wanted to get her home and keep her safe. I wanted to talk to her and tell her what happened before anyone else did. I wanted her to know from the very beginning that he took his own life. I didn't want her to have to learn about this years later and then find myself explaining why I'd kept it secret from her."

Once they got home, Alison sat down with Rachel and started explaining. "She was only four, so I told her that some people's bodies get sick and they die and some people's minds get sick and they die. I explained to her that her father's mind was sick, and that it wasn't his fault. I said, 'He was very sad, and he took some drugs and drowned himself.'" Rachel listened carefully to her mother, and her eyes filled with tears. When her mother was finished, Rachel said simply, "I just wish I could have said good-bye."

Rachel didn't have a lot of questions initially, but in the years since her father's suicide she's come to her mother on many occasions to ask questions. "She knows that she can ask me anything anytime and that I'll give a straight answer," Alison said. "I'm grateful for that—that she feels she can ask me anything."

Sachiko was eight years old when she and her mother found her aunt's body slumped over the kitchen table. Now fifty, the Japanese-born literature professor vividly recalled what would normally have been an unremarkable visit to her aunt's apartment: "There was no answer at the door, so we went in—the door wasn't locked. It was during the day, so my uncle, who was a policeman, was at work and my two cousins were not home either (they are older than I am). We went into the kitchen, where there was a little table with four chairs. She was on the table, as if she were sleeping. And there were opened medicine bottles around her."

From Sachiko's past experience of seeing her older brother fall asleep while doing his homework, Sachiko thought nothing of what she saw. Her mother, who was a nurse, remained calm and took Sachiko into another room. "She told me to wait and went back into the kitchen," Sachiko recalled. "My mama was a nurse, and I thought she was helping my auntie. After a while I got scared not hearing anything—it was so quiet—but then I heard my mother talking to somebody on the phone. A long time after that my uncle and my cousins came back, and then it became chaotic. My cousins were so upset."

At first Sachiko didn't understand what had happened, but with all the upset it was clear that her aunt had died. "My aunt was always a sad person," she said, "so I thought that maybe she just didn't like being alive. Then at the funeral I wondered, *Was*

Auntie sick? Is that why she died? But it wasn't until after everything was over, after the funeral, that I asked my mother. And she told me, 'She killed herself.' "

From the beginning Sachiko's mother wanted to make certain that her daughter understood that "if you choose to kill yourself, that's a no-no. I'm sure my mother wanted me to understand that killing yourself is not good," Sachiko said. "She explained to me that if you kill yourself your spirit will get stuck—it will not go anyplace peaceful. Your spirit is dead and will always suffer. I don't know if this is Japanese culture or just my mother's philosophy. In general, when my mother speaks about suicide, she always says that it doesn't solve any problems."

Sachiko never thought to question her mother. She said, "I never asked her why it was bad to kill yourself, beyond what she told me. She was right in so many ways, and I never questioned her. I guess I was the good daughter, and I have to agree with her that suicide doesn't solve any problems. Also, for everyone left behind it causes problems."

Although Sachiko said she never speaks about her aunt's suicide, "seeing my aunt like that had a big impact. It was shocking. But I let go of that experience. I've never had a depression, and because of the experience I had with my aunt it would never occur to me to end my life. It's sad to lose somebody in that way, but I wasn't my aunt's child, so the impact is different than it was for my cousins because they were more directly affected."

If you're not sure what approach to take with your child, get advice from an expert. You have a tremendous responsibility to help your child through this experience, and what you do and say can have an enormously positive—or negative—impact. Talk to a social worker at the hospital where your spouse or loved one died to get advice. Call a crisis hotline for guidance or to find a bereavement group for children who have lived through the suicide of a parent. However you do it, get the help you need to help your child as best you can.

How do people react to the suicide of a sibling?

How people react to the suicide of a sibling depends a lot on the age of the surviving siblings, their stage in life, and the nature of their relationship with the person who died. For example, my uncle's experience of my father's suicide was intensified by the fact that my father, his brother, was twelve years older and was more of a father to my uncle than a brother.

During my uncle's formative years my father was his best buddy, his teacher, and someone my uncle could always count on to protect him. So, added to the crushing blow of losing a brother who had been like a father to him was the overwhelming guilt my uncle experienced because he had failed to save the brother who had protected him from harm while he was growing up.

Although adult siblings have many different kinds of complex reactions to the suicide of a brother or sister, the siblings who are affected most profoundly and predictably are generally those who are still living at home. For example, Jennifer was sixteen when her twenty-one-year-old sister took an overdose of pills while she was away at college. Now twenty-six, Jennifer told me: "Everything changed. My parents were so caught up in Cindy's death that they seemed to forget that I was alive. I began to wonder if maybe I'd get more attention if I were dead."

In retrospect, Jennifer now realizes that she deliberately started getting in trouble at school to get attention from her parents. She said, "I didn't know how else to let them know I needed them. It was a good thing that my idea of trouble was staying out past my curfew and failing a couple of tests. My parents were so oblivious that I could have really gotten in a lot of trouble if I'd been more fearless. Looking back, it seems so obvious that I was suffering too. Cindy was my sister, and we shared a room until I was thirteen years old. Her death was horrible for me too, but my parents were so destroyed that for more than a year they couldn't see beyond their own suffering."

In contrast to Jennifer's experience, surviving siblings sometimes find themselves the focus of intense parental attention because the parents fear that their other children will follow the lead of their dead sibling. In that case the surviving sibling may rebel against parents who are suddenly overly protective.

Like other siblings who have lost a sister or brother to suicide, Jennifer found that despite her grief over Cindy's death, she felt resentful toward her dead sister. "That made me feel even worse," Jennifer said. "But she ruined everything. I genuinely had a happy family. We all got along. I loved my parents, and my parents loved me *and* Cindy. That's what made the whole thing so shattering. And it was all her fault, or at least that's how I felt."

Surviving siblings also sometimes find themselves switching roles with their parents and wind up being parents to their own parents while they struggle through their grief. For Sandra, whose brother hanged himself, the experience of stepping into the role of a parent was sadly all too familiar. Fifteen years earlier, when her father took his life, Sandra found herself being a mother to her mother at the age of twenty.

Sandra recalled, "My mother went through a period of infancy where she couldn't function or even eat. So basically I took on the role of monitoring her, being her confidante, making sure she was eating, that she got out of the house, and I also helped her deal with the financial mess that my father left behind. I was very angry at my father for what he did. He was supposed to support and take care of my mother always. He was supposed to be there looking after her. What loomed large was that now she was my responsibility *forever*."

While Sandra was angry at her father, she wasn't angry or resentful toward her mother, in no small part because of their close relationship. "We always had a very heart-to-heart relationship," Sandra said. "My mom was wonderful. But when she was needy after my father died, I had to be there for her because that's what she had done for me my whole life up until then. But then she couldn't do it anymore, not in the same way. She tried, but her need for consolation was greater than my need for consolation. It seemed that her loss of her husband was greater than my loss of my father, because of the way he died and because it was perceived more as a rejection of her than of me. My mother's loss was more profound, and I responded to that by taking care of her."

By the time Sandra's brother hanged himself fifteen years later, Sandra and her mother were back on more equal footing, but her brother's suicide changed that. "In this situation it was insult to injury for her," Sandra said. "I stayed in Los Angeles after my brother's funeral to look after her. I had to resume my active role as the parent to help guide her through that first year. She didn't go through the same depth of grief as she did for my father, but like the first time her need for consolation was much greater than mine."

Sandra said that in the years that followed, her mother was

never really able to resume her role as the parent. "Sure, she was my mom, and she was very generous with me, but that ineffable aspect of the mother-daughter relationship that we'd had at one time was never visited again. Some parents are their children's parents until the day they die. Because of these compounded tragedies, in my case it was the other way around."

How do people react to the suicide of a teenager?

In addition to the usual range of reactions to any suicide, people feel an acute sense of a young life needlessly cut short when they learn of a teenager's suicide. How, we ask, could someone with so much life to look forward to end it before it's really started?

Besides the terrible impact on the immediate family and loved ones, a teen's suicide also affects other parents, who can't help but wonder, *Could this happen in my family?* Young friends ask themselves, *Could this happen to me? Is that the answer to my problems?* And both friends and teachers are left wondering, *Is there something I could have done to prevent it?*

To get a sense of what it's like for one family that experienced the suicide of a teenage child, I highly recommend Dana Perry's compelling documentary about her son Evan, *Boy Interrupted.* You'll find it listed in the appendix.

How do people react to the suicide of a colleague or acquaintance?

Any suicide sets off a shock wave that travels far and wide. Even if the person who died is someone you knew only casually or someone who worked in your office, news of the suicide can have a surprisingly big impact.

I recently received a call from a friend who arrived at work on a Monday morning to discover that one of his employees had taken his life over the weekend. He was shocked by the suicide and even more shocked by the reaction of the rest of his staff, who were dazed, emotional, and almost incapable of doing anything other than talk about their colleague—what he'd done, how shocked they were, what signs they might have missed, the impact on his family, the terrible waste of a life.

This was a new job for my friend, who had recently left a hard-charging Wall Street investment bank to head up an arts-focused nonprofit. He explained: "In the world I come from, you just suck it up and keep on going. One of the reasons I love my new job is that my staff is so much more human and humane. They really feel things, so this suicide shook them up in a profound way, but it wasn't something I was prepared for."

To help his staff, my friend called in a grief counselor who specialized in dealing with suicide. And he told his staff that they were welcome to take a day or two off in the immediate aftermath of the suicide so they could deal with their feelings about what had happened.

I've been shocked over the years by how stunned I am when I've learned about the suicide of an acquaintance or colleague. It hasn't happened often, but each time I find myself asking the same kinds of questions: *What happened? Didn't anyone see it coming? Why didn't they stop him? Why did he do it?* And I find myself asking those questions even though I know all too well that satisfying answers to questions about a suicide are generally in short supply.

Perhaps there are people who can brush aside the death of a colleague or acquaintance, but I can't. Maybe because of my family history I have to accept that it's just impossible not to be shaken by such a death. I was reminded of that just a few months ago when I received an e-mail about the suicide of Rodger Mc-Farlane, a man four years my senior whom I'd met for the first time in the early 1980s and with whom I'd crossed paths and conversed on many occasions in the years that followed. We were not friends, but we knew each other and worked in professions that sometimes overlapped.

From the first, Rodger left a big impression on me, as he did on many people. He was larger than life in every way, direct to the point of being rude, and a no-nonsense doer who headed up the first AIDS organization in the early and terrifying days of the AIDS epidemic. Rodger's response to that confounding time was to take action.

News of Rodger's suicide shocked me and left me asking all the inevitable questions. And because Rodger and I shared some common ground, I wondered: *If it could happen to someone like Rodger, could my life suddenly go off a cliff and leave me at the same precipice where he found himself at age fifty-four?*

The e-mail announcing Rodger's death, which was written by a group of loyal friends, left a lot unsaid and gave the impression of a man who was making a rational and reasoned decision in the face of chronic back pain and a newly diagnosed heart ailment (not potentially fatal, as I later learned). I didn't buy it. I wanted more details to satisfy my need to make some sense of what Rodger had done and to put distance between who I am and who Rodger was. I was surprised by my own need to know and my wish to establish that distance, and I was also surprised by the shock and despair I felt over Rodger's death, especially because he was only an acquaintance. But in my conversations with friends about Rodger's death, I found that I wasn't alone in how I experienced it. A lot of us who knew him, even if only as an acquaintance, were asking the same questions and wrestling with the news of his suicide.

As I discovered when I did a little digging, Rodger's life and his path to suicide were far more complex than the public statement suggested. The details I uncovered with a little research filled enough blank spots in Rodger's story to satisfy my need to know and to ease my anxiety over the possibility that our experiences were alike. Still, even as I was able to put distance between the trajectory of Rodger's life and my own—a distance in which I took comfort—I couldn't help but feel a deep sadness that at fifty-four one of my contemporaries who contributed so much and helped so many had felt compelled to take his life.

How do mental health professionals react when clients or patients kill themselves?

From what I've read, approximately one-third of the people who take their lives each year have had contact with a mental health provider within a year of their death. That translates into ten thousand psychologists, psychiatrists, social workers, and counselors who experience the suicide of a patient or client every year.

Because these professionals are no less human than the rest of us, their response is much the same as anyone else's. But added to the usual list—shock, grief, denial, and so on—is the impact of such a loss on their professional identity, their relationships with colleagues, and their clinical work. For example, mental health professionals are supposed to help their clients get better, so a suicide can be experienced as a colossal failure. And while colleagues know that the suicide of a patient is not necessarily any reflection on a mental health professional's abilities, it can be difficult in the wake of a suicide to avoid making judgments about a colleague's competence to do his or her job effectively.

Dr. Aaron Kheriaty, assistant clinical professor of psychiatry and human behavior at the University of California–Irvine and founder of that school's Psychiatry and Spirituality Forum, didn't feel at all judged by his fellow mental health professionals when one of his patients took her life. Quite to the contrary, he found that his colleagues were uniformly supportive. The death of his patient came early in his career, and he just happened to be at the hospital with his wife for the delivery of their third son when he got the news. He recalled, "This was a woman I treated while I was a resident and saw her for a year for psychotherapy. She had stopped seeing me for a time—I think it was an insurance issue—and sought treatment elsewhere. A year later she came back to the clinic where I worked and was being seen by one of the attendings after she had an electronic device surgically implanted for treatment of severe depression. She was seventy-two when she committed suicide."

Shortly before the suicide, Dr. Kheriaty saw his former patient one last time. He said, "She was very friendly, seemed happy to see me, and was clearly depressed and now on top of that quite anxious." Dr. Kheriaty didn't anticipate that his former patient would kill herself, but he said that in his training he and his fellow students learned that this was something they could expect to encounter during the course of their careers. "There's a dean at our medical school who said there are two kinds of psychiatrists," he explained. "There are those who've had patients commit suicide and those who *will* have patients who commit suicide. It happens to all of us eventually because of the high-risk populations we treat."

Following the suicide of his former patient, Dr. Kheriaty's boss told him, "Cardiologists who treat people who have heart disease have people die from heart attacks. You can't prevent all bad outcomes." Nonetheless, Dr. Kheriaty found that he was second-guessing himself. He said, "That analogy can be helpful, but in some sense it limps. With suicide, because it is a motivated behavior, it appears that a person chooses to do this, so the analogy to cardiologists breaks down. Their patients don't choose to die. So I think psychiatrists second-guess themselves more than cardiologists do when their patients have heart attacks."

However much he might have second-guessed himself, Dr. Kheriaty didn't have to worry about his colleagues second-guessing *him*. He said, "No one looked down on me or questioned me. I felt like I could speak freely to them about it without being stigmatized." And, he added, it helped that the patient's family didn't blame him for her death. "Her husband called, and said he was grateful for the care she'd been given. He was aware that his wife had been suffering for a long time and we'd been treating her with various methods that were unsuccessful. He seemed to be somewhat prepared for what happened."

While Dr. Kheriaty found it "difficult to accept and deal with" his former patient's suicide, a couple of things lessened the blow. First, he hadn't been seeing the patient for a year. "If I had still been seeing her on a weekly basis," he explained, "it would have been much easier to second-guess myself. Did I miss something? Should I have hospitalized her? Those feelings were there, but it was such a brief encounter after such a long period, it made it easier not to ruminate about what I could have done, which is the typical thing you do after a suicide."

A second factor was that just a few years before, one of Dr. Kheriaty's very close high school friends took his life. He recalled, "Matt had been diagnosed with bipolar disorder while I was in medical school, and I saw how he struggled with the illness. I had been home a month or two before he died, and he had called to ask if I wanted to get together. We used to go waterskiing and swimming all the time. I was fighting a cold and was leaving in a couple of days and never saw him on that trip. It was his effort to reach out one last time knowing what he was going to do. So I regret not having seen him again. Watching his family suffer in the aftermath was quite difficult."

The death of Dr. Kheriaty's friend in no small part inspired his interest in suicide prevention. "I studied it more than I would have," he said. "If anything, Matt's suicide made me dive more deeply into the issue professionally than try to avoid it." Dr. Kheriaty told me that one of the lectures sponsored by the Psychiatry and Spirituality Forum at UC Irvine was on spirituality and suicide prevention. And during that lecture, he said, "I spoke about Matt and that patient in the context of presenting data."

I recommend that anyone who would like more information on this topic visit the Web site for the American Association of Suicidology, where you can find information specifically for clinicians who have lost patients or family members to suicide. Please see the appendix for contact information.

What should you say to friends, family, and colleagues when you've experienced the suicide of a loved one?

You should do what's comfortable for you, whether that means full disclosure of exactly what happened, hiding the truth, or doing something in between.

According to Alison, whose ex-husband drowned himself when their daughter Rachel was only four, her daughter is very straightforward about explaining what happened. She said that Rachel, who is now ten years old, says, "My father committed suicide when I was four." Alison told me, "That's the easy part for her. The part she hates is when people say in response, 'I'm sorry.' I asked her why she hated that, and she said, 'Mommy, they didn't do anything wrong, so why are they saying they're sorry?'" Alison asked Rachel what she thought people should say, and Rachel said, "They should say, 'I can't imagine how you felt.'"

Sandra, whose father and brother both killed themselves, is also forthright in disclosing what happened. She said, "I'm very open. I tell people I come from a suicidal family. Forty percent of my immediate family committed suicide. I tell people this mostly in the context of discussing how I've created a healthy lifestyle and maintain a manageable level of stress in my daily life. And I explain that I do this because I'm afraid of ever repeating what my father and brother did. There's joy in me that I can talk about this and that I'm not mired in a dark lifestyle."

I believe strongly that those of us who can talk about the suicide of our loved one should do so. I think it helps to diminish the stigma of suicide, and talking about it often gives the people we talk to the opportunity to share their own experiences. Ideally, everyone winds up feeling better. Still, no one should feel obligated to talk about a loved one's suicide if they don't want to.

My grandmother never told anyone how her son died, and

for her that was less painful—and less shameful—than having to talk about it. If anyone pressed her, she would say that my father died of pneumonia—not terribly believable for someone who was only forty-four, but my grandmother always made it pretty clear that she wasn't going to say anything more.

In general, I tell people when asked, and usually I'll volunteer the information if it comes up in conversation. But even all these years later, I find that I still tense up in anticipation of the reaction I might get when I disclose that my father killed himself. And as I discovered recently, if I don't have the chance to prepare myself, even *I* get tripped up over my own residual discomfort, shame, and embarrassment.

It happened at dinner one evening with new friends at a hotel in Mexico where we were the only guests. The four of us—two middle-aged couples—had already spent plenty of time talking about our parents, although I never talked about my father. I don't know if this was conscious or not, but Molly noticed and said out of the blue—or what felt like out of the blue—"Eric, we've never talked about *your* dad." Without pausing to think, I said, "He died very young," and changed the subject.

When we got back to our room that night, my partner asked me, "What was *that* about?" I knew what he was asking and said, "I choked. Molly caught me off guard, and I couldn't say it." I was shocked by what I had done. Or *not* done. It had been years since I'd done anything like that, and I was very upset with myself.

After a sleepless night, I decided that I had to come clean. So at dinner the next night with Molly and her husband Tom, I took advantage of the break between the salad course and main course and apologized to Molly for giving an abrupt answer about my father and went on to explain that he had indeed died young, but by his own hand. And I explained that it was normally something I didn't hesitate to discuss, especially given all the practice I'd had as the author of a book about suicide. Molly smiled, nodded, and said, "Well, you and Tom will have a lot to talk about. His brother committed suicide six years ago." I was sorry for Tom and Molly, but relieved to know that I was in good company.

From the start, Patricia was direct about her twenty-year-old daughter's suicide and called her colleagues in her department at work from the hospital, explaining that her daughter had shot herself. She said, "I told everyone in my department that I didn't want them to lie. I didn't want anyone to think I was hiding the truth about what Elizabeth had done. And after Elizabeth died, I called and sent out e-mails to other friends telling them that my daughter took her own life after a lifelong struggle with severe depression."

At Patricia's company, where she worked as an attorney, she had to decide what would be included in the companywide notice about Elizabeth's death. "By custom, the notices never say how the person died," she explained, "so I added in the notice that if anyone wanted to make a donation, that in lieu of flowers they could make a donation to NARSAD [National Alliance for Research on Schizophrenia and Depression], which the notice identified as a mental health charity. So it was pretty clear. We did that in the obituary too."

Not everyone in Patricia's family was comfortable discussing the truth. She recalled, "My former mother-in-law, whom I adore, told her family members that Elizabeth died in a car crash. I was stunned and horrified. I'm a very truthful person. It wouldn't occur to me to be ashamed of it. I knew Elizabeth had a chemical imbalance, and it wasn't her fault. I didn't want to be ashamed about anything about her."

By being as open as she was, Patricia discovered that she wasn't the only suicide survivor at her office. "Several people in the company came up to me and told me that they had never told a soul," she said. "They were shocked that I was so open about it. Everyone thinks it just happened to them. If we don't tell the truth, that's what everyone is left to believe. And that's why whenever I'm asked directly, I say that my daughter killed herself."

Why do people feel the need to keep secret the suicide of a loved one?

There are many compelling reasons why people feel the need to keep secret the suicide of a loved one. The primary reasons are a wish to protect oneself, one's children (or elderly parents), and the deceased loved one from potentially hurtful judgments, comments, or negative reactions. Given that society has long viewed suicide as something shameful and embarrassing, it seems perfectly natural for those of us left behind to feel the need to hide the truth.

Even nearly four decades after my father's suicide, I find that

I instinctively brace myself whenever the subject of his death comes up in conversation with people who don't know that he killed himself. What I'm preparing myself for is the almost inevitable reaction of surprise or shock that my father died by his own hand. If the conversation doesn't come to an abrupt halt, which has happened plenty of times over the years, then there are the inevitable questions: What happened? How old were you? Why did he do it? And so on. After all this time, I don't find the questions particularly painful, although I can't help but feel hurt when the conversation simply dies in an uncomfortable silence.

For someone just beginning to cope with the suicide of a loved one—or for someone like my grandmother who always found discussion of my father's death painful— keeping the suicide secret is a way to avoid the potentially painful questions, silence, or occasionally insensitive remarks that are meant to be comforting but can be hurtful nonetheless.

People also wish to guard against being judged for being a deficient spouse, parent, or sibling. When first disclosing the suicide of a husband, child, or sibling, it's impossible not to worry that the person standing in front of you will wonder: *What kind of terrible wife were you that your husband felt compelled to kill himself? What kind of neglectful parent were you that you couldn't keep your child from ending his life? What kind of sibling were you that you didn't get help for your brother or sister?*

When the person who took his life has left behind family members who are perceived to be vulnerable, such as young children or elderly parents, there will inevitably be family members whose first instinct is to shield them from the truth. For example, a parent may wish to protect the children from what could be confusing and upsetting information (on top of what is already inevitably traumatic news). The surviving parent may also wish to protect the children from feeling that they've been rejected by the dead parent. And the parent may hope to save his or her children from the potential stigma of having had a parent die by suicide and to save them, as well, from the judgments of other parents who might now view these children as coming from a defective family. Or the surviving parent may choose to hide the truth, at least in the short term, simply because they're personally overwhelmed by grief and shock and not able to imagine talking to young children about their parent's suicide and having to answer their questions about what happened.

In the case of elderly parents, particularly if they are in ill health or suffering from dementia, a wish to protect a loved one from terrible and shocking news may easily outweigh the desire to be entirely honest. Later in this chapter, Sandra, whose brother and father both took their lives, discusses what she decided to do in just such a circumstance.

And finally, some people feel compelled to hide the nature of their loved one's death to protect that person's memory or reputation. A suicide is such a dramatic and surprising death that it can easily overshadow whatever good things a person accomplished in life. Any number of people I've spoken with about the suicide of a loved one have said, "I don't want this to be the only thing he's remembered for." And some people who feel this way believe that the best way to protect their loved one's memory is to hide the truth.

I like to think that how we view suicide has evolved in the years since the original edition of this book was published and that the stigma long attached to suicide has diminished sufficiently that we no longer feel compelled to hide something that is sad and tragic rather than shameful and embarrassing. But I also believe strongly that you have to consider what is best for yourself, given your own circumstances, and that no one should feel compelled to disclose a loved one's suicide if they don't want to.

Why not just keep a loved one's suicide a secret? Why talk about it?

If you don't talk about what you've been through, it can be difficult to come to terms with the experience of losing a loved one to suicide. And if you can't come to terms with what happened, it is likely to burden you in some way for the rest of your life. This doesn't mean you have to feel compelled to discuss your loved one's suicide with everyone and answer every question. You can talk about what happened in the context of one-on-one therapy, in a support group, or just with your family and friends.

John generally never talks about his younger brother's 1996 suicide, although he's talked about the experience in therapy. And on rare occasions he has felt compelled to say something when someone else has brought up the subject. John explained, "I do still think there's some residual shame. It feels awful to say it, but it feels shameful because it reflects badly on me. So it's not something I bring up casually."

One time when John decided to talk about his brother's suicide was in 2001, while he was on vacation in the Baltics. John and his partner Jim had hired a car and driver for the day. In conversation with the driver, he recalled, it came up "that *his* brother had taken his life just a year before. I remember looking at Jim and Jim looking back at me, and I volunteered that I knew where he was coming from. I told him that my brother had committed suicide.

"As a Good Samaritan–type thing, I felt I *had* to talk about it. I know that there are hundreds, thousands of us out there, who have had this done to them. This was *done* to me. And it was *done* to others, including this man. So in a way we're a brotherhood and understand each other. I said to the driver, 'This must be extraordinarily painful for you.' I was trying to say to him that it would take a long time for the dust to settle. He wanted graphic detail about what happened to my brother, but I didn't want to go there."

There's another reason not to keep a suicide secret besides letting others know that you have something in common. Despite how attitudes have changed in recent years, there is still tremendous stigma attached to any suicide. By talking about what you've lived through, you can help lessen the stigma—for yourself and for future generations.

Telling the truth can be frightening. It can be embarrassing. It can be awkward. You can never be certain how someone will react. But if you hang on to the secret and never give people the chance to learn, understand, and grow from knowing more about your experience, then the stigma of suicide has the potential to poison your life and the lives of your children. So at the risk of sounding like a broken record, for those of us who are comfortable talking about a loved one's suicide and have the wherewithal to answer questions about it, we should try our best to be honest about what happened. Of course, being this open is not for everyone, and even those who manage to be open about their loved one's suicide don't necessarily feel that way all the time.

I like Alison's attitude about how she dealt with her child Rachel. From the very beginning, she told her daughter the truth about her father's suicide. She explained, "I didn't want Rachel to feel this was something that she had to hide, that she had to be ashamed of. Because she was four, she didn't know anything about the stigma of suicide, and I wanted to help her avoid that burden. As she's grown older, she's learned from others how difficult this whole issue is. I've worried a lot about how she would handle it. But I don't think I have to worry. Next year she starts middle school, and she's told me how she wants to start her own support group for other kids like her. That gives me hope."

Are there times when it's best to lie or hide the truth about a suicide?

Yes, there are times when it's best to hide the truth—or flat-out lie (or lie by omission)—to avoid a conversation that you think may be hurtful to you or the person you're keeping the truth from. There are no hard and fast rules about this, so you have to use your own judgment.

Kevin can hardly remember anything that happened in the days immediately after Craig, his partner of thirty-four years, drowned himself in their backyard pool. But despite the shock and grief that left him in a haze, there were decisions he had to make. One of them was what to say in the death notice, which simply said that Craig died "at his home in East Hampton." As Kevin explained, "We didn't deny it was suicide, but I just didn't want to go into it. I didn't want people asking me the details of what happened. I was still in shock and couldn't imagine having to answer questions."

The most poignant example of a circumstance when hiding the truth turned out to be the best course of action came from Sandra, the theater director from northern California whose father and brother both killed themselves. Sandra's mother was devastated by the loss of her husband and son, and Sandra believes that it was the second suicide—her brother took his life fifteen years after her father—that triggered her mother's slide into dementia.

Over time, Sandra's mother's memory slipped away to the point where she no longer remembered key events in her life. Sandra wrote in a personal essay that was published in the *San Francisco Chronicle* about what happened when her mother asked how her husband—Sandra's father—had died. Earlier in the book we learned from Sandra that after her father's death her mother lied about the circumstances and said he'd had a heart attack, a lie she held fast to for several months before disclosing the truth about what really happened. Here's an excerpt from Sandra's essay:

> She held her wedding picture and stared at it for a long time, a puzzled look on her sagging skin.
> "I still miss him," she said.
> "Me, too," I agreed.
> "How did he die?," she asked.
> "You don't remember?" I was incredulous.
> "No, I really don't." She looked so lost.
> In the pause that followed, I thought about truthfulness, a value she instilled in me, a value we both held strongly. I thought about the twenty-plus years of her grieving incomprehensibly, losing the love of her life by an act of his choice. And I thought that in this case, the truth had found a better home among the forgotten sorrows of a lifetime.
> "He had a heart attack," I whispered.
> She neither contradicted nor disbelieved my quiet assertion. And incredibly, the answer stuck—fact twisted into a greater irony than this writer might ever have invented, something I never could have foreseen in all the years we wrestled with the painful truth of his departure, an abandonment she had never gotten over.
> During her lengthy decline, her memory continued to function although what was retained and what discarded defied the logic of our linear comprehension, a more mysterious process at work in the jumbled transmissions of her shrinking brain. From the woman she used to be, living an eternally felt rejection, she became a freer being and in her new limitation, she was given something the rest of us struggle toward. No longer a survivor-victim, my mother, blessed with her lack of memory, lived very much moment-to-moment in a peaceful present.

How do people react to someone who has lost a loved one to suicide?

People react in a variety of ways, depending on the circumstances. But in general, reactions range from compassion and understanding to shock, extreme discomfort, and awkwardness. And if it's your child or spouse who died, some people can't resist making judgments about your parenting skills or the state of your marriage.

In the four decades since my father's suicide, I've found that there is no better conversation stopper than to disclose that someone in your family died by suicide. But in recent years I've been pleasantly surprised to find that more often than not the initial surprise or shock is followed by compassionate remarks and questions. And of course, if the person I've "come out" to about my father's suicide has been through a suicide as well, then my disclosure gives them permission to come out about their own experience of suicide—and often they do.

One thing to keep in mind is that not everyone who responds with silence or awkwardness is passing judgment. Some people may genuinely care yet not say anything—or simply change the subject—because they fear they'll add to the upset or because they simply don't know what to say. Or they might just be shocked, whether the suicide occurred recently or long ago. That's what Sandra finds when she talks about what happened with her father and brother, both of whom hanged themselves. She said, "How do people react? They look shocked because if they thought *they* had a fucked-up family . . ."

What should you say and do when someone you know has lost a loved one to suicide?

When someone you know loses a loved one to suicide, you need to give her enough room to grieve, but not so much room that she feels abandoned or shunned. If you withdraw, for whatever reason, your absence will be noticed and not easily forgiven. However you do it—by phone, in an e-mail or letter, or in person— you need to convey that you care and that it's okay to talk about it. For example, to a coworker you can say: "I heard the news. I'm so sorry. This must be terrible for you. How are you doing? I'm here if you need me." Even a simple "I'm so sorry" will do.

On the first Mother's Day after Patricia's twenty-year-old daughter took her life, Patricia hoped that her colleagues and relatives would take note of the holiday and say something. She explained why: "My mother died when I was a teenager, so I've been very conscious of how to treat people who have lost someone. So I wish that they had said, 'Happy Mother's Day.' If they had a lot of courage, they might have said, 'You must miss Elizabeth.'" No one other than Patricia's ex-husband, however, said anything. She added, "I like it on the rare occasions when people ask and want to know what happened. Every time I talk about it, it lessens the power of what happened. I want to be asked. If people seem comfortable, I tell them everything. That's when people feel free to share with me what's happened to them."

Keep in mind that the person who is grieving will need support over a long period of time. Compassion and understanding are key. Even if months have passed since the suicide and your friend or colleague seems just fine, it never hurts to ask, "How are you doing?"

Although there is no one right thing you should say to someone dealing with the suicide of a loved one, there are definitely things you should avoid saying and asking. For example, don't ask, "Didn't you see it coming?" Most likely, the survivor already feels guilty for not having seen it coming and doesn't need anyone implying that he or she wasn't paying attention. Also avoid asking, "Why?" There is almost never an adequate answer to that question, and asking just accentuates that fact. Besides which, most survivors have asked themselves that question a thousand times a day since the suicide, so why make it a thousand and one?

I also strongly recommend not saying, "It was God's will." Even if the survivor is religious, such a statement is not likely to be of any comfort and will probably only generate anger. In the same vein, don't say, "Suicide is sinful, and your loved one will suffer in damnation." Even if you sincerely believe this, keep it to yourself. Expressing this belief will only hurt your friend or loved one and will drive him or her away.

People say other things with the hope that what they say is of comfort to the bereaved. Especially if the person who took his life was ill or had suffered from mental illness for a long time, it may be tempting to look on the bright side and say, "At least the person is out of pain." Such a statement is not likely to be of any comfort to the survivor and is best not shared.

Sometimes friends and family can get impatient when they feel the survivor is not moving along through the grieving process or returning to normal routines as quickly as they think that person should. You may have legitimate concerns that your friend or loved one has been grief-stricken longer than expected. But saying to the survivor that it's time to "get over it" or time to "move on" is not a constructive way of dealing with this concern. Consider encouraging your friend or loved one to see a counselor or join a support group. You can even track down the information yourself. Or consult a counselor to find out how you might be of help.

And finally, never say, "I know how you feel," unless you really know how the survivor feels. You can be terribly sorry. You can even know what it means to lose someone you love. But unless you've been through the suicide of someone you know, you can't genuinely know what your friend or loved one is going through and what he or she is feeling. Though it may seem like an inno-cent thing to say, unless you've experienced the suicide of someone close to you, don't attempt to offer comfort by saying this or by suggesting that a recent loss you've lived through—fired from a job, a divorce, the death of a pet—is in any way equivalent. One woman I spoke with whose sister killed herself said that one of her colleagues said to her when she first returned to work, "I know how you feel, my cat just died."

If you have firsthand experience with the loss of a loved one to suicide, by all means, share it. Your friend or loved one will appreciate talking to someone who understands completely what he or she is going through.

Above all, however uncomfortable you may feel about dealing with someone who has lost a loved one to suicide, don't pretend it didn't happen. Otherwise, the person will feel abandoned at a time when he or she needs you most.

Is there something practical you can do to help someone who has experienced the suicide of a loved one?

There's plenty you can do, from bringing a meal to the survi-vor and volunteering to babysit to providing information about suicide survivor support groups or even accompanying a friend or neighbor when they go to the hospital or coroner's office to identify the body of their loved one.

I generally live by the rule that it's better to ask specifically what help is needed—"Can I go with you to the hospital? Can

I help you make the funeral arrangements? Can I take you to dinner? Can I take your kids to a movie?"—than it is to simply say, "Let me know if there's something I can do." People are often embarrassed to ask for help, and if you offer a list of things you can do and ask them to choose one, they're more likely to accept the help. At least that's been my experience.

Patricia said she was "touched by people's generosity" in the aftermath of her daughter Elizabeth's suicide. She recalled, "A friend drove me to the hospital. And while I was at the hospital, my next-door neighbor went in after we left and he cleaned Elizabeth's whole room. He took out the rug and the padding and cleaned everything. It's not like he left the rug at the curb—it was gone. And he had to move all the furniture to get it out. There was no blood anywhere by the time I got home. I was very touched by that."

When I expressed surprise that Patricia's neighbor would assume it was okay to clean up the room and remove the rug while Patricia was out, Patricia explained, "He asked my friend who was taking me to the hospital if he thought it would be okay, and he said it was—and it was okay with me."

Patricia was also surprised by how her colleagues responded after she called them from the hospital to tell them that her daughter had shot herself. "They all came to the hospital in the middle of the night to be with me," she said.

The generosity Patricia experienced extended even to the funeral home. She recalled, "We went to the funeral home, and we were going through the list of things we needed them to do, and it turned out there would be a day when Elizabeth's body would be at the funeral home when no one was there to be with her. My ex-husband asked if we could come by the next day to see Elizabeth and say good-bye. They warned him she would look horrible because of the autopsy."

Patricia's ex-husband insisted that he wanted to see Elizabeth, so the next day Patricia went with him to the funeral home. She planned to wait outside while her ex-husband went in to see Elizabeth. Patricia told me, "On their own and without charging us, the funeral home people had completely fixed her up and made her look gorgeous. We got to spend an hour with her. I still can't believe they did that, but I'm grateful because that was my last image of my daughter. It looked like she was sleeping."

One of the lasting memories I have from the immediate aftermath of my father's suicide is when my best friend's father came over the evening of the day my father died to bring me back to their apartment for dinner. As we left my apartment, Mr. Loeb put his arm around my shoulder and said, "I'm sorry." I didn't know quite what to say in response, so I said, "I'm sorry too." Other than the fact that my father had just died, it was a normal dinner, and I greatly appreciated that the Loeb family reached out to me that evening and invited me into their home for a meal. It was a simple and kind gesture, and one that I'll never forget.

What is it like for someone who finds a loved one who has killed himself—or witnesses a loved one's suicide?

Traumatic. Shocking. Horrifying. No adjective adequately describes the experience, although these are the words used by people I spoke with who found their loved one's body, witnessed the suicide, or, like Patricia, whose twenty-year-old daughter shot herself, discover their loved one still alive but mortally injured. For one mother I spoke with, the image of her son shooting himself was the last thing she saw every night before falling asleep and the first thing she saw in the morning. She said, "It was like being battered by a wave on the shore. It was all I could see for years."

For people like Daniel, whose brother had shot himself six months before I first spoke with him, just visiting the place where a loved one took his life can be extraordinarily painful and traumatic. Daniel was relieved that he wasn't the one to find his brother's body, but within days of the suicide he and his parents went to the house where the suicide took place. Daniel said, "We were advised by everyone not to go to the house, but my mother and her husband, and my father and his wife, and I went to the house to search for clues in the hopes we'd find something that would make his death more clear."

Walking into the house, Daniel recalled, "I couldn't hear anything but the sound of blood rushing through my ears. We went through every room searching for clues and went into his bedroom last. When I saw the dried-up puddle of blood, I just wanted to get us all out of there, but it was too late. My parents crumbled. Dad knelt down and touched the stained floor and started sobbing. Mom screamed and collapsed onto the bed.

They were my parents. They were supposed to be the strong ones, but now I had to be the parent, and I told them this was too much and escorted them out to the yard."

With his parents safely in the yard, Daniel went back into the house and returned to his brother's bedroom. He explained, "I was more calm this time, and I had a chance to look around. He must have shot himself downward because there was a bullet hole by the bottom of the window. I cried for the rest of the day. Given how awful it was seeing the room where my brother shot himself, I think if I'd been the one to find him, I'd still be throwing up."

What is it like for someone to identify the body?

Having to identify the body can also be traumatic, especially when the suicide has been a violent one that leaves the victim disfigured.

In my family it was my uncle—who was thirty-two at the time of his brother's suicide—who was the one who identified my father's body. Before my uncle and I talked about the details regarding my father's suicide—twenty-five years after it happened—it hadn't occurred to me that someone would have had to identify the body.

What I learned from my uncle was that because of the nature of my father's death, an autopsy was required. Then, following the autopsy, before the body could be released to the funeral home, someone had to identify it. My uncle's description of the scene at the morgue and the condition of my father's body—the word "horrifying" doesn't do justice to what my uncle described—has left images in my mind's eye that haven't faded even a little since we had that conversation nearly fifteen years ago. Nothing made me understand more clearly the trauma my uncle lived through than hearing his description of identifying his brother at the morgue. If I harbored any feelings of blame before that conversation, I had only compassion for him afterward.

I'm glad that my uncle and I talked. For me, learning about the details of my father's suicide, the aftermath, and everyone's role has been important.

Are people at greater risk of suicide following the suicide of someone they know? Are the children of people who take their lives at special risk?

There are statistics and studies showing that those who are left behind are at greater risk for suicide, especially the family members and children of those who have taken their lives. I have known this for a long time, and knowing it always made me a little nervous, as if I were fated or genetically programmed to repeat what my father did at the same age he was when he took his life. Was it possible that I inherited his depressive nature and at forty-four years of age would be driven by pain and despair to do the same as he did?

For many years before I turned forty-four, I said that when I was forty-four I'd be in therapy because I was afraid of that ominous number. Several years before that fateful birthday, I decided to get a head start and began seeing a therapist. Much to my surprise, I sailed through forty-four without a hiccup. And long before I reached the age my father was when he died, I came to recognize that, while he was my father, I'm not him and the trajectory of my life has been different from his. I was also very fortunate not to inherit his mental illness, which left him so vulnerable to suicide.

Now that I'm well past that once-ominous number, I view my father—who, of course, never grew older than forty-four—very differently and with more compassion. He was so terribly young to give up on life and so clearly in pain when he ended it. I wish it had been otherwise.

The fact is that there's no clear agreement on why the family members of someone who dies by suicide are at greater risk of suicide themselves. The grief and depression that may follow a suicide (or any death, for that matter) are certainly contributing factors. Genetics may be involved, since depression and schizophrenia, which can put people at greater risk of taking their own lives, can be passed on to the next generation.

There is also the example set by someone who dies by suicide. In other words, "if this is how my father (or sister or husband) dealt with his (or her) problems, maybe it's an option for me too." I always remind myself that not choosing suicide is an option as well, and a far more constructive one. For anyone interested in this particular aspect of suicide, I highly recommend a book called *Blue Genes: A Memoir of Loss and Survival*, by Christopher Lukas, whose mother, brother, and other relatives killed themselves.

On the flip side, I also think that the suicide of a loved one can be a deterrent—or an antidote—to suicide and suicidal thoughts. On those occasions when I've had thoughts of suicide, these thoughts are almost instantly followed by the thought: *Given what my father did, I could never do that to my family.* Remembering the devastation that can follow a suicide is a clear reminder that your family will not be better off after your death and that even if you're in extreme pain, you will inflict even greater pain on those you love and leave behind.

Sandra, whose father and brother both hanged themselves, also sees her family's history of suicide as a deterrent. She told me, "If I ever did commit suicide, everyone would say, 'Well, of course, look at her family!' That's a deterrent. I don't want to be like them. And I know the suffering it causes. Therefore I would not want to cause my husband that pain."

What can the survivors of suicide do to lessen the risk of following in the footsteps of their loved one?

In talking to suicide survivors, especially the children and siblings of people who took their lives, I was surprised by how aware and concerned these people were about taking action to avoid the same fate as their loved one. Two things came up repeatedly. First, how important it is to seek professional help in the wake of a loved one's suicide. Most of the survivors I spoke with have sought counseling with a mental health professional, in no small part because of fear about themselves in the aftermath of their loved one's suicide and their wish not to follow in those footsteps.

And second, as Sandra, the freelance director from northern California, and several of the other survivors told me, it was important to "create a good life" in the wake of a loved one's suicide. Sandra explained, "For me, I now live a very purposely and deliberately healthy existence, so that I can flourish despite my family history. I eat what I do and go to the gym and am married to the wonderful man I'm married to and do work that I love because I have to be very careful. I tell people all the time I come from a suicidal family. For me, the option of suicide comes up quickly when things fall apart, so I have to be very careful. It helps that I got the happy gene in my family, but that's not enough."

What can you do to cope with a suicide?

There's a lot you can do. You can talk to a school counselor, a member of the clergy, or a psychologist, psychiatrist, or social worker. You can also call a crisis hotline to talk to a counselor, or you can attend a support group for people who have lived through the suicide of a loved one.

You can even take a class, which is what Sandra did in 1971, a couple of years after her father's death. Sandra recalled, "I took a course with Edwin Shneidman [one of the pioneers in the study of suicide] called 'Death and Suicide' at UCLA. I took it because after my father killed himself, I wanted to understand more. It was a terrific course."

For people who like to read, there are many books on the subject of suicide at the local library or bookstore. And there are articles and other information available online through a range of organizations, including the American Foundation for Suicide Prevention.

In the course of researching this book, I read a lot about suicide and its aftermath that has helped me better understand what my father did, my own reactions, and the reactions of my family members. It's been a comfort to learn that I'm hardly the only person who has been through this experience and that how I responded to my father's death was perfectly normal. It was nice to discover that I wasn't crazy after all.

Once past the initial shock and grief, some people find that doing volunteer work for a local suicide prevention hotline is a way to help others while they help themselves. Other people facilitate bereavement groups, write a book (like this one), start a nonprofit foundation dedicated to suicide prevention—like the Jed Foundation—or even make a documentary film, which is what Dana Perry did following the suicide of her fifteen-year-old son Evan, who had suffered for years with bipolar disorder.

Perry recalled, "It's such a profound experience to lose someone to suicide that you feel moved to do something, anything. Of course, the first thing you have to do is get out of bed in the morning, and that's really quite challenging. But even once I got into that routine, I still felt so overwhelmed with grief. That experience of grief is so profound that we survivors have to find something to do. I'm a filmmaker, so I made a film. I was just trying to unravel why this happened. I wanted to know, 'What did I miss?' 'What didn't I know?' It wasn't about, 'What should I have done?' I just wanted to examine every aspect of who Evan was. That's why I was eager to ask questions of everyone who had spent time with him—his friends, his teachers, his psychiatrist—when I wasn't there, and by doing the film I had the chance to ask them."

Although Perry has heard from hundreds of people who were helped by the film, providing such help wasn't what motivated her in the first place (although she is glad that the film has had a positive impact). She said, "I made the film really for myself, to say I had looked this in the eye firmly and at length to understand what my son felt and what it felt like to be him and what it felt like for my family to experience this. I wasn't thinking I was doing a film as a prevention piece. I thought maybe it would spare one family what we've experienced. But I'm hearing from teens that the film saved them from suicide by showing the impact it has on the people left behind. The film is providing a push for them to come forward and talk about how they're feeling. I really didn't want teenagers to watch this, but they are so vocal about wanting to talk about it. That's been gratifying."

For more information about Perry's film *Boy Interrupted*, please see the appendix.

Can you give an example of a suicide survivor doing something to make the life of a loved one who died by suicide seem like it was not a "total waste"?

It was through the experience of donating her daughter's organs that Patricia and her ex-husband "were able to feel that [their daughter] Elizabeth's life wasn't a total waste," as Patricia explained it to me. Elizabeth was twenty at the time of her suicide, and she survived long enough after shooting herself for her organs to be harvested. Elizabeth's organs went to four people, and Patricia wrote to each of the recipients through the organization that had arranged the organ donation.

Patricia recalled, "About a month after Elizabeth passed away,

I sent each of them a short letter and enclosed a photograph of Elizabeth." Patricia was told which organs went to which people, although the actual identities of the recipients were withheld, so she wrote the letters accordingly. Here is what Patricia wrote to the man who received Elizabeth's liver:

> *Dear liver recipient:*
> *I understand that my daughter's liver was donated to you in early July. I would like to tell you about my daughter Elizabeth. She was twenty years old when she passed. She was very pretty, and smart, and funny. She was a junior at UNC Ashville at the time of her passing. She was majoring in anthropology and loved animals, movies and music. She was a computer wiz. I have enclosed a photograph of her.*
> *Although I grieved when she passed away and I am still grieving I want you to know that . . . knowing that several people were getting wonderful phone calls from their doctors informing them that there was an organ available for them, it was comforting to me that you and your families received such happy news. . . .*
> *My entire family and I pray for your continued recovery and good health. I am so happy that part of my daughter lives on in you.*

Patricia chose not to include in the letter that her daughter had killed herself because, she said, "I thought that might be too upsetting to them. I had zero shame about what happened and never hesitate to speak about how Elizabeth died, but in this case it didn't feel right."

Patricia heard back from three of the four recipients. (One recipient died almost immediately after he received one of Elizabeth's lungs.) The man who received Elizabeth's liver explained in his response to Patricia that he'd been infected with hepatitis C from a transfusion when he was sixteen and could no longer work by the time he received the liver transplant. He included with his letter a photograph of himself with his wife and two young sons. Choking back tears, Patricia recalled, "Behind them in the background, blown up, framed, and hanging on the wall was the photograph of Elizabeth that I'd sent with the letter."

I asked Patricia why she felt compelled to send letters to the people who received Elizabeth's organs. She replied, "I think partly because I wanted them to write back. I wanted to know they were alive and that Elizabeth's life wasn't a total waste. At least her organs would help these people live. When you get the letters from the people who wanted to live so badly . . . Elizabeth never wanted to live. It really is great that her body parts have made such a huge difference in the lives of these three people."

What can a family do to cope with a suicide?

Talk with one another. Ask questions. Don't hide your feelings. Go to a counselor or support group. And take your kids with you. There is no need for your family to experience the hurt and isolation that mine did.

I like something that the filmmaker Dana Perry told me her stepson said when he spoke at his brother's memorial service. He said, "If we as a community take on the pain that Evan left behind, we can distribute it and not each individually have to take on the whole burden." This is such a simple and powerful idea. And hopeful too. This is something that no family or individual needs to experience—or should experience—alone.

Can you get over the suicide of a loved one?
Is there such a thing as closure for suicide survivors?

I don't know about you, but I don't like the word "closure." For me it implies that there is a point at which the death or trauma you've been through can be labeled "case closed," when you "put it behind you," when you "move on." Nice to think so, but I don't believe that this is the reality for most of us. And we're potentially setting ourselves up for disappointment if we set as our goal or expectation the idea that the suicide we've lived through won't be a part of us for the rest of our lives.

In an interview the filmmaker Dana Perry did with the *Wall Street Journal* about this subject, she said something that struck a chord for me: "The process of dealing with this grief is something like taking a teaspoon to an ocean of tears. You can spoon a little, but if you keep on going at it you might actually make a dent in it."

It was the process of making the film that helped Perry begin working through her grief. As she explained to me when I spoke with her about the film, "All I could do was use the means that I have to try to process this experience in bite-size pieces. So day upon day upon week upon month of looking at movies, considering editorial choices, helped me process it. Will the ocean of tears ever be emptied? Of course not. I would never say I thought that that process is done or will be done. I don't think it will. But I have other children in the family. It's certainly worth sticking around for them. And I have no intention of giving up on life."

Still, for Perry the immediate aftermath was a struggle, as it is for most of us. She recalled, "During the first six months I remember thinking I might just as well go in the grave with him. There's a great Samuel Beckett quote from *Waiting for Godot*: 'I can't go on, I'll go on.' That really summed it up for me. I don't have a choice. There are choices as to the degree you choose to examine the suicide or not. By making a film, I chose the extreme in exposing my family, and that was good for me. I see mourning as something active. It's something you do, not something that just happens to you."

There's no question that over time you can learn to live with the loss of a loved one to suicide, but the fact that your loved one died by suicide is something you never forget. And there are plenty of reminders. Inevitably, your loved one will come up in conversation. Also, there are anniversaries, birthdays, and holidays. For years I got depressed around the time of year my father died, but it wasn't until a decade after his death that I made any connection between the depression and his suicide. During the first few years, Father's Day was the worst. All the other kids at school talked about the gifts they were getting or making for their fathers, and all I could do was joke that I was lucky I didn't have to worry about that. For other people, the worst time of year may be Christmas, Thanksgiving, or the anniversary of their loved one's death.

For my Uncle Richie, who never needed a holiday or anniversary as a reason to think about his brother's suicide or to feel guilty about it, the passing of four decades has made a difference. He said, "With time, the guilt has dissipated. I don't think about it every day, and I don't beat myself up every day over it, but there's a lot of stuff still there. I have trouble saying his name. I still have a hard time talking about him and the circumstances of his death. I don't hide it, but I don't bring it up. It's still something I prefer to keep deep down inside, and it probably costs me. I think that a lot of the pain is sublimated, and it rears its ugly head every once in a while. I'm sure that was no small contributing factor to the depressive sequences in my life. It's in there, and it's something that will be in my soul until I die. I'm resigned to that."

Yet the passage of time has also given my uncle the chance to reflect: "In retrospect, I look at thirty-two-year-olds, which is how old I was when my brother died, and think they're kids. At the time, I had two young children, and I was going to a job where I was doing my best just to get through every day. So therein I may cut myself some slack."

In the three years since his long-term partner killed himself, Kevin has gone from a state of complete shock and paralysis in the immediate aftermath to functioning quite well independently, and he is even considering the possibility of a new relationship. But as Kevin told me—and as I know from my own experience—it's not a quick process, and you're inevitably changed by your experience. He said, "Over time some of the worst feelings recede, but I can't imagine that this won't ever be with me. My theory is that some of my friends want me to be over this and don't want to deal with it at this point. I'm not how I was before Craig committed suicide, and they want me to be who I was. I can't be who I was. I still often act for people and hide my feelings because a lot of people just don't want to spend a lot of time talking about it."

It's a cliché to say that time heals all wounds, but even in the case of suicide, in time you will feel better. I'm not suggesting that you will ever be able to put the experience behind you as if it never happened. That is impossible. But eventually you may even be able to talk about the experience without feeling as if you've been punched in the stomach.

How long does it take to get over the suicide of a loved one?

I don't know if you ever "get over" the suicide of a loved one. That phrase implies that it's over and done. Finished. Book closed. The end. I think a better question is, "How long will I *grieve* over the suicide of my loved one?" And add to that, "How long will it take to *accept* the suicide of my loved one?"

This is not something you put behind you in six months. Even people who have been through the death of a loved one from an accident or natural causes aren't through grieving so quickly. For any loss, after an initial period of intense grief lasting weeks or months, it is perfectly normal to grieve for a year to a year and a half or more. Fully accepting the loss and integrating the experience of that loss inevitably takes longer.

I wish I could say that there's a clear-cut answer to this question, as in, "After one year you will feel . . . ," but there isn't. I've interviewed people who were able to get through their grief and accept the suicide of their loved one in just a couple of years. For me it was more than two decades before I even had all the details of what happened, and then nearly another decade went by before I accepted and felt relatively comfortable with the reality of my father's suicide. I still get instinctively uneasy when I'm asked about my father by someone who doesn't know my history, but that usually doesn't keep me from talking about what happened and it doesn't ruin my day. I'm guessing I'll feel less uneasy as the years pass.

There is no formula for how long the grieving process should last or how long it will take to accept the suicide death of a loved one. Circumstances are different. People are different. But if you or someone you love seems unable to get past the initial grief and acceptance seems like an impossibility, it is important to get help from a support group or a mental health professional.

Given that "getting over" a suicide, "putting it behind you," or achieving "closure" are either overstatements or misnomers, can you give another example of something someone did to find some degree of peace in the aftermath of a loved one's suicide?

I was intrigued by something Sandra did years after her father killed himself to make right something she didn't feel right about. Sandra recalled, "We buried my father in Mt. Sinai in Los Angeles, which is part of Forest Lawn. I didn't go back for seven years. We didn't unveil him or anything." (In the Jewish faith, it's customary to return to the grave one year after the burial to "unveil" the gravestone, and a rabbi leads a prayer service, usually just for the family. This is called an "unveiling.")

Sandra continued, "We didn't do an unveiling because we were just too devastated. I couldn't forgive my father for killing himself, for depriving me of him. I was angry enough at him to not honor him. And the anger did not abate for seven years. Then I went back and told him that I forgave him. There's a part of us that never forgives them for that, but I forgave him."

Still, it wasn't until 1996, twenty-seven years after her father died, that Sandra decided to hold an unveiling. She explained, "I decided to make burial arrangements for my mother while she was still alive and found that the closest plot to my father was a football field away. So I bought a crypt for her and moved my father there so they could be next to each other. After I moved him, that's when I unveiled him. I used a lay rabbi and invited my relatives and everything. I did that because it was unfinished. There was no closure. He was a Jewish man and studied the Bible. It felt like the right thing to do, and I'm glad I did it."

How do therapy and support groups help people cope with a suicide?

For many, if not most, people who have experienced the suicide of a loved one, it is helpful to talk about their experiences, their feelings, and their anguish, whether it's in the context of one-on-one therapy with a psychologist or psychiatrist or in a support group specifically for people dealing with suicide.

Donna Morrish, a marriage and family therapist who has served as a consultant to crisis and suicide agencies, is a big proponent of support groups. She said, "I think the groups are very beneficial. If I were forced to choose between individual counseling and a group, I'd take the group every time. For one thing, being with a group of people who have been through the same thing works to dissolve the stigma. Here you are, sitting with this group of perfectly nice people, and the same thing happened to them. Also, people who have been through a suicide feel so alienated and isolated and experience subtle blame. In this group you can talk about all of this, and there are people who can identify with what you're going through."

Also, because people in a group know what you're going through, it's a place where you can tell people things you fear other people might think were crazy, like how you've kept your deceased loved one's voice mail message for six months or how you get in your car, close the doors and windows, and scream until you're hoarse.

Another advantage of a group, Morrish explained, is that there's a mix of people. Some are new and just beginning to deal with their feelings, and others are further along. "So the new people can see a path," she said. "If you can see that people come through their grief, then it gives the griever some courage."

Vanessa McGann, a clinical psychologist in private practice who runs bereavement support groups for suicide survivors in New York City, considers this to be the top benefit of participating in a group. She said, "When you see people who are a few months further along in the grief process, you realize that you can survive." And there are additional benefits. "People also learn from the other participants ways of coping that feel good to them," she said, "like the practical aspects of responding to colleagues and how to handle things like holidays and anniversaries." McGann knows about suicide from personal experience. Her forty-two-year-old sister took her life in 2004.

Getting help isn't just for people who have recently experienced a suicide. I can personally testify that you can start talking about it with a therapist many years after the fact—as I did—and benefit enormously from the experience of understanding what you've been through, why you feel the way you do, and how your loved one's suicide has affected your life.

Alison didn't take her daughter Rachel for any kind of professional help until six years after Rachel's father drowned himself. She recalled, "I had some concerns over the years that she never really cried much about what happened to her father, but I just assumed she'd dealt with it well." Then one summer Rachel was watching a television show where one of the characters died. "It was the grandparent, and Rachel became hysterical," Alison said. "The emotion came out for the first time, and she really cried."

After that experience, Alison enrolled herself and Rachel in a bereavement program run by a local hospice. She told me, "There were six children in Rachel's group, and they were all about the same age and had all lost a parent. The person leading the group taught them that they were allowed to express their feelings. So the children talked together about how this made them feel. It was great because it was the one place where they didn't feel different from other kids. They all had a parent die. The counselor told me several weeks into this that he thought Rachel had dealt well with the death of her father and was helping some of the other kids get through their grief."

Support groups are not for everyone. After her daughter's death, Patricia continued to see the counselor she'd already been seeing because she found that it helped, even though "she's not a trained grief counselor." So she also contacted a counseling center near her home in the Atlanta, Georgia, area that had support groups for suicide survivors several times a month.

Patricia went to the support groups "two or three times," but stopped "because it wipes me out for weeks," she said. Vanessa McGann, the psychologist, explained, "For a few select people, groups have the potential to be re-traumatizing, so it is important to honor your own reactions and needs if you find that a support group is not helping you." There are also people who are simply not comfortable sharing their feelings in a public forum.

Once Patricia stopped going to the support group, she started seeing one of the therapists at the counseling center. "He put things in perspective for me," she said, "because he's a trained grief counselor. He gives me ways to think about what happened and ways to get on with my life. I found him a couple of months ago and see him weekly."

Sometimes the difficulty people have with a support group isn't with the support group per se but with the kind of people they find there. A half-year after his partner of thirty-four years took his life, Kevin decided he would go to a suicide bereavement support group sponsored by the Samaritans. He recalled, "There were three people and a facilitator. All three people had brothers who committed suicide, and for different reasons all felt enormous guilt over what happened. But I didn't feel guilt, so none of their experiences resonated with me. Then I went to a bereavement group for gay people sponsored by the gay center in New York City. There were six other people in the group, all of whom had drug addiction issues. I couldn't relate to any of their experiences either and didn't go back."

Although frustrated by what he found at the first two support groups, Kevin didn't give up, and eventually he found a bereavement group near his house on Long Island sponsored by East End Hospice for people who had lost spouses. He said, "It was seven widows and me, and there was total acceptance that I had lost as much as they had. Even though none of their husbands had killed themselves, they were just as angry at being left as I was, and we all needed to talk about these feelings. The group went on for twelve weeks, and it was amazing to see how they were able to evolve in just the first *four* weeks. And I evolved along with them."

Kevin offered this bit of advice for anyone in search of a bereavement group: "Look for a group until you find the group that's right for you. They may not be people just like you, but that doesn't matter. I had spent thirty-four years with my partner, just as they had spent decades with their husbands. We had a lot in common, and they treated me as an equal, which surprised me."

What happens at a support group for people coping with the suicide of a loved one?

More than anything, people talk. The group may be organized and run by people who have experienced the suicide of a loved one, or it may be organized through a local hospital or mental health center and run by a mental health professional.

Carolyn, whose seventeen-year-old son killed himself, started a support group in an attempt to come to terms with her son's death. The monthly meetings, held at a local hospital, draw anywhere from a handful to three dozen people. She said, "We have people from every walk of life, every profession, and all ages from fourteen on up. At the start of the meeting I introduce myself, and I explain what the support group is about and that everything said in the room stays there. Confidentiality is very important in making people feel comfortable to speak honestly. Then we go around the room—people are seated in chairs arranged in a circle—and people introduce themselves and briefly talk about their circumstances. Some people are in such pain that they can't yet talk about it, and so they simply listen to the discussion."

There is nothing mysterious or exotic about these support groups. They're simply a place where people can gather to talk about what they've been through, share their feelings, help one another cope with their experiences, and begin the difficult process of healing.

How long do people attend bereavement groups?

Psychologist Vanessa McGann runs a free drop-in bereavement group led by clinicians. She said that, in her experience, "people sometimes come once. Sometimes they come a couple of times and stop and then come back later. I find for my group that the average is four to six times, with a wide range in between." McGann added, "I would never tell anyone they had to go, but if people are feeling isolated, feeling crazy, or having increasing difficulty in their ability to cope, I would suggest trying it for a few months. You don't even have to speak if you don't want to. Just listening can help."

How can you find a support group or bereavement group?

The fastest way to locate a suicide survivor support group or bereavement group is to go to the Web site for the American Foundation for Suicide Prevention (AFSP) and search for the group nearest to where you live. If you don't live near a support group, there are online nonprofit support groups and survivor Web sites that you can link to from the AFSP Web site. See the appendix for contact information for AFSP.

Does everyone need the help of a mental health professional or support group to cope with the suicide— or attempted suicide—of a loved one?

There are plenty of people who have managed to cope with the suicide or attempted suicide of a loved one without seeing a mental health professional or going to a support group. And I know there are experts who believe it's not necessary. Nonetheless, I think that some form of counseling is essential, especially for children and young people, who don't have the same coping skills and support networks that adults have. Even for adults who

are doing a good job of coping, seeing a mental health professional or joining a support group can help speed the healing process.

In chapter 5 ("Attempted Suicide"), Luke, who is now in his
midfifties, spoke about what it was like for him when he was
fourteen and found his mother just after she had cut her wrists.
He recalled the experience being traumatic, but didn't speak
with anyone about it, or about his mother's mental illness, until
he was in college. For someone like Luke—and anyone who has
lived through the experience of having a suicidal loved one—
working with a psychologist or other mental health professional
can be beneficial.

I asked Luke whether anyone recommended that he see a
counselor after he witnessed his mother's suicide attempt (or following any of her subsequent attempts and hospitalizations). He
laughed and said, "Counseling? Of course not! What kind of
enlightened world do you think I lived in? That's absurd! When
you look at it from the perspective of today, it's crazy to think
that someone was *not* sent to counseling, but back then no one
in my town would have sent their kid to therapy. You just didn't
talk about it. We were told—consciously or unconsciously—not
to tell anyone and to just bear it, which I did for years."

When Luke was in his late twenties and experiencing a period
of emotional distress, he decided to see a therapist. He recalled,
"I spoke a lot about that time and my mother's mental illness.
I probably could not have healed to the extent that I feel that I
have without the help of a therapist." Although he might have
been able to heal "to some extent" without this help, he said,
"going to a gym for the mind helped me stretch those muscles
and achieve the emotional flexibility I now have."

What books do you recommend for people coping with the suicide of a loved one?

Please see the bibliography for a list of books.

What services are available to suicide survivors?

Support services for suicide survivors are available all across the United States through local organizations, community mental health centers, and hospitals. Many resources are also available online. The fastest and most efficient way to find out what's available is to call or visit the Web site of the American Foundation for Suicide Prevention (AFSP). You'll find the contact information for AFSP, as well as for many other organizations and support services, in the appendix.

What is National Survivors of Suicide Day?

National Survivors of Suicide Day, which is sponsored by the American Foundation for Suicide Prevention (AFSP), is an annual event held at scores of locations in the United States and around the world.

Here's how AFSP describes the event on its Web site: "National Survivors of Suicide Day is a day of healing for those who have lost someone to suicide. It was created by U.S. Senate resolution in 1999 through the efforts of Sen. Harry Reid of Nevada, who lost his father to suicide. Every year, AFSP sponsors an event to provide an opportunity for the survivor community to come together for support, healing, information and empowerment."

I attended my first National Survivors of Suicide Day program in New York City in 2008 shortly after my sister-in-law took her life. I was still in a state of shock and welcomed the opportunity to participate in a program that was for people like me.

I'm a little embarrassed to admit that I had never gone to any kind of suicide survivor group before, which I should have, if only as part of my research for the original edition of this book. Although I was nervous about going, I found the program to be both moving and informative. But the best part was simply meeting with and talking to fellow suicide survivors over lunch. It was a revelation to be in a room with so many other people who had lived through the suicide of a loved one. At a moment when I was feeling very alone, I suddenly didn't feel alone at all.

When it came time for the afternoon program to begin, the organizers had to work hard to get our attention because we

were all so deeply engrossed in conversations. The daylong program proved to be a surprisingly uplifting experience, even for a
suicide veteran like me.

Is it ever too late to repair the damage done by a suicide?

My Uncle Richie was the inspiration for this final question. After
showing him how I used our conversations in this book, he wrote
to me: "Our family can never fully recover from the devastation
of losing Irwin, but we have made significant strides in our attempts to repair the damage. Perhaps we can talk about that, as
well. It might make for a somewhat hopeful and uplifting ending
to a book filled with sadness."

This is a book that is indeed filled with sadness and heartbreak. Given the subject matter, it couldn't be otherwise. But
many of us survivors know that there is hope for getting back on
our feet, going on with our lives, and repairing the ties to our
loved ones that may have been frayed or broken by the searing
experience of a suicide.

There is no one road back from a suicide, but I thought I
would ask my uncle what he thought worked for our family, how
we've repaired some of the damage, and what advice he might
have for others who have had the misfortune to live through the
suicide of someone close to them. This is what he said:

*After reading what you wrote, I was left with a sense that we
were back where we were right after Irwin's suicide four decades
ago. Certainly you're not making anything up about what happened, and I know it's hard not to remain focused on the negative, because that's what it is. A suicide like the one we lived
through was a disaster. But you and your brother and sister built
a life out of that morass, lives you can be proud of. And as a
family, I think that ultimately the experience of what happened
drove us to embrace what we had left.*

*It's true that there are things that can't be repaired. You were
denied a father for the most formative years of your lives and
that can never be replaced. You guys were innocents in this and
you lost a lot. That certainly is a hole. And, of course, I can't
forgive myself for certain things that I wasn't able to do at the*

time. But I am very proud of how my nephews and niece turned out. And I'm proud of my relationship with the three of you. We look out for and care for one another.

You kids—and each of you is very different—always rise to the occasion for each other. When there's a crisis, everybody seems to pull together. For whatever reason, there was a sense of family that drove all of you to embrace what you had left—each other, Grandma, and me. None of you gave up on me, so I couldn't give up on all of you. I recognize that for the most part we didn't talk about what happened, especially in the early years, but that hasn't kept us from looking out for one another and caring for one another.

Would I do things differently if I had a chance? Yes, knowing what I know now I wouldn't make the same mistakes. I would have been more proactive and stepped into the breach with you kids.

I would advise anyone who finds himself in the position I was, don't remove yourself. Don't let your own hurt and anger get in the way of digging in and stepping in in the ways you're needed. By stepping in I would have helped my nephews and niece when they needed me most and I would have spared myself a lot of guilt and grief down the road for having failed to do so. Since I didn't prevent my brother's suicide, at least I could have taken over the role he had. So don't withdraw. Don't remove yourself. If anything, work on getting closer together.

My uncle and I agreed that he would have benefited from some kind of professional help at the time of his brother's suicide to help him "step in" in the ways he was needed. He said, "I was very young myself and it certainly would have helped to have had a counselor of any kind who could point me in a more positive direction. But I didn't and there's no going back. So the best you can do is go forward. And when you consider what we've all been through, there's a lot to feel good about."

When I asked my uncle if he had any final words of encouragement for people who have lived through the suicide of a loved one, he said, "There is life after suicide—it's worth living and in spite of it you can build good relationships and a family can stick together."

APPENDIX

Suicide Prevention and Crisis Telephone Hotlines

General

National Suicide Prevention Lifeline
1-800-273-TALK (1-800-273-8255)
www.suicidepreventionlifeline.org
The National Suicide Prevention Lifeline (NSPL) provides free and confidential access to trained telephone counselors 24/7 for anyone in suicidal crisis or emotional distress. You can call for yourself or on behalf of someone you care about. Comprising more than 140 crisis centers nationwide, the Lifeline will route your call to the center nearest you. NSPL also provides extensive information on its Web site about suicide, suicide prevention, and specific information for veterans (see below).

Military/Veterans

Veterans Suicide Prevention Hotline
1-800-273-8255
www.suicidepreventionlifeline.org/Veterans
The Veterans Suicide Prevention Hotline, which is part of the National Suicide Prevention Lifeline (see above), provides access to counselors who are specifically trained to work with veterans of the U.S. military and their friends and family. After calling the 800 number, simply press 1 on your keypad, and your call will be routed to one of these counselors. You'll also find extensive resources on the NSPL Web site specifically for veterans.

Gay, Lesbian, Bisexual, Transgender Youth

The Trevor Helpline
1-800-850-8078
www.thetrevorproject.org
Trained peer counselors are available 24/7 for gay, lesbian, bisexual, and transgender youth (up to age twenty-five) who are in a crisis or thinking about suicide.

Organizations and Web sites

General

American Association of Suicidology
5221 Wisconsin Ave., NW
Washington, DC 20015
202-237-2280
www.suicidology.org
The goals of the American Association of Suicidology (AAS) are clear and straightforward: to understand and prevent suicide. Founded in 1968 by Edwin Shneidman, AAS promotes research, public awareness programs, public education, and training for professionals and volunteers. In addition, AAS serves as a national clearinghouse for information on suicide. The organization's extensive Web site offers a range of information and referrals, including a suicide survivor support group directory and information for clinicians who have lost a patient or a family member to suicide.

American Foundation for Suicide Prevention
120 Wall St., 22nd Floor
New York, NY 10005
212-363-3500
1-888-333-AFSP
www.afsp.org
The American Foundation for Suicide Prevention (AFSP) supports research, education, and treatment programs with the goal of preventing suicide. AFSP also maintains an extensive Web site that provides information on everything from suicide prevention

to listings of local support groups for survivors of suicide. And the organization publishes a newsletter for people concerned about suicide and for those who have lost a loved one to suicide.

Some of the special events run by AFSP include "Out of the Darkness" community fund-raiser walks and annual National Survivors of Suicide Day conferences, which are held across the United States and around the world.

Canadian Association for Suicide Prevention
870 Portage Ave.
Winnipeg, MB, R3G 0P1
204-784-4073
www.casp-acps.ca
The Canadian Association for Suicide Prevention (CASP) works to reduce the suicide rate and minimize the harmful consequences of suicide by advocating, supporting, and educating. Its Web site offers extensive information and resources on suicide, suicide prevention, and suicide survivor support groups across Canada.

International Association for Suicide Prevention
IASP Central Administrative Office
Le Barade
F-32330 Gondrin
France
011-33-562-29-19-47
www.iasp.info
The International Association for Suicide Prevention (IASP), a nongovernmental organization affiliated with the World Health Organization (WHO), is dedicated to "preventing suicidal behavior, alleviating its effects, and providing a forum for academics, mental health professionals, crisis workers, volunteers and suicide survivors." IASP sponsors an annual World Suicide Prevention Day and provides extensive resources on its Web site.

National Organization for People of Color Against Suicide
PO Box 75571
Washington, DC 20013
202-549-6039
www.nopcas.com

The National Organization for People of Color Against Suicide (NOPCAS) was founded with the goal of stopping "the tragic epidemic of suicide in minority communities." Its mission includes improving knowledge for counselors and educators, providing insight on depression and other brain disorders, sharing coping methods with survivors, educating bereaved family members and friends, improving training for those who work with young adults, and sharing information on suicide prevention and intervention. The NOPCAS Web site provides a range of resources and information.

Suicide Prevention Action Network USA
1010 Vermont Ave., NW, Suite 408
Washington, DC 20005
202-449-3600
www.spanusa.org
The Suicide Prevention Action Network USA (SPAN USA) serves as the public policy and advocacy division of the American Foundation for Suicide Prevention (AFSP). The organization was created to raise awareness, build political will, and call for action with regard to creating, advancing, implementing, and evaluating a national strategy to address suicide in the United States. SPAN USA merged with AFSP in 2009. SPAN USA's Web site provides extensive information and resources on a range of issues, from how you can get involved in suicide prevention efforts to how to find online or in-person survivor support groups.

Suicide Prevention Resource Center
Education Development Center, Inc.
55 Chapel St.
Newton, MA 02458
877-438-7772
www.sprc.org
The Suicide Prevention Resource Center (SPRC) provides prevention support, training, and information resources to individuals and groups, including health and human service professionals, community leaders, survivors and advocates, coalitions and prevention networks, prevention professionals, researchers,

and policymakers. SPRC's resources include an extensive Web site, an online library, and an e-newsletter.

College Students

The Jed Foundation
220 Fifth Ave., 9th Floor
New York, NY 10001
212-647-7544
www.jedfoundation.org
http://ulifeline.org/main/Home.html
Donna and Phil Satow launched the Jed Foundation in 2000 following the loss of their son Jed to suicide. The Jed Foundation works to "reduce emotional distress and prevent suicide among college students" by providing information and resources for colleges, students, and parents. The organization's first program, ULifeline, is a widely used online resource for college mental health services that provides campus-specific information for more than 1,250 schools.

Military/Veterans

U.S. Army Suicide Prevention Program
www.armyg1.army.mil/hr/suicide/
The stated mission of the U.S. Army Suicide Prevention Program is to "improve readiness through the development and enhancement of the Army Suicide Prevention Program policies designed to minimize suicide behavior, thereby preserving mission effectiveness through individual readiness for Soldiers, their Families, and Department of the Army civilians." On the prevention program's Web site you'll find extensive listings for suicide prevention materials, programs, and other resources.

U.S. Army Center for Health Promotion and Preventive Medicine
http://chppm-www.apgea.army.mil/dhpw/readiness/suicide.aspx
At this site you'll find suicide prevention resources, including

printed materials, briefings, and videos, as well as information for survivors of suicide.

Army Behavioral Health: Suicide Prevention

www.behavioralhealth.army.mil/sprevention/index.html
This Web site offers information, news, and videos about suicide prevention and the Army's efforts to prevent suicide.

Marine Corps Community Services: Suicide Prevention

www.usmc-mccs.org/suicideprevent/
Established specifically for the Marine Corps, this Web site provides links to news, information, and resources.

Air Force Suicide Prevention Program

http://afspp.afms.mil/
As noted on the Air Force Suicide Prevention Program Web site, this resource is "designed to provide information and tools to members of the Air Force community (Suicide Prevention Program Managers, commanders, gatekeepers, IDS members, etc.) in their efforts to help reduce Air Force suicides."

Navy Suicide Prevention Program

www.npc.navy.mil/commandsupport/suicideprevention
This Web site provides links to news, information, and resources specifically for Navy personnel.

Survivors of Suicide

Many of the organizations listed under the "General" subsection of the "Organizations and Web sites" section of this appendix provide resources for survivors of suicide. For example, on the American Foundation for Suicide Prevention (AFSP) Web site (www.afsp.org), you can search for a suicide survivor support group in your area.

Documentaries and Educational DVDs and Videos

Boy Interrupted
www.boyinterruptedfilm.com

Boy Interrupted, a compelling and heartfelt documentary film about a teenager named Evan, asks how a boy can end his life at the age of fifteen. The filmmaker Dana Perry, Evan's mother, made this film by gathering home movies, photographs, and a variety of different documents to tell the story of her son's bipolar illness, his life, his death, and their impact on those who loved him the most.

Fatal Mistakes: Families Touched by Suicide
www.afsp.org

Fatal Mistakes chronicles the recovery of several families in the aftermath of suicide. These suicide survivors share their experiences with the hope that what they say will be of comfort to others who are experiencing similar grief. And they hope to prevent those who haven't yet experienced such a loss from ever knowing the pain of losing a loved one to suicide. The film includes interviews with researchers and clinicians on the latest advances and trends in suicide prevention research, as well as information about warning signs, risk factors, and appropriate treatments for suicidal patients.

More Than Sad: Teen Depression
www.morethansad.org

The American Foundation for Suicide Prevention (AFSP) partnered with the New York State Office of Mental Health on this film, whose aim is to educate high school students about depression. Since the majority of suicides are caused by untreated or inadequately treated depression, it is AFSP's hope that teaching adolescents to recognize the signs of depression in themselves and in others will help to bring down the number of suicide deaths among teenagers in New York State and nationwide.

Struggling in Silence: Physician Depression and Suicide
www.doctorswithdepression.org

Struggling in Silence is a one-hour public television documentary that sheds light on the hidden and perplexing phenomenon of physician suicide. The film is part of an American Foundation for Suicide Prevention (AFSP) national campaign to explore the professional policies and the culture of stigma that prevent physicians and medical school students from seeking help for the common and treatable mood disorders that can lead to suicide.

The Truth About Suicide: Real Stories of Depression in College
   www.afsp.org
   The aim of this film, which was developed by the American Foundation for Suicide Prevention (AFSP), is to present a recognizable picture of depression—and other problems associated with suicide—as they are commonly experienced by college students and other young adults.

SELECTED BIBLIOGRAPHY

In addition to the works cited here, you can also consult the organization Web sites listed in the appendix for their most current book recommendations.

Clinical and Academic Books

Jacobs, Douglas, ed. *The Harvard Medical School Guide to Suicide Assessment and Intervention.* Hoboken, NJ: Jossey-Bass, 1998.
———, ed. *Suicide and Clinical Practice.* Washington, DC: American Psychiatric Press, 1992.
Maris, Ronald W., Alan L. Berman, and Morton M. Silberman. *Comprehensive Textbook of Suicidology.* New York: Guilford Press, 2000.
Shea, Shawn Christopher. *The Practical Art of Suicide Assessment: A Guide for Mental Health Professionals and Substance Abuse Counselors.* Hoboken, NJ: Wiley, 2002.

Coping with Suicide, Suicide Survivors, and Memoir

Bolton, Iris. *My Son, My Son: A Guide to Healing After Death, Loss, or Suicide.* Atlanta: Bolton Press, 1983.
Cain, Albert C., ed. *Survivors of Suicide.* Springfield, IL: Charles C. Thomas, 1972.
Fine, Carla. *No Time to Say Good-bye: Surviving the Suicide of a Loved One.* New York: Main Street Books, 1999.
Flyer, Karen. *Loss and Found: A Memoir.* Bloomington, IN: Xlibris Corp., 2008.
Hammer, Signe. *By Her Own Hand.* New York: Vintage Books/ Random House, 1992.
Hewett, John H. *After Suicide.* Philadelphia: Westminster Press, 1980.

Hsu, Albert. *Grieving a Suicide: A Loved One's Search for Comfort, Answers, and Hope.* Downers Grove, IL: InterVarsity Press, 2002.

Kuklin, Susan. *After a Suicide: Young People Speak Up.* New York: G. P. Putnam's Sons, 1994.

Linn-Gust, Michelle. *Do They Have Bad Days in Heaven? Surviving the Suicide Loss of a Sibling,* 2nd Edition. Albuquerque, NM: Chellenhead Works, 2001.

Linn-Gust, Michelle. *Rocky Roads: The Journeys of Families through Suicide Grief.* Albuquerque, NM: Chellenhead Works, 2010.

Lukas, Christopher. *Blue Genes: A Memoir of Loss and Survival.* New York: Anchor, 2009.

Lukas, Christopher, and Henry M. Seiden. *Silent Grief: Living in the Wake of Suicide.* Philadelphia: Jessica Kingsley Publishers, 2007.

Meyers, Michael F., and Carla Fine. *Touched by Suicide: Hope and Healing After Loss.* New York: Gotham, 2006.

Rappaport, Nancy. *In Her Wake: A Child Psychiatrist Explores the Mystery of Her Mother's Suicide.* New York: Basic Books, 2009.

Requarth, Margo. *After a Parent's Suicide: Helping Children Heal.* Sebastopol, CA: Healing Hearts Press, 2008.

Robinson, Rita. *Survivors of Suicide.* Franklin Lakes, NJ: New Page Books, 2001.

Rosenfield, Linda, and Marilynne Prupas. *Left Alive: After a Suicide Death in the Family.* Springfield, IL: Charles C. Thomas, 1984.

Smolin, Ann, and John Guinan. *Healing After the Suicide of a Loved One.* New York: Fireside/Simon & Schuster, 1993.

Taylor, Beth. *The Plain Language of Love and Loss: A Quaker Memoir.* Columbia, MO: University of Missouri Press, 2009.

Wertheimer, Alison. *A Special Scar: The Experience of People Bereaved by Suicide.* London: Brunner-Routledge, 2001.

Wickersham, Joan. *The Suicide Index: Putting My Father's Death in Order.* Boston: Mariner Books, 2009.

Gay and Lesbian

Aarons, Leroy. *Prayers for Bobby: A Mother's Coming to Terms with the Suicide of Her Gay Son.* San Francisco: HarperOne, 1996.

Ford, Michael Thomas. *Suicide Notes.* New York: HarperTeen, 2008.

Remafedi, Gary, ed. *Death by Denial: Studies of Suicide in Gay and Lesbian Teenagers.* Boston: Allyson Publications, 1994.

Rofes, Eric E. *I Thought People Like That Killed Themselves: Lesbians, Gay Men, and Suicide.* San Francisco: Grey Fox Press, 1984.

General

Colt, George Howe. *November of the Soul: The Enigma of Suicide.* New York: Scribner, 2006.

Durkheim, Emile. *Suicide (Le Suicide).* Translated by John Spaulding and George Simson. New York: Free Press, 1997.

Farberow, Norman L., ed. *Suicide in Different Cultures.* Baltimore: University Park Press, 1975.

Farberow, Norman L., and Edwin S. Shneidman, eds. *The Cry for Help.* New York: McGraw-Hill, 1965.

Heckler, Richard A. *Waking Up Alive: The Descent, the Suicide Attempt, and the Return to Life.* New York: Grosset/Putnam, 1994.

Hendin, Herbert. *Suicide in America.* New York: W. W. Norton & Co., 1996.

Jamison, Kay Redfield. *Night Falls Fast: Understanding Suicide.* New York: Vintage, 2000.

Lester, David. *Questions and Answers About Suicide.* Philadelphia: Charles Press, 1989.

Nuland, Sherwin B. *How We Die: Reflections on Life's Final Chapter.* New York: Vintage, 1995.

Quinnett, Paul G. *Suicide: The Forever Decision.* New York: Crossroad Publishing Co., 1987.

Shneidman, Edwin S., and Norman L. Farberow. *Clues to Suicide.* New York: McGraw-Hill, 1957.

Stengel, Erwin. *Suicide and Attempted Suicide.* New York: Jason Aronson, 1974.

Literature and Poetry

Alvarez, A. *The Savage God: A Study of Suicide.* New York: W. W. Norton & Co., 1990.

Goethe, Johann Wolfgang von. *The Sorrows of Young Werther.* New York: Vintage Books, 1973.

Levi, Primo. *The Drowned and the Saved*. New York: Vintage, 1989.

Middlebrook, Diane Wood. *Anne Sexton: A Biography*. New York: Vintage Books, 1992.

Miller, John, ed. *On Suicide*. San Francisco: Chronicle Books, 1993.

Plath, Sylvia. *The Bell Jar*. New York: Harper Perennial, 2006.

Styron, William. *Darkness Visible: A Memoir of Madness*. New York: Modern Library/Random House, 2007.

Teen/Youth Suicide

Aarons, Leroy. *Prayers for Bobby: A Mother's Coming to Terms with the Suicide of Her Gay Son*. San Francisco: HarperOne, 1996.

Klagsbrun, Francine. *Too Young to Die: Youth and Suicide*. New York: Pocket Books, 1985.

Kuklin, Susan. *After a Suicide: Young People Speak Up*. New York: G. P. Putnam's Sons, 1994.

Leder, Jane Mersky. *Dead Serious: A Book for Teenagers About Suicide*. New York: Atheneum, 1987.

Lezine, DeQuincy, and David Brent. *Eight Stories Up: An Adolescent Chooses Hope over Suicide*. New York: Oxford University Press, 2008.

Young Adult Novels

Asher, Jay. *Thirteen Reasons Why*. New York: Razorbill/Penguin, 2007.

Ford, Michael Thomas. *Suicide Notes*. New York: HarperTeen, 2008.

Peck, Richard. *Remembering the Good Times*. New York: Laurel Leaf/Random House, 1986.

INDEX

parents: adult children reacting to suicide of, 164–65; reacting to child's suicide, 160–62; surviving children and, 161; young children reacting to suicide of, 162–64
Perry, Dana, 153, 195
Petersen, Melody, 48
Plotkin, Daniel, 81
politics: suicide method and, 55–56; suicide motivation and, 34
Pollack, Andrew, 37
prescription medication: side effects of, 32–33, 46–48, 66, 142, 153–55; suicidal patients' refusal to take, 111
prevention: age-appropriate resources for, 112; of bullying, 106–7; elderly suicide, 81–82; failures of attempted, 99–100; getting help after attempted suicide, 88, 91–92; issues to consider for, 103; of jumping off bridges, 117–18; professional development of resources for, 111–12; teen/youth suicide, 71. *See also* suicide hotlines; treatments
psychological issues: suicide method, 54–55; suicide motivation, 31–33, 42–49
Psychology Today (journal), 103
public humiliation, 36

Quang Duc, 55–56
"Quest for Evolutionary Meaning in the Persistence of Suicide," 33–34
Quinnett, Paul, 45, 84

racial/ethnicity differences: the elderly and, 77; suicide rates and, 19
refusing medical treatment, 3
Reid, Harry, 205
rejection, 132
relief reaction, 135, 143–45
religious issues: Bible stories on suicide, 9; Christianity, Judaism, and Islam on suicide, 9–11, 28

revenge motive, 32
Reynold, Charles, 22
Rivers, Joan, 39
Robinson, Rita, 9, 13, 14, 104
Roh Moo-hyun, 36
Rosenberg, Edgar, 39

sacrificing for others motive, 33–34
sadness. *See* depression
Salazar, Eusebio, 8
Saunders, Cecil, 80–81
Saunders, Julia, 80–81
The Savage God: A Study of Suicide (Alvarez), 24–25, 27, 28
scandal motive, 36
schizophrenia, 31, 45
seasonal suicide rates, 24–25
secrecy reactions: appropriate times for, 182–83; "official" denial as, 128–29; reasons for, 178–80; talking about it instead of, 180–82; wish to forget, 152–53
self-recrimination, 139–42
seppuku (Japanese ritual suicide), 28
September 11, 2001, 34
sexual orientation, 36, 67–69, 112
shame reaction, 89, 90, 147–48, 177–78
Shneidman, Edwin, 13, 15, 103, 104
shock reaction, 121–25
sibling suicide, 168–71
situational clues, 104
slow suicide, 2
Social Psychiatry and Psychiatric Epidemiology (journal), 25
The Sorrows of Young Werther (von Goethe), 69
spouse's suicide, 158–60
Stuckler, David, 5
Styron, William, 31, 43
suicidal crisis: as situational clues, 104; suicide hotlines for help, 51, 68, 114–16; suicide risk following, 15
suicidal feelings: clinical depression and, 45; clues to someone's, 12–13, 103–4, 108; fear of, 151–52; passage